D1480747

LITERATURE

AND

PHILOSOPHY

*Structures of
Experience*

RICHARD KUHNS

Routledge & Kegan Paul   London

First published in Great Britain 1971
by Routledge & Kegan Paul Ltd
Broadway House, 68–74 Carter Lane,
London EC4V 5EL
Printed in Great Britain by
Lowe & Brydone (Printers) Ltd, London

ISBN 0 7100 7086 1

For Peggy and Frederick

Professor Eucalyptus said, "The search
For reality is as momentous as
The search for god." It is the philosopher's search

For an interior made exterior
And the poet's search for the same exterior made
Interior . . .

WALLACE STEVENS,
"An Ordinary Evening in New Haven"

Preface

Philosophy takes as one of its tasks an account and analysis of the grounds of experience; literature takes as one of its tasks the presentation and realization of specific experiences. What philosophy explains, literary art realizes or makes. Philosophy asks "What makes experience possible?" and "What makes *this* kind of experience possible?" Literature establishes the realities for which philosophy must seek explanations. Although philosophy and literature have always been coordinate modes of articulating experience, enmity and ignorance have kept them apart. Most philosophers lack literary power; most writers find philosophy puzzling. The affinity between philosophy and literature is the origin of this book.

Philosophy devotes itself to argument and to truth, while literature seems the least argumentative and most false kind of statement we tolerate; yet literary works have long been esteemed for their value as teacher and truth-teller. Is it simple-minded to believe a literary work can make a truth claim? How can congeries of false statements culminate in truth? These questions were asked by philosophers when they turned to consider literature, and one can see the Platonic dialogues as efforts to create philosophical literature, that is, literary forms whose content would be, in a defensible way, true. Plato's obstinate arguments to show literary statements without philosophical critique false were answered by Aristotle's reconsideration of how literary forms create valid experiences. Their arguments need to be examined in terms of our enlarged sense of literary possibilities. I shall ask in the opening chapter what meaning we can give to the claim that the literary art of tragedy is true.

The original inquiry into the philosophy of literary art established by Plato and Aristotle has undergone only a few revolutionary turnings in the history of philosophy, and I shall discuss these as the argument develops. In my view, Augustine, Hegel, and Freud are the thinkers who radically changed the ways we read and use literature. Their conclusions not only force us to think differently about art, but also compel art to take note of itself and to reform itself in new ways. Each one of the chapters to follow takes a forceful philosophical account of literary art and shows its affinities to the experiences realized by the coordinate literary works.

One such relationship, important to the conditioning of modern literary values, occurs in the eighteenth century and in the early nineteenth century. Chapter 2 shows how the accounts of experience given by Hume and Kant are realized in the writings of Sterne and Goethe. Together, these philosophers and literary artists suggest the possibility that literary values—indeed perhaps all values —are ultimately aesthetic, and in making this move they challenge traditional literary values of truth and morality.

Hegel and Wordsworth took another step toward modernity in their creation of forms of philosophy and art in which a phenomenology of awareness is explored; Chapter 3 considers their common concerns.

Chapters 4 and 5 take up this development in two novels which self-consciously consider the purposes and capacities of literary art, making a defense of the moral and historical truthfulness of art. Tolstoy's *Resurrection* accepts the attack on art's moral capacities as its greatest problem and defends the position that art can be morally and ontologically true. Lampedusa's *Leopard* enlarges that defense by setting the experience of his protagonist against the claims of history. Taken together, the two novels compel us to think seriously about the question Wittgenstein asked while he was writing the *Tractatus*: "Was geht mich die Geschichte an? Meine Welt ist die erste und einzige!" (What has history to do with me? Mine is the first and only world!). This anxious question might stand as an epigraph to which this book is a partial answer. In Chapter 6 I shall show that philosophy, in the early writing of Wittgenstein, and literary art, in the movements we refer to as symbolism and imagism, formulated an answer to this question. Rather than impugn the truth of literary art, philosophy ends in becoming itself a work of literary art.

RICHARD KUHNS

New York
June 1970

ACKNOWLEDGMENTS

Exhortation and support have come in various ways. Professor Ralph Freedman gave patient, painstaking, constructive criticism to the whole; Professor Edward Said gave exhortation when most needed and introduced me to new ideas; Professor Robert Wolff gave a new perspective to Chapter 4; Mr. Erwin Glikes returned grammatical bread manyfold by carefully reading and improving the completed manuscript. University seminars at Columbia University provided the occasion for learned, contentious discussions of several chapters. I am grateful for all these gifts and hope the givers will not be disappointed in what I have done with their help. From the American Council of Learned Societies I received a grant which enabled me to undertake this work. Chapter 5, somewhat expanded, is reprinted with permission from *Contemporary Psychoanalysis*, Vol. 5, No. 2 (1969).

I would like to thank the original publishers for permission to quote from the following works:

Goethe, *The Sorrows of Young Werther*, trans. Victor Lange (New York: Holt, Rinehart and Winston, Inc., 1949). © 1949 by Victor Lange.

Giuseppe di Lampedusa, *The Leopard*, trans. Archibald Colquhoun (New York: Pantheon Books, 1960). Reprinted by permission of Pantheon Books, a Division of Random House, Inc.

Acknowledgments

Wallace Stevens, "An Ordinary Evening in New Haven," *Collected Poems* (New York: Alfred A. Knopf, Inc., 1954).

Leo Tolstoy, *Resurrection,* trans. Louise and Aylmer Maude (London: Oxford University Press, 1966).

The Collected Works of Paul Valéry, ed. Jackson Matthews, Bollingen Series XLV, volume 7, *The Art of Poetry,* trans. Denise Folliot (Princeton: Princeton University Press, 1958). © 1958 by the Bollingen Foundation. Reprinted by permission of Princeton University Press and Routledge and Kegan Paul Ltd.

Ludwig Wittgenstein, *Notebooks, 1914–1918,* ed. G. H. von Wright and G. E. M. Anscombe (Oxford: Basil Blackwell, 1969). Ludwig Wittgenstein, *Tractatus Logico-Philosophicus,* trans. D. F. Pears and B. F. McGuinness (London: Routledge and Kegan Paul Ltd., 1961). Reprinted by permission of Routledge and Kegan Paul Ltd. and the Humanities Press, Inc.

William Wordsworth, *The Prelude,* ed. Ernest de Selincourt, 2d ed. rev. Helen Darbishire (Oxford: The Clarendon Press, 1959).

William Butler Yeats, "The Tower," *Collected Poems* (New York: The Macmillan Company, 1928). © 1928 by The Macmillan Company, renewed 1956 by Georgie Yeats. Also reprinted by permission of Mr. Michael B. Yeats, Macmillan & Co. Ltd. (London), and The Macmillan Co. of Canada.

Contents

STRUCTURES

OF

EXPERIENCE

Chapter 1

Truth as a Value
of Tragedy

I

Although philosophical thought extends the range of art and opens ways to its restructuring, there has always been competition and antagonism between art and philosophy. A contemptuous dependency was expressed in the first confrontation between art and philosophy, that which occurred in Athens. The central issue in that dispute—carried on right down to our own time—was whether or not literary art in general, but more specifically drama, could make a truth claim. All philosophic theories of literature, whether imitation theories or expression theories, must work out this question, and therefore it is one to take up at the beginning of an essay ⸱on the relationship of philosophy and literature.

The easiest formulation of the problem can be found in Augustine's painful musing on the theater, for it reflects the widespread confusions about "truth" in drama. He wonders how an audience can be moved by—more, can actively seek—scenes of suffering. Since drama is not true, the affect is inappropriate, and were it true, the pleasure

B

would be sinful. Therefore, either way, representations of human suffering are panderings to human baseness. However, the rhetorical tradition in which Augustine was schooled taught him that the human means of imitation —language—was capable of truth. For Augustine the truth of dramatic language, if it were possible, had to be measured against the truth of scripture, while for his teachers in the tradition it had to be measured against the truth of philosophical inquiry. Both classical and Christian, then, assumed that drama, if it were to be justified, had to be tested against a competing mode of statement. This leaves drama in a secondary position, in any case, because it is thought of as adventitious, or perhaps as a parasite, deriving its goodness from a more fundamental human capacity and exercise of intelligence. So considered, drama remains puzzling for it holds our attention and gives more pleasure than either scripture or philosophy. That fact led Aristotle to ask in the *Poetics* what the truth of tragedy might be, led Plato to defend philosophers as truth-tellers against literary men as misperceivers, if not liars, and led Augustine to defend inspired books against pagan wickedness. In all cases, though, the problem is the same: if we claim truth to be a value of drama, wherein does the truth reside? For in one obvious sense drama is false: it is the work of creative imagination which erects traditional stories or private fantasies into shows. The audience then responds to what is shown by having all the emotions, involvements, beliefs that they would have if the representations were true, that is, actual happenings. Yet they are not actual happenings, though much that occurs in drama is real if by "real" we mean likely or probable; and some things that

4

occur in drama are unlikely or even impossible. So how is it that within the framework of a stage so many events can evoke strong emotions and genuine belief?

When the audience leaves the theater questions of emotion and belief are put aside: no one pretends he witnessed historical events; no one would tell the events of the theater as if they were events of the day. And yet everyone will come to know the events depicted in drama as if they had the reality of history, for every generation shall see the same dramatic representations. There is a sharing in drama not unlike the sharing in the "real" past. This sense of sharing, and the feeling, among peoples who share a tradition, that all ought to see the same plays, elevates the drama to a special eminence. To be a participant in a culture is, by definition, to have experience of the community established by literary statements. For the Athenians these were the *Iliad* and, later on, certain dramas whose authority became proverbial. By Plato's time the power of drama was such that he had, as a first task, to challenge its authority before he could make a case for philosophy.

I do not think conditions are very different for Augustine who lived in a city where theatergoing clearly took precedence over churchgoing. Both philosopher and apologist for scripture had a similar task: to show that if truth were a value of tragedy—at best dubious—then at least it was insubstantial, capricious, evanescent, and unsure of itself as contrasted with philosophic thought, whose excellence lay in care of thought and formulation of argument, and scripture, whose truth was guaranteed by a divine being. But these claims are highly intellectual, that is, dependent on concepts whose meanings must be

5

grasped in talk alone, while the drama gives us action, something to look at, and excites us through our eyes and ears. No wonder the audience at a drama finds it easy to "believe," while the philosophical student and the scriptural hearer are lost in unsureness and doubt. In conclusion though, it must be stated that the philosopher and the hearer of scripture leave their respective "theaters" with a belief unshaken and undiminished. They do not go out into "the real world"; they have rather come into contact with "the real world" and can take that with them into the marketplace. So drama seems to fade on leaving the theater, but the conclusions of philosophy and scripture seem to persist.

This difference was not lost upon Aristotle who still wanted to defend drama as delivering something permanent, analogous to the truths of philosophy. In saying poetry is more philosophical than history he hints at this, but he has another argument far more powerful that goes to the heart of the difference between philosophy and drama.

His argument is this: If the drama produces merely a "catharsis" in the banal sense of relieving emotion, then it is evanescent and has little claim to truth, for then the drama is to be compared with religious celebrations. In religious celebrations what is most remarkable is that there is a resolution of action and passion very like that we see in drama: the participants find themselves "purged," that is, they enjoy a diminution of strong feeling and become quiescent. But in those cases we notice a further fact: a repetition of the violence must follow the quiescence. In our terms, religious and some dramatic experiences are like a repetition compulsion. The partici-

6

pant enjoys the relief they give only to be forced to repeat the experience because once the exhaustion passes
the tensions and conflicts are exacerbated and must be
dealt with through the same "medicine." If this is all the
drama delivers, then it is little other than its root and origin, namely religious celebration. The early chapters of
the *Poetics* explore this origin to make the point that although drama began in primitive ritual and religious celebration, it soon moved beyond that to a higher, more
complex, and biologically "evolved" form. Therefore, although we see the origin of drama in religion, it does not
mean that we ought to commit the genetic fallacy and
say it is the same as religious celebration. Aristotle's
whole point is that it can be distinguished as a mode of
performance from all other modes of performance—
including religious celebration and philosophical "agonis-
tic" exercise—and therefore is in its claim to truth different and unique. The *Poetics* is an effort to tell us what
the claim to truth amounts to.

The claim to truth is this:

Drama is philosophical in the sense that it reveals a
truth in the totality of its exhibitive form, not in the individual statements which make it up. It matters not that
poets may be dreamers and "possessed" as Plato depicts
them, nor that the drama deals with myths and with "unreal" characters; all that is its claim to falsehood, if you
will, and we readily admit that its content is not historical. But it is, if it has any merit, poetical, and poetry is a
different mode of statement from history and from philosophy. It is, however, like philosophy in that it aims at general statements of a theoretical kind, even though it is unlike philosophy in rejecting argument. But if it lacks

7

argument, then what is its structure? How does it go from premises to conclusion?

Aristotle's answer is that it has a motion and a progress of its own peculiar to itself: the progress of what I shall call *affective rhythm*. Drama, again when rightly constructed, moves from a beginning through a middle to an end in a form analogous to an extended argument. Now just as we can analyze an argument—and Aristotle devoted several inquiries to this mode of development in language—so we can analyze the affective rhythm of a drama. This is what Aristotle does in the *Poetics*. He gives names to crucial points in the developing rhythm, for example, "reversal," "recognition," "pathos." These are terms that denote both cognitive and affective nodes in the plot. The plot then can be thought of as a structure in which these nodal points are clearly articulated. I shall briefly describe this structure according to Aristotle's sense of how drama moves from its first statements and actions to its last statements and actions.

The central argument of the *Poetics* is aimed at an account of dramatic experience, that is, how the experience in the theater is possible, and how it should be evaluated. Thinking of the *Poetics* in this way, we might say that Aristotle is raising the question posed by Kant as *the* philosophical question: "How is experience possible?" In this case the question is narrowed to "How is dramatic experience, and of that, experience in the case of tragic drama, possible?" The answer is complex in detail but simple in basic formulation. Dramatic experience occurs as it does because of the structure given the drama; that is, plot determines both dramatic form and the organization of experience. If the drama is well constructed and has the right plot, the audience will be led through the right kinds of feelings, beliefs, and affects to the appropriate conclusions. There will be a dramatic experience of a valuable kind.

By taking the arguments in the *Poetics* and placing them together for purposes of exposition, the following summary of Aristotle's views can be given. Let us think of a dramatic situation as a performance within which we can distinguish the plot, the characters, and the audience; Aristotle wants to give these three aspects in their *functional* interrelationship. By "functional" I mean simply that the way in which each affects the other must be shown, for drama is a complex situation in which an audience is led through a series of states as a consequence of a play performed before them.

A drama can be divided into a beginning, a middle, and an end. The beginning shows us an action begun: a person (protagonist) aims to bring off action A_1, but in reality, unknown to him but known to the audience, is going to bring off A_2. A_1 and A_2 are causally and morally related, to be sure, but that they are is hidden from the protagonist. The plot is in effect his coming to see this relationship, known all along to the audience. Because of his unknowingness the protagonist is happy, or relatively so, when the drama begins. But the audience cannot be said to share his feelings, for they know, or sense, the depths of the complication he is about to reveal. Thus in the beginning of the well-made drama there is an interesting complicity: an unknowing person, aiming at A_1 is about to bring off A_2 in the belief that what he is doing is right and just and of little consequence to him personally. The audience sees his situation quite differently, knowing

9

he must fail, that he is unknowing, and that he stands in relationships of deep culpability to others who as far as *he* is concerned are of no morally compromising significance. This disparity is essential to the success of the well-made drama.

The middle of the drama introduces two complicating events and structures to which Aristotle gives the name "reversal" and "recognition." These refer to the coalescing of A_1 and A_2 as the protagonist furthers his actions, and they culminate in his recognizing the distinction as well as the moral incongruity of A_1 and A_2. The distinction as well as the incongruity forces a radical change in his affective state: he ceases to be happy and now is filled with fear, dread, guilt, and other emotions which may become destructive. Reversal and recognition lead to the possibility of violence. The protagonist suffers an affect reversal which is a function of plot reversal; and a cognitive re-cognition dependent upon the plot uncovering. For the audience, his seeing this and responding to it are the occasion for deep and disturbing emotions, as well as a satisfaction in having a prediction borne out. There is no doubt but that for Aristotle the pleasure of tragedy— though it be of suffering—is genuine because it grows out of a situation where one knows what must happen and then sees it happen. Something godlike descends upon a person so honored. This sense of knowing, and seeing the inevitability of what works itself out, prepares the audience for the truth of the drama. The audience is prepared because it has had its sense of certainty reconfirmed. It is otherwise when tricks and foolings go on, for then the audience, though titillated, cannot trust itself. The sense of rightness over events and the doom-filled assumptions of

the opening scene, realized in the protagonist's coming to
see and know what the audience sees and knows, is essential to bring the audience and actors into the same world.
The irony of fallibility and ignorance is erased. Now protagonist and audience are in the same dramatic situation.
Hence both share in the suffering or pathos, that passivity
in which the protagonist fully realizes what he has done
and how a moral incongruity can dash his world of satisfaction and moral stability. The protagonist is pushed
now to a total reorganization of his social and moral condition. He is no longer morally acceptable, nor centrally
placed politically; rather, he is now morally unacceptable
and politically anathema. Here he is left, but here the audience is encouraged to take a step beyond that of the
protagonist; for just as the audience is one step ahead of
him in the beginning, so in the end they continue one
step ahead, and in fact leave the theater having given the
ending, as it were.

Thus when we say a plot has a beginning, middle, and
end, the dimensions of these three parts are not to be
found solely within the structure of the text as such. The
incongruity of audience and protagonist persists outside
the action in this sense: what the audience must do,
where the best tragedy is concerned, is to confer upon
the protagonist the resolution his situation cannot confer
upon him. They must accord him the acceptance that he
cannot accord himself. This audience responsibility is
what distinguishes tragedy in the best sense—true
tragedy—from the serious drama of political consequences, or from the drama of pathos in which a resolution is accorded by the state or by the gods. So distinguished, the tragic suffering of Oedipus is quite different

from the pathos and the forgiveness accorded Orestes. In the *Oresteia* acceptance is accorded by the supernatural, and all this occurs within the drama. In *Oedipus the King* the drama ends without the according of anything other than exile upon the protagonist; the gods are most remote, justice is obscure, and yet the moral issues are clear. The audience accords respect and acceptance. This is an *affective* realization, and comes closest to giving a sensible dramatic meaning to the concept of "catharsis."

That catharsis has many meanings is clear; that it has a special and right dramatic meaning is the reason, I believe, for bringing it into a discussion of drama. That it may be similar or analogous to its meanings and functions in other contexts is probably true; but the dramatic sense is not reducible to or interchangeable with any other sense.

The conclusion Aristotle reaches is that we can meaningfully say that truth is a value of drama, at least of a species of drama to which he gave the name "tragedy of reversal and recognition." It is a drama of a serious kind, of a certain magnitude, with a plot containing reversal and recognition elements, with a first actor of great but not perfect or evil nature, whose actions move him from good to bad fortune, and it is so structured that the conclusion deals with emotions by means of a term that Aristotle employs very rarely, that is, "catharsis." In representations of this special kind there is a truth claim that can be defended. This is what the *Poetics* is about, and we are now ready to consider the truth claim and what sort of defense we can give it.[1]

[1] The view presented here is dependent upon three discussions of the *Poetics:* Jeanne Croissant, *Aristote et les Mystères.* Bibliothèque de la

We need to go beyond anything worked out in the *Poetics*, for that fragmentary work gives us hints and bits of argument, but does not complete its case. Can we complete the case? If we can, we have at least made sense of the claim to truth of one kind of literary statement, and it then might be possible to extend it to other kinds. But I have another thesis that I do not want to lose sight of: namely, that the claim to truth of literary statement has itself been variously understood at different times in our history. And one of the great changes that took place in the years since say 1730 was the rejection by some poets and philosophers of the possibility of truth in literary statement, and a conviction that the value of literature was, if anything, aesthetic. Thus the claim to truth is a traditional and, if you will, a classical claim. It is also a claim made over and over again by various writers and critics in our tradition. But it is a claim violently challenged in the eighteenth century (and before too, in isolated cases like that of Rabelais) and fought over continuously to our own time. It appears again in the expression theories of Hegel, Nietzsche, and Freud. But before we can understand the attacks on the claim to truth in literature, we must see how the most powerful defense of it is made, and I think that defense is in the *Poetics*.

What, then, is the "truth" to which Aristotle was pointing, and that both Plato and Augustine either could not see or would not admit? To answer this question it is necessary to ask how Aristotle thought of literature in its re-

faculté de philosophie et lettres de l'université de Liège, No. 51 (1942); G. F. Else, *Aristotle's Poetics: The Argument* (Cambridge: Harvard University Press, 1957); Richard Kuhns, *The House, The City and the Judge: The Growth of Moral Awareness in the Oresteia* (New York: Bobbs-Merrill, 1962).

13

lation to "reality," in the sense of events and processes in the world which might be investigated by philosophy (or, as we would say, science). The first relationship that he establishes is one of "likeness"; that is, events we see on the stage, especially violent events, are like events in ordinary life. People attack one another, hurt one another, find themselves in grievous circumstances, are dealt with cruelly by fate, enjoy unmerited reward, and so on. In short, tragic drama gives us "the world" in all its moral rightness and wrongness, its fairness and unfairness. But of course it concentrates on the misfortunes rather than the good fortunes. We respond to dramatic narrative because of this likeness. Aristotle even gives an "explanation" of why we respond: first, we are by nature imitative, and second we are by nature learners, and the second follows from the first. Therefore drama satisfies a natural, indeed a definitional, human trait. But we do not therefore go on to confuse the drama with natural philosophy or with everyday experience, even though Plato likes to pretend we might do this. We might, however, go on to say that the dramatic narrative shows us something *about* life, and this both Plato and Aristotle agree is a consequence of dramatic representation. Plato makes the further claim that the dramatic might become the substitute for reality; whereas Aristotle never considers this a danger because he knows—as Plato does too—that this is not the human use to which drama is put. Nobody basically is confused about such things. Even Augustine has to agree, though he is appalled at his friends' attachment to theatrical experience.

The relation to reality, as Aristotle sees it, is one of what we might call double imitation: that is, there is the imitation of the words in their literal meaning, and there is the imitation of the structure of the whole as an action in the sense of a plot and a character working out the plot. There is a duality of the meaning process which enables us to say that the sentences are false yet the drama is true. The sentences are false in the obvious sense that they do not refer to actual persons or events, but together they delineate a true action in the sense that what makes the plot come out as it does, and therefore our feelings follow the route they follow with the shape they have, are realities of life and thought whose confirmation lies not in the mythic characters but in the qualities and movement of their actions as human beings. Thus Oedipus is both a mythic person and a human being; his killings are both legendary actions, and, by moral assumptions, wrong and reprehensible actions however and wherever they occur.

This is made possible by the nature of language, for though the characters make assertions that are false in the sense that they do not refer to events that occurred outside the drama, they are in a quite legitimate sense true in that they state conditions of choice, deliberation, and actions whose reality lies in the nature of human beings as such, not in a specific mythic representation of imaginary beings. We therefore are justified in using mythic traditions, Aristotle argues, because in myth we have a fund of material open to all, and, further, such material describes actions of a most doleful, painful, conflicting kind which *in real life* produce the greatest affective response. Why the myths contain this material Aristotle does not say, but Freud did try to say. In both cases, though, a fundamental aspect of literary statement is defended: both Aristotle and Freud characterize language in its literary use as dual. That is, the language of literary statement is at once literal, saying something which refers to events in the world, and metaphorical, saying something whose meaning is understood through a process of interpretation. That is why Aristotle spends so much time in the *Poetics* analyzing language usage as it occurs in literary statement. Metaphor is the key because it opens up this duality. And this duality is what distinguishes literary from philosophical statement. Parenthetically, it is most important to remember that the meaningfulness of scripture was only evident to Augustine when he learned the art of interpretation from Ambrose. It is not that Augustine rejects literary statement because it cannot be true; he rejects it as not rich enough for the interpretive ingenuity of a brilliant man who, when dealing with scripture, finds much to interpret. Augustine was quite capable of turning around and applying the exegetical method he learned from Ambrose and used on scripture to classical philosophy and even classical drama. Thus Plato is "scripturized" and the drama made less offensive.

The great insight of the *Poetics* is not only in the analysis of drama as such, but in the way language, put to literary uses, makes assertions. Aristotle sets out to make the *Poetics* more than a "how to write a good play" handbook; he puts into it a theory of interpretation, answering Plato's attacks on the truth of drama by giving, in brief, suggestions for how drama should be responded to as well as how it should be constructed. In taking the *Poetics* as an interpretive as well as a "how to" manual, I place greater emphasis on Aristotle's theory of how language functions than is usually the case. I believe he has started an inquiry into the complexities of language which is continuous throughout our tradition.

II

In the *Poetics*, both the discussion of language and the comments on how one ought to understand a drama make a basic assumption that literary language functions by means of a dualism of literal and what we would call, broadly, symbolic meaning. Whether it be strictly metaphorical, exaggerated, impossible, implausible, and so on, the language has to be tested on a two-dimensional scale: one dimension is that of literal matter-of-factness, the other is that of poetic purpose. Now we admit that poetic language has its own purposes that are different from philosophical or historical usage. Aristotle sums this up by saying, "In poetry itself there are two kinds of flaws, one of which is intrinsic, the other incidental." [2] Intrinsic flaws come from failure to succeed in the art one attempts, but incidental flaws come from representations that are, from the point of view of literalness, inaccurate. We must be careful to test flaws against poetic purposes, for we may admit their propriety if we understand the aims of poetry. Of course the whole of the *Poetics* sets forth these aims. Poetic language is characterized by its two-dimensional meaning system. All dramatic

---

[2] Aristotle, *Poetics*, trans. G.M.A. Grube (New York: Bobbs-Merrill, 1958), Ch. 25.

events have a literal meaning, that is, they are recognized as events whose possibility and plausibility are tested through everyday experience. This dimension begins with the simplest identities—that man is Oedipus—to the much more complex identities—Oedipus is a man accursed, or, Oedipus is filled with divine potencies. Our willingness to accept plausibility over possibility is the condition for response to the drama. If we are unwilling to make that concession, we cannot respond to poetry at all. But our willingness is a function of something essentially human, not some flaw or perverseness in us. Here Plato and Aristotle differ, for Plato wants to argue that it is our lacks and instinctual immaturities which lead us to long for the drama, while Aristotle wants to demonstrate the naturalness and continuousness of dramatic experience with everyday experience on the one hand and theoretical thinking on the other.

We go, therefore, by a series of natural steps from seeing the masked figure on the stage to beliefs about the figure which are wholly dependent upon the poetic situation. *Poetic reality* is the consequence of a complicated situation whose structure develops as the drama develops, bit by bit through the time of the performance. At the end we can accept statements whose meaning is determined now solely by symbolic dimensions.

However, the poetic structure is a man-made structure, and to understand it we must understand something about human beings. Therefore the *Poetics* has a lot to say about the so-called tragic hero and his nature. A dualism is once more asserted to account for the dualism of language. That is, the literal-symbolic dimensions of language are related to, or if you wish are an expression of, a duality of the human which defines the peculiarities of human life. I shall sum up this twofoldness by calling it the distinction of the private and the public. And it is this double aspect of human nature which provides the central reality in drama and the reality out of which tragic conflicts develop. For this twofoldness is expressed in communal life on the one hand and individual need on the other.[3]

Aristotle notes that the subject of most serious drama is traditional families in which irreconcilable conflicts of a mortal kind occur. They are the best source of dramatic plots. I interpret his choice of plot source to suggest that these family stories turn on an essential conflict between the political needs of individuals and therefore of communities ruled, and the private needs of those into whose hands the ruling has been committed. I shall term this conflict that between *private psychic needs* and *public political needs*. All the Greek tragic dramas turn on this conflict. One need only consider the extant plays to see that this is true. I call attention particularly to the *Oresteia* and the Oedipus plays. But it is true as well of the Euripidean plays and even of the Aristophanic comedies. Political and psychic realities generate those conflicts through which individuals are destroyed and the greatest suffering descends upon the community. This is recognized in the *Poetics*. And further, this duality of human life is pervasive: all that man says as well as all that he does reflects this dualism. This, I repeat, is an extended interpretation of my own, but one that is solidly supported by the text of the *Poetics*.

[3] This theme is taken up and enlarged in Chapter 4, "Art as a Defense of Moral Values."

C

The above discussion enlarges the doctrine of "imitation." I suggest not only that there is a representation of "life" in the drama, but, more importantly, a representation of a pervasive reality in the structure of the means as well as of the subject of representation. Aristotle distinguishes the means or instrument of representation, language, from the stuff or subject of representation, human beings acting in purposive ways. That the subject reflects life we do not doubt, but it is more difficult to show that language itself reflects in its meaning dimensions a duality of human consciousness, that is, a duality between public and private, or what I have called psychic and political reality. I want to enlarge the concept of imitation by suggesting that the instrument of poetry, language, is itself "imitative" in this metaphorical sense.

This helps us to make a first approach to the question we are trying to answer: "What does it mean to say that truth is a value of tragedy?" First, there is a correspondence between the subjects of drama and of everyday life, and second, there is a structural duality in poetic language which reflects or grows out of a duality of psychic and political reality in the awareness of the individual. It is the latter which is "truer" than the former in the sense that the subject of drama may be mythic, but the function of language, whatever it takes as subject, is still revelatory of the psychic and political realities out of which the mythic stories grow. I postulate a human condition in this root sense and argue that this condition determines the stories as imaginative projections or descriptions of that condition; that the condition is one of basic conflict, and finally that the instrument of making known or formulating the description, language, itself embodies or reflects the two aspects of reality which are in conflict, that is, the reality of psychic needs and the reality of political needs. This then is simply a way of saying that drama deals with a fundamental conflict, and that whatever else it may contain, and however it uses language, this conflict is one source of the tragic, and the language insures that the conflict will be present in every part of the structuring material, not just in the gross plot.

Looking at the *Poetics* this way opens up the possibility of interpreting the statement that a plausible impossibility is preferable to an implausible possibility. Drama can tolerate "unreality" or inconsistency with everyday experience, but it cannot accept the implausible. The substance of such impossibilities but plausabilities are assertions of a special kind which we find only in poetic language. They are assertions about identities whose reality is not to be tested by reference to everyday experience. What I refer to are identities about persons and actions, identities that lead to critical disputes. They really have to do with the symbolic interpretation of character and action and fill the literature of commentary. The mechanism for this type of assertion which Aristotle singles out is that of reversal and recognition, to which he gives a rather mechanical plot analysis. But reversal and recognition have a purpose beyond that which he sees, important as that is for both the plot and the affective rhythms set up in the audience. Reversal and recognition are means of making identities which we could not otherwise make, identities such as "Jocasta *is* aware of the true situation but refuses to admit it," "Oedipus, in blinding himself, *is* castrating himself," "The messenger coming to Clytemnestra *is* death." These are odd sorts of statements to which there is no exactly corresponding evidence, and therefore they are what we call "interpretations." But interpretation is a natural and necessary response to language in its poetic uses since the language is the instrument by means of which a fundamental human conflict generated in the grounds and purposes of action is revealed to an audience. The identities of a symbolic kind are explications of linguistic presentations whose full meaning is not grasped without such explications. This is not to say that they are without meaning unless interpreted, but simply that they are impoverished in meaning if not explicated or do not have the identities asserted, and therefore that they are diminished in their imitative power.

The *Poetics*, considered in these terms, proposes a thesis whose truth I hope to defend in these essays: that there is a deep and important relationship between philosophical thought about art and art itself; namely, that what philosophers analyze as the way in which experience is possible has its necessary counterpart in the kinds of experience actually realized in art itself. The paradigm for this relationship is the drama, for it is most obviously a representation of human beings in action, and so most closely fits and complements philosophical theories of action. That this was so for Plato and Aristotle is in part a fortunate cultural concern: in Athens philosophy and drama grew up together. Later philosophical thought also explored the relationship between art and philosophy, in many cases without the self-conscious complement that Plato and Aristotle brought to their commentaries. In the chapters to follow I shall extend this complementariness into other moments.

III

The position defended in the *Poetics* was challenged by two different conceptions of literary truth, one formulated by Augustine in his reassessment of classical art, the other implied by the Augustinian critique. The first establishes what came to be a Christian interpretation of literature, the second, surprisingly, a structuralist treatment of literature. Augustine's radical views on the nature of art place him along with Hegel and Freud as one of three revolutionary postclassical theorists in the philosophy of art.

For Augustine, the status of art, its truth and power, are judged by reference to the faith; scripture, not philosophy, is the standard for any truth claim. The production and consumption of art are not a communal but a sacerdotal concern, overseen by spiritual leaders, not the city administration. What the artist produces is to be evaluated by its approximation to the truth of scripture, and its excellence determined by its spiritual content. The art work itself is to be understood by comparison with God's creation, the cosmos, and its goodness determined by the degree to which it manifests the goodness of the original creation. The process of production, that is, the creative act artistically considered, is to be understood through its likeness to and difference from the act of the Deity in his role of Creator and Begetter.

Augustine's treatment of the imitative relationship is complicated by his concepts of creating and begetting, introduced on the basis of scripture, but elaborated to cope with theological problems the ancients did not have to contend with. Not only is God the creator responsible for all creation (there is no antecedent stuff), but he is at once the creator of the cosmos and the begetter of Christ. The complexity of such distinctions makes Augustine more sensitive to some modes of artistic creativity than the theories he inherited and found overly simple in their analysis of imitation. Because the demands of Christian theology lead one to analyze imitation through the related and subsidiary concepts of creativity and begetting, Augustine is able to offer a more complete analysis of art structures than the rhetoricians from whom he learned so much. In this case, it seems to me, theological complexity enlarged the awareness of philosophical problems that a theory of art had to face. Augustine's theological needs encouraged his philosophy of art to be fairer to art itself.

Initially Augustine learned his method, in rather crude form, from his teacher Ambrose. He relates the awakening in the *Confessions:*

I was glad that the old scripture of the Law and the Prophets were set before me now, no longer in that light in which they had formerly seemed absurd, when I criticised your holy ones for thinking this or that which in plain fact they did not think. And it was a joy to hear Ambrose who often repeated to his congregation, as if it were a rule he was most strongly urging upon them, the text: *the letter killeth, but the spirit giveth life.* And he would go on to draw aside the veil of mystery and lay open the spiritual meaning of things which taken literally would have seemed to teach falsehood.[4]

[4] Augustine, *Confessions,* trans. F. J. Sheed (New York: Sheed and Ward, 1942), Book VI, 4.

As he became more familiar with this method of exegesis, Augustine found he could, with the power of his intellect, "draw aside the veil of mystery," revealing to the perspicacious the truths within. But the method need not be limited to scripture; hidden truth can be found in pagan literary products which, though at first they might endanger the soul, can be used to indicate the truthful way. Indeed, the writings of Plato and Virgil, Augustine believed, could be shown to point clearly to truths of Christianity after their own time: marvelous presence in the written word, another evidence of God's providence. But what of human making in general, since we make imitations in paint, in stone, in sound? Music and the material arts too were able to point to the hidden mystery of things, and in exploring these possibilities of the arts, Augustine was led to the adumbration of a structuralist position.

The sovereign art of God Almighty, which is called Wisdom and by which everything was made from nothing, operates through the intermediary of the artists, and is what enables them to make beautiful and well-designed works. But the artist does not create out of nothing, but from a given material, such as wood, marble, or ivory, and other kinds of material which can be shaped by the hand of the artist. And this is why the artists are incapable of bringing something out of nothing: it is because they work with what is physical. Nevertheless, the proportions and linear harmonies which they realize in a physical thing by physical action, they discover in the intellect of that highest Wisdom which, through an art of a different order, realized the proportions and harmonies of the whole physical universe created from nothing. And in that we find among other things the bodies of animals composed of cosmic elements, but with a higher power and perfection than that of human artists who reproduce in their works the same silhouettes and bodily representations. Indeed, one does not find in the statue all the proportional details of the human body, but all which is found there, through the intermediary of the artist's effort, derives ultimately from the Wisdom which in the natural realm brought the human body itself into being. When we realize this, it is not necessary to make so much of the authors and amateurs of this kind of work: because the soul which is attracted to these lesser objects, produced by the body in a physical medium, is attracted all the less to the highest Wisdom from which it takes its powers. It misuses its faculties when it exercises them on these externals because its attachment to things makes it lose sight of their essential and external form, and it thereby loses its value and power. As for those who have made a cult of this kind of work, one can see the extent to which they have turned from truth to these lesser objects; for if they dedicated their cult to the original bodies of animals (a composition more perfect, and one of which these artist's works are copies), would we think anyone more miserable than they? [5]

In Augustine's view music, even more than plastic structures, can mirror the divine harmony, for of all the arts music comes closest to realizing a true image of that beauty which is the proportion of God's handiwork. However, like the other arts, it too must remain at best a semblance, the image of God in most developed earthly manifestation being reserved for the relationship between man's intellect and God. Augustine spends considerable

---

[5] Augustine, *De Diversis Questionibus*, 83, no. 78, "De Pulchritudine Simulacrorum." My translation.

thought on the problem of image relationship, as the following meditation makes clear.

1. Exterior and Interior Man

The holy Scripture speaks of the outer man and the inner man, and notes a distinction of which the Apostle says (II Cor. IV, 16): "Though the outward man perish, yet the inward man is renewed day by day."

One can ask if only one of these two was created in the image of God. But it is absurd to ask which, since only one was. . . . Is there need of both? Absurd question, because if Adam is the outer man and Christ the inner, there is need of both. . . . These are the two men whom the Apostle distinguished in indicating one as the old man to strip off, and the other as the new man to put on (Coloss. III, 9–10). The first he called the image of the earthly man, because it is under the influence of the sin of the first man who is Adam; and the other, the image of the heavenly man (I. Cor. XV, 49) because he is under the influence of the sanctity of the second man who is Jesus Christ. But the outer man, which is corrupted in the present, will be made over by the resurrection [*futura resurrectione renovabitur*] when he will pay the debt of natural death and enter into heaven.

2. But is it not offensive [*incongruum*] to say that the body was made in the image of God? This is easy to understand if one pays close attention to the word: "And God saw every thing that he had made, and, behold it was very good" (Gen. I, 31).

. . . One can say with good reason that all beings resemble God: some which are created in strength and wisdom, because in Him force and wisdom resides; others simply because they are living, because in Him is the highest life and the source of life; and others insofar as they exist, because He exists eminently and is the cause of all existence. That is why those things which simply exist, without having life or knowledge, are in his image, not perfectly, but in a certain measure, because even they are good in their proper place inasmuch as He is good above all else and from Him comes all that is good. . . . Beings which know are closer to Him than all other created things. For they participate in knowing, in life, and in existence. Also, since man is able to participate in knowing in as much as he is the inner man, to that degree is he "in the image," in the sense that he is formed without an intermediary of any other nature, and nothing is more intimately united to God. . . .

3. We mean by the outer man that life which we realize in bodily sensations by means of the five well-known senses and which we possess in common with animals. It is not unreasonable to say that this man also participates in a resemblance to God, not only because he has life as do animals, but especially because he is under the domination of intellect which leads him by the light of wisdom, something impossible among animals deprived of reason. Further, the human body is alone, among bodies of terrestial animals, in not having a hanging belly [*non pronum in alvum prostratum est*].

The front is open and upright so that the heavens can be contemplated. . . . It is in this adaptation for the contemplation of the heavens that it can be said it is in the image and likeness of God; and because of this it has the best claim to that of all the other animal bodies. . . .

4. And it is necessary to distinguish on the one hand the image and likeness of God which we call the Son, and on the other that which is made in the image and likeness of God by which we mean created man. There is an intention in the use of two expressions, "in the image" and "in the

likeness," on the ground that for a single characteristic a single word suffices. It expresses the fact that the intellect was created "in the image of," for it is formed without an intermediary or any substance by Truth itself, and it is therefore called "spirit": not the Holy Spirit which is identical in substance with the Father and the Son, but the human spirit. The apostle has distinguished them in these terms: "For what man knoweth the things of a man, save the spirit of man which is in him? Even so the things of God knoweth no man, but the Spirit of God" (I Cor. II, 11). And he says of the human spirit: "And may your whole spirit and soul and body be preserved" (I Thess. V, 23). . . . Thus that spirit is held by all to be created "in the image of God," thus capable of knowing the truth without the need of any intermediary. The other parts of man can be considered as created "in the likeness" because all images are no doubt semblances, but that which is a semblance cannot be strictly called an image except occasionally by extension.[6]

It is on the foundation of the theory of imitation just sketched that Augustine goes on to build his theory of literary interpretation. If we understand the relationship of God to man, and of creator to created in the way Augustine suggests, then the problems of interpretation are clear: the way into the inner truth of a text, an image, a musical composition is our obligation, and requires a developed method as well as a recognition that most human products are special kinds of symbols whose secrets can be revealed to the less gifted. The best source for Augustine's directions to successful interpretation is his book

---

[6] Augustine, *De Diversis Questionibus*, 83, No. 51, "De Homine Facto Ad Imaginem et Similitúdinem Dei." My Translation.

De Doctrina Christiana, a handbook, as it were, of critical procedures. There Augustine elaborated two sets of four-dimensional interpretive procedures, the first giving directions for how to interpret a symbolic presentation in its largest relationships, the second how to interpret that most dense symbolic order of meaning, the allegorical. Taken together they offer a schema like this:

There are four ways of interpreting a symbolic presentation.

1. Historical: what it recounts as historically true
2. Etiological: what it recounts as the cause of an event
3. Analogical: what continuity it exhibits as holding between the Old and the New Testament
4. Allegorical: what inner, spiritual, truth is to be found through figurative interpretation

The last can be analyzed into its four moments.

a. What is literally said or presented (literal)
b. What truth for humanity as a whole is to be found within (allegorical)
c. What truth of morality it reveals (tropological)
d. What ultimate spiritual truth it leads us to see (analogical)

We can now ask, what new dimensions of human products has Augustine's philosophy of art made available? Consider the implications of his way of seeing art: Augustine holds a double-aspect view of art, that there is an inner and an outer meaning, an esoteric and an exoteric content. This double aspect is readily apparent to the human mind which is itself, as it were, a metaphor, since within the universe as God has created it there is an inner structure of divine order clothed in the appearance of the flesh. Because God has expressed himself in this way—hiding his truth within a physical husk—man, in imitating God, as God's creature, expresses God's inner truth through an instrument outwardly clothed as the created order is clothed, inwardly ordered as the created is ordered. The inner structure and the outer shape are given through the power of the ideas in the mind of God.

Just as God's power inhabits the universe—we might say the universe is an expression of his power—and therefore exhibits itself in beautiful relationships, so this power can come, by God's deputies, to inhabit words and images. The best example is to be found in the Bible, the word of God, for once we *see through* to the inner truth, we no longer can simply stare, but must always interpret. In like manner, the artist creates a transparent sensory thing through which the order of beauty, an imitation of divine beauty, is discovered. With this the theory of imitation inherited from Plato is transformed, for what man makes does not imitate directly, but only indirectly, as a kind of analogy. No longer is art a mirror held up to nature, but a sensory key given the mind which it uses to open the deep mystery of divine order. An outer imitation therefore exists only for a possible inner imitation: an order of the senses becomes meaningful only when transformed through thought into an order of the intelligible.

This suggests that there is in Augustine's philosophy another sense of imitation: the artistic imitates the prototypical, the most masterly art object, that is, the life of Christ. This offers to human making a tested order of imitation, for the avenue of God's truth has already been explored in the scriptural stories, chief of which is the life to be a model for all lives. The truth is therefore found, if one has but the way to its revelation; and art is defined by its taking up this truth and re-presenting it for others to know it, though dimly and inadequately. All art, therefore, leads back to scripture.

Augustine has opened the way for a thoroughly iconographical art, an art of intentional allegory. But this does not mean he advocates an art whose formal and stylistic aspects are dead and repetitive; quite the contrary. It is in formal relationships themselves that the highest, most abstract, and most nearly godlike relationships are revealed. This is the theory of Beauty, no less difficult for Augustine than for us, which he proposes. Beauty is realized in that which we can best refer to by the term "number" (*numerus*). Grasping the nature of number is the work of intellect, mysterious in its origin and in its power. Let us be content to see it as a sense of rightness in the order of things made, a sense which grows and deepens through prolonged contemplation of God's work.

This doctrine, that it is through the grasp of the nature of number that man realizes the spiritual content of art, is sufficiently vague to be encouraging to artistic experimentation, as it proposes a position which would defend the uses of art in the Church. But Augustine is ambivalent about the power of art, offering consolation to both the iconodule and the iconoclast. His intellectual formulation, though, is clear.

Out of several pieces of material hitherto lying around in scattered fashion and then assembled into one design, I can make a house. If indeed I am the maker and it is made, then

I am the more excellent; and the more excellent precisely because I am the maker. There is no doubt but that I am on that account more excellent than a house. But not on that account am I more excellent than a swallow or a small bee; for skilfully does the one build nests, and the other construct honeycombs. I am, however, more excellent than they, because I am a rational creature.

Now if reason is found in calculated measurements, does it follow that the work of birds is not accurately and aptly measured? Nay, it is most accurately and aptly proportioned. Therefore, it is not by making well-measured things, but by grasping the nature of numbers, that I am the more excellent. What then? Have the birds been able to build carefully constructed nests without knowing it? Assuredly, they have. How is this shown? By the fact that we, too, accommodate the tongue to the teeth and palate by fixed measurements, so that letters and words rush forth from the mouth; and when we are speaking, we are not thinking of the oral movement by which we ought to do that. Moreover, what good singer, even though he be unskilled in the art of music, would not, by that same natural sense, keep in his singing both the rhythm and the melody known by memory? And what can become more subject to measure than this? The uninstructed man has no knowledge of it. Nevertheless, he does it by nature's doing. But why is man superior to brute animals, and why is he ranked above them? Because he understands what he does. Nothing else ranks me above the brute animal except the fact that I am a rational animal.[7]

·I think it fair to say that though Augustine moved often toward iconoclasm, he bestowed upon his successors, and the Christian artistic tradition in particular, a

[7] Augustine, *De Ordine*, trans. Robert F. Russell (New York: Cosmopolitan Science and Art Service Co.), Ch. 19, par. 49.

liberating doctrine, though it came, eventually, to perversions for which it is still blamed. I think we ought to recognize its contribution to the enlargement of artistic possibilities, to the new possibilities it gives for symbolic subtleties, and the joy it takes in the truly aesthetic side of art.

Of course, Augustine's allegorical emphasis was not new, not a discovery, since art had always been allegorical, given the natural human propensity to the creation of symbols. But it did make conscious a technique and an artistic goal, and it encouraged artists, as well as beholders, to grow more subtle in their apprehensions and their exploitations of traditional material. Art grew in what it might attempt and in what might be seen in it. The art of the whole pagan world was thus enlarged, put into a new perspective from which it suffered but from which it also drew new life; a new way, lifting the pagan inheritance to the purgatorial renovation of Christian exegesis. Philosophy can claim to have made a difference here, working in the world on behalf of what was thought to be otherworldly.

Augustine's interpretive method explained the possibility of linguistic complexity, its exploitation and its power to open up awareness. But his theory of literary truth appears inadequate when the object of literary art is human action, since for Augustine action opened up the truth only when it took as its model the actions of a single, paradigmatic life, that of Christ. How different the dramatic situation in its concern for human depravity and its addiction to the perverse! The truth of drama can be a reasonable claim only when the drama imitates something essentially nondramatic, at least nondramatic from

34

the classical point of view. Augustine's answer, therefore, to the question, in what sense can drama make a claim to truth is this: insofar as it is not drama.

It is at once a cruel and fortunate fate suffered by imitation theories of literary art, for Augustine's rethinking of the relationship between art and reality introduced two changes: first, a change from Aristotelian naturalism to neo-Platonic realism; and second, a suggestive theory on how the medium of literary art itself can be a symbol. The unfortunate loss of the sensible side of the *Poetics* was compensated for by a new and powerful enlargement of literary formalism. Augustine, steeped as he was in the rhetorical tradition, could not reject the literary as such; sensitive to art in all its forms, he was driven by his remarkable intellect to find defensible values in those most exalted products of human ingenuity. If literary art could not compete with scripture on the level of moral and spiritual truth, it could on the level of structural sufficiency to God's creation. Since literary art cannot be true unless it is scripture, as scripture it ceases to be literary. Yet literary art exhibits a set of formal properties which can be evidence of the truth in the sense of God's truth of creation. This shifts "truth" from moral and ontological content to structural orders in the language. Thus, although literary art cannot be said to be true in the Aristotelian sense, it can be said to be true in an enlarged sense of "metaphor." Literary art, like music—the best exemplar —and like painting and sculpture, bodies forth the order, structure, and therefore the beauty of God's mind. As a beautiful artifact it comes to be a symbol of divine potency and God's created order. Human art can be understood as a structural counterpart to the truths of scrip-

D

ture. In their art, human beings realize God's order and power insofar as art can be a symbol for finite awareness. But the possibilities of a structural theory of truth is not fully developed until considerably later, and I shall turn to the recent interest in that side of truth in literary art in the last chapter.

IV

The question I have been asking, "In what sense can we say that the assertions of tragic drama are true?" has so far been answered by applications of theory which shift the values of literary art from aesthetic to moral or religious. In doing this they answer the question by offering sentences about literary art; they have value for us because they show us how literary art can be part of a larger philosophical undertaking. They allow us to formulate many orders of true sentences about literary art which follow as deductive consequences from the theories, but they still leave us with the sentences of the literary work itself. The question, therefore, needs to be reformulated for the next step in this inquiry: "Is there any sense in which the literary work, considered as total performance, itself produces sentences that are true?"

In this form the question brings us closer to our interest in the value of literary art, by shifting from the moral and the ontological to the aesthetic as the most important value of literary performance. I have argued that Augustine, in his eagerness to reject the Aristotelian possibility of tragic drama being true, suggested a position of literary formalism which sought the value of literary art in the structure of the work insofar as that structure exhibited beauty. In the next chapter I shall refer to Nietzsche as a philosopher who took most seriously this possibility for the aestheticizing of art and enlarged it into a total ontology by insisting that aesthetic values are the only ultimate values. However, in saying this he was simply making explicit a theory of literary value anticipated by Augustine and further explored in the eighteenth century.

In asking about the truth values of the sentences making up literary works, I shall limit the discussion to dramatic literature. A dramatic work is read or acted from a set of sentences which constitute the text. One of the performers' tasks is to discover truths of the text in the sense of what the text means, and truly means. Since meaning of the text depends upon the whole, unity is sought in the voice of the work as if it were an utterance from a central consciousness. When the text "sounds" and only then do we, the audience, derive satisfaction from the performance. Our understanding apprehends an adequate instance of the text. An adequate instance possesses, among other things, a specific and determined sense of what the utterer of the drama means. I shall refer to this sense of adequacy in one's experience of a text as a nonmediated understanding of what it means to say that a dramatic work is true. The truth of the work in this sense is not found in reference to an external reality to which all literature may be believed to aspire; rather, the truth of the work is found in saying what the work says. This sense of the truth of the work I call the nonmediated sense because the evidence for truth, the test to which the work must be put, is in the organization of the medium in the work. This sense of truth is distinct from the truth of theoretical interpretations of the sort I have examined above; I shall call this the "truth of literary immediacy."

Truth of literary immediacy refers to the meanings to be found in the text without invoking theories of a nonliterary kind. When we talk about the meaning of a literary text as such, and ask if there is any sense in saying truths can be found in literary art, we need to know what kinds of events are presented in a literary work. Where the text is a drama, Aristotle was correct in pointing out that the most important event is human action, that is, human choice, and choice introduces moral values, for one chooses between the better and the worse. But we all know that a dramatic treatment of moral choice is quite different from a philosophical treatment, so that in saying one central event in drama is moral choice, we ought not to assume it will be treated as a subject of philosophical argument. Rather, it is conveyed by means of characters who speak and act. It is in this relationship between thinking and doing, between language and action, that the drama comes into our awareness as something possibly true.

Theories of literary immediacy are concerned to show the relationship between a language as a whole and the particular selection from the whole for the purposes of the individual text. The individual text then is a set of sentences whose semantic and syntactic relationships can be systematically explored. We come to understand the sentences of a literary text as meaningful within the semantic and syntactic relationships defined by the language and by the selection made for purposes of the individual dramatic work. We recognize the sentences as "true" in a special sense which is contextually determined, as distinct from a theoretical sense of "true" which follows from the interpretation of the text by means of large-scale theories. When we want to know if the sentences of a text can be true, we hope they can be understood to be true without requiring that there be a reality outside the text to which reference must be made to determine truth.

One way we do this is by establishing the well-formed expressions in a text, that is those sentences whose terms and syntactic relationships are consistently meaningful throughout the text as a whole. Just what the well-formed expressions in a given text may be is one of the fundamental problems for criticism, and opinions differ at any one time and at different historical moments. But the rules of sense in terms of which well-formed expressions are established and recognized remain fairly well fixed over long periods of time. In contrast to the sentences established by the rules of sense discovered for a text, there are those sentences which are rule-violating expressions, and they may be given prominence where literary force is needed. The kind of literary text—tragic or comic drama, novel, lyric or epic poem, and so on—helps us to recognize the central sentences, both those admitted as well-formed expressions, and those admitted as rule-violating.

Confronted with a text, such as *King Lear,* we respond to particular actions and thoughts. A term such as "bequeathing" carries a much more complicated set of sentential and action implications in *King Lear* than it does in, say, *Bleak House.* In both, "begetting" and "bequeathing" are functions of one another, and in both, these terms contribute to larger well-formed expressions. In the text of *King Lear* "bequeathing" is found to be meaningful in the context of what Lear says and does, that is, bequeathing a kingdom to daughters, on behalf of peace and in the hope of political marriage, and in the expectation of being cared for by his favorite child in his old age. As we consider all these conditions under which bequeathing takes place, we come to see more and more in the expressions which at first appeared to be of background importance only. Certain terms, sentences, and actions may then leap into prominence, and the implications of these sentences and actions become real for us, as the theorems of a deductive system of sentences become meaningful as we perform proofs.

An example of emergence from background into prominence occurs in the case of a sentence uttered by Edgar when he feigns madness. After a certain chattering of demonological lore he says, "Frateretto calls me, and tells me Nero is an angler in the Lake of Darkness. Pray, innocent, and beware the foul fiend" (*King Lear*, III, 6, 6–8). Nero had become a model of ingratitude, since, according to Suetonius, he was said to have devised cruel designs to kill his mother. Like Lear's daughters, he destroyed the source of his life; like the children in Lear's fantasy world, he dwelt in the darkness of sexual depravity and lust. Like Lear, Nero "plumbed" the depths of the waters where he hoped to catch fish with devices of intricate design. Lear, like Nero, was driven by an urgency to pull out what was in the depths. In this context, reflecting on the thoughts and actions of Lear, the seemingly mad remark of Edgar reveals currents in the drama to which we may have been responding all along. By suddenly bringing out the name "Nero" and describing him as "an angler in the Lake of Darkness" the text makes us see something, like catching a movement out of the corner of the eye, or touching a cold current beneath warm water. In hearing the sentence uttered by Edgar we experience the presence of something previously hidden, now breaking through the text and through our consciousness. And so too, the character of Edgar breaks out upon Lear, revealing himself in all his fantastic garb, as the sentence breaks out of the language, forcing itself upon us.

The sentence uttered by Edgar cannot be considered alone, but in the context of the whole drama and its relevant environment. The reference to Nero directs us to think about the political and private conflict out of which Lear's trial develops, for the opening of the drama shows us a person beset by opposed and irreconcilable needs. On the one side is kingship, its obligations, restrictions, problems, subjection to frailty, time, and family inheritance; and on the other, family affection, sexual demands, the moral obligation of persons united by blood. The conflict of affection and political obligation is displayed in the opening scene, for from the first sentences it is clear that Gloucester and Albany know the kingdom has already been divided by Lear, with the larger third going to Cordelia, and equal parts to Goneril and Regan. The reason for this, we see as the action develops, is preservation of a peaceful kingdom. Cordelia with her large share geographically between the two other shares, with her father in residence with his hundred knights (a considerable military adjunct) shall be placed above her sisters in power, and they subjected to her and her father in vassalage. Therefore, the profession of love demanded by Lear has a clear political motive: to record publicly oaths of filial obedience and allegiance before the distribution of land takes place. Lear's darker purpose is feudal canniness; but, perhaps unknown to him, it also responds to private urgencies.

Lear struggles to overcome two crippling restrictions: that which comes from the need for political unity and peace where only daughters inherit; that which comes from a father's love where the only object is his own child. Lear's anger is therefore a realistic response to the destruction of his political and private plans. Were he to keep politics uppermost, he would never have allowed the two "loving" daughters to "digest" Cordelia's larger share, since then two equal forces eager to conquer one another hold the kingdom. Were he truly convinced of Cordelia's falling away, he would have made one of the supposed true daughters vassal to the other. He is rendered politically ineffectual by his keen disappointment in Cordelia, and losing self-control, he proposes the absurd plan of living alternately with one and the other daughter, thinking that the presence of his hundred knights can keep the power where he resides.

The old man's destructive disappointment goes further: he tries to spoil Cordelia's marriage by advertising her poverty; how could a king want "this little seeming substance"? Against Lear's scheme France takes Cordelia, and with that the aged king's hopes are nothing.

After this initial revelation of Lear's private and public struggle, his private world is further revealed as he moves toward madness, and in sentences such as "Nero is an angler in the Lake of Darkness" we become aware of a hiddenness in Lear's nature. This aberrant sentence draws our attention to a deeper object of the protagonist's awareness, and we discover, through a structural deviation, a substance into whose presence we are led by the unexpected utterance. In our first encounter with this sentence we recognize a violation of the linguistic expectations the text has established, and we suspect a purposeful enlargement of the rules for well-formed expressions established by the text up to that point. Introducing this sentence is like introducing a theorem in a logical system and asking for a proof. If we can work the proof, we establish the validity of the sentence, and in that sense we are able to introduce the concept of truth as a property of the text. As a system of well-formed expressions according to rules of sense the text can be understood, can be said "to make sense," can be seen as exhibiting rightness in every part and to that extent to be "true," that is, valid. We are justified in according validity to a literary work provided we can show that the sentences making up the text are interpretable by the rules of sense for well-formed expressions. Since there are complicated criteria in terms of which validity is accorded or withheld from a literary text, the term "truth" may seem misleading, but I think it the most satisfactory term we have if we recognize that traditionally truth as validity names a property of related sentences, and that in the case of a text we use it to refer to the perceived and experienced rightness we have of the text. In saying a work of literary art is "true" in the sense of valid, we establish a property of the sentences of the text. This is distinct from sentences about the text which are formulated by theories of art. The sense of truth I want to establish may be called the truth of literary immediacy, and it is most important to literary art as a structured object creating through its powers specific kinds of experiences.[8] Later, in Chapter 3, I shall discuss literary validity in terms of synaesthesia.

V

I have tried to answer the question, "In what sense can we say a work of literary art, particularly dramatic art, is true?" At one time dramatic art was opposed to other modes of discovering and publishing the truth, but this is no longer the case because the social function of art is so changed. Yet we persist in according literary art the value truth. I have suggested the ways we may meaningfully do this, but there is yet one sense of "truth" relevant to literary works that has not been mentioned. For the artist, and for a considerable sector of his audience, the literary creates an aesthetic reality within which questions of truth, untruth, reality, illusion, beauty, and ugliness can be raised. Literary art can be taken as part of a totality within which human awareness may find all that is needed to constitute a world. Hence distinctions we apply to everyday experience can be properly applied to that world; such distinctions as illusion, reality, dream, imagination, make-believe, the real, the commonplace, the exotic, the sublime, and so on. So considered, the aes-

[8] The discussion in section IV is dependent upon several arguments by Albert Hofstadter. See his *Truth and Art* (New York: Columbia University Press, 1965).

thetic reality offers itself to endless exploration. Every literary work contributes to that seeking and finding, every performance adds to the definition of that reality. Reiteration defends this reality against the claims and encroachments of other realities, such as the scientific and the philosophic. One aspect of the aesthetic reality is its need to be sustained by repetition. Indeed, art is born out of a compulsion to repeat; to the artist, once done is ill done. The overwhelming sense of the artistic is that no individual work exhausts the aesthetic reality. Each work is a fragment of an infinite totality; and so considered, each work discloses at best *a* truth, a truth about reality, not *the* truth of art. Every work suggests the possibility of further exploration. As a recent writer, Borges, has said, any work of art is a groping within a reality we believe might be revealed, but which in fact never is. That sense of many artistic truths is the one I want to explore in this book.

Classical thought about literary art rightly seized upon the fact that the clarification of aesthetic reality occurs for us through performance. Yet that insight was part of a larger theory that placed art in an imitative relationship to natural events. This seems inadequate to us because it presupposes an antecedent reality from which the art work draws its value as something true. Our interest in truth as the truth of literary immediacy has led us to seek structural solutions to these problems, and we have been helped to clarify these problems by theories, especially prominent in the nineteenth century, which stressed the expressive nature of art. Expression theories opened up the possibility that the art work itself is part of the aesthetic reality and need not derive its value from a distinct

45

and separate natural reality. This development, which derives much force from the art theories of the preceding century, changes the way we think about art, and I shall take up this revolution in the next two chapters.

Under the possibilities opened up to us by expression theories we have come to think of performance not as an imitation of an antecedent reality, but rather as a revelation of the self in the sense of an objectified person. We respond to the aesthetic reality as to a performance of one whose presence is realized and recognized by his style in the performance. The aesthetic reality is known as personification.

The recognition of style as a personification is especially relevant to the experience created by literary art since the structure of the text creates a structured experience in which we apprehend the presence of a person but a person externalized as object. For this reason, the object appears invested with human concern of a particular sort to which I shall give the name "care." Since I shall return to this concept later, I simply want to point out here that literary performance reveals to us an aspect of care which has to do with the manifestation of the person in language. So we say the artist, in creating literary art, "expresses himself," but what we mean is, the self is expressed in a linguistic object. And the object exhibits a self caring for the medium shaped into an object with a specific style. In this presentation we become aware of the self established permanently in a styled presence which opens up to the beholder some small part of the aesthetic reality.

But care, as an intention of the aesthetic reality, is not fully realized in one act, one performance, one work. The literary artist realizes his concern by creating an *oeuvre*, and that in turn is but a contribution to a larger literary reality. This reality is not established by one instance any more than a moral character is established by one act. All the instances, and all the possible instances to come, suggest the possibility of an aesthetic reality in which we may have our being. In contributing to this reality, literary art helps us to know it, and in that sense we can say a particular exploration of it is "true." This sense of truth is not that of sentences about art, nor is it the truth of literary immediacy, but rather "truth" as a setting before ourselves of a part of reality. Here is where the image of God as artist comes from; a simple reversal of the realization all human lives have that the artist is a god, and art the only created reality. Once we see this interchangeability, we are able philosophically to examine the possibility that forms of art define the structure of human experience.

Chapter 2

Forms of Art as Possibilities of Experience

I

Plato, Aristotle, and Augustine all assumed that truth is a possible value of literary art, although each took an original stand on whether or not literary art realized truth in fact. They shared a belief in the imitative origins and functions of literary art, that literature re-presented events in the world, and that literature derived its validity from truthful writings such as philosophy and scripture. Yet the aesthetic values of literary art were appreciated by traditional theory which established an easy distinction between the content of literature and its embellishment, essentially a rhetorical conception since literary art was considered to be strengthened if it possessed powers of persuasion sufficient to compel assent. Ornamentation then was in part the servant of truth, in part the instrument of conquest, but in neither case was it the center of artistic value.

The case is quite different today. While we have rejected the rhetorical distinction between content and ornamentation, we have accepted, often without sufficient

48

skepticism, the shift of literary values from the valid to the aesthetic. We define modernity by defending aesthetic values as ultimate and artistically more important than the logical and moral values attributed to literature in the past. Discomfort at the removal of literature from traditional values has been the cause of much recent debate over literary values especially on the part of young scholars and teachers who see "the establishment" using literature as an aesthetic screen to hide both the genuine content of serious literature and its relevance to the problems of a disturbed society. But the interest in aesthetic values has itself a rooting in the past, and in this chapter I shall explore one aspect of the thesis that insofar as literary art is concerned, "modern" refers to a condition in which action moralized is gradually eroded and replaced by action aestheticized; action as a demonstration of responsibility is replaced by action as performance. In this replacement, moral criteria of judgment are subordinated to aesthetic criteria of judgment. So considered, the modern is not a state entered into as if one crossed a boundary into a new country; rather, it refers to an evolving set of beliefs, attitudes, assumptions which determine the shape and content of literary art.

One consequence of this change is the way we think about the past and about the future, for to think of human actions as morally determined and as morally meaningful points action toward the future; outcomes matter, and the present is incomplete without the future. The future we await is believed to be determined in its qualities by the actions responsible for it. The disruptions we suffer because of this shift is the subject of a later chapter, in which I consider Lampedusa's *Leopard*.

Actions aesthetically considered are valued not for their towardness but for their structure in the present, their contribution toward a whole to be grasped by one given. This totality, whose validity is determined by the relationship of its parts, is structured so that a coherent, interesting, and pleasing affect is induced. Its rightness is determined by qualities of feeling rather than by calculations of future events, or by rational arguments of either a deductive or an inductive sort.

The difficult task of stating how human actions are to be appraised both morally and aesthetically was undertaken by David Hume. He argued that events, logically considered, cannot be said to be determined by necessary relationships. He concluded that morality, as part of the life of feeling, and its underlying passionate base that was responsible for judgments of taste as well as judgments of morals, could be understood only if we possessed a clear understanding of causal relationships, that is, sequences of events in relation to one another in time and space. Since both the sciences and the moral life depend upon concepts of causation, clarity about them would inevitably help us gain insight into our actions and the explanations we give for natural phenomena. The analysis of causation Hume offered is in fact a step toward the subordination of the moral to the aesthetic, since from a strictly rational analysis of event and event relations, any event might be joined to any other. Logically there can be no necessary relations in the natural world. "Reason is and always ought to be the slave of the passions" is simply Hume's paradoxical way of giving a psychological interpretation to an epistemological principle. In moral actions as well as in the behavior of billiard balls, no consequent can be said to follow with necessity from a prior event;

and therefore man as acting animal is determined by feeling and habit. These are indeed the "cement" of our lives, but a cement whose source is sensibility, not divine fiat or reason.

Similar and more powerfully aesthetic interpretations of actions and events are provided by a later philosopher, and one whose similarity to Hume is much closer than is usually recognized. It is Nietzsche who can be said to make fully conscious the modern attitude to which I refer and for which Hume provided the initial analysis. Nietzsche makes the final transforming step which turns all actions into performances. In his late introduction to *The Birth of Tragedy* he asserts: "Nur als ästhetisches Phänomen das Dasein der Welt *gerechtfertigt* ist" (Now existence could be justified only in aesthetic terms). He goes on:

I attributed a purely aesthetic meaning—whether implied or overt—to all process: a kind of divinity, if you like, God as the supreme artist, amoral, recklessly creating and destroying, realizing himself indifferently in whatever he does or undoes, ridding himself by his acts of the embarrassment of his riches and the strain of his internal contradictions. Thus the world was made to appear, at every instant, as a successful *solution* of God's own tensions, as an ever new vision projected by that grand sufferer for whom illusion is the only possible mode of redemption. That whole aesthetic metaphysics might be rejected out of hand as so much prattle or rant. Yet in its essential traits it already prefigured that spirit of deep distrust and defiance which, later on, was to resist to the bitter end any moral interpretation of existence whatsoever.[1]

[1] "A Critical Backward Glance," from Nietzsche's autobiography written in 1886. From *The Birth of Tragedy* and *The Genealogy of Morals*, trans. Francis Golffing (New York: Doubleday Anchor, 1956), pp. 9–10.

E

"Illusion is the only possible mode of redemption" might stand as the maxim for the shift in concern that Nietzsche defends; it sums up the transformation which blurs distinctions between life and art, and it offers a definition of "modernity." Easy as this is to say, the difficulty comes in trying to make clear what this change amounts to, and in order to give form to these thoughts we must consult specific cultural attitudes and acts in regard to performances.

II

The vision of reality as aesthetic phenomenon which begins to take shape in Hume's analysis of causation, and concludes in Nietzsche's self-conscious interpretation of all reality as a mode of illusion, has its counterpart in the art of the eighteenth century. Indeed, every important move in an effort to clarify the nature of experience has both philosophical and literary counterparts. Forms of art and thought directed to the analysis of the possibilities of art reinforce one another. Art forms themselves are instances of aesthetic experience in the sense that they are demonstrations of possible experience realized through a set of artistic conditions. Those artistic conditions— conditions which make aesthetic experience possible—are explicitly thought about in the philosophies of art which constitute the speculative and critical practice of the time. This close interdependence of art forms and art theories is especially evident to us because we have lived through the period of manifestoes, a period in which both artists and critics talked about what art ought to be, and what kind of experience it seeks to establish. We have come to expect art theory to accompany art.

This same explanatory-exhibitive relationship existed in other times as well, but we are less aware of the mutual reinforcement art and philosophy offered one another on other occasions because, first, we are not close to the time and tend to separate in scholarship what was close together in the past; and, second, because we assume the ancient enmity of poetry and philosophy of which Plato spoke. But separations are artificial; in fact the forms of art and the explanations of what makes aesthetic experience possible are—in the past as in the present—functions of one another.

I shall show one such interrelationship in the eighteenth century, the period when there was renewed and vigorous talk about art, and when there were new directions in the making of art that at once illustrated and confirmed art theory. The examples I shall take are defined philosophically by accounts of experience offered in the thought of Hume and Kant, and artistically by Sterne's *Sentimental Journey* and Goethe's *Sorrows of Young Werther*.

The philosophical question put by Kant defines the quest of epistemology: "How is experience possible?" Kant argued that the answer is to be found in an analytical examination which breaks down the various aspects of experience into the theoretical, practical, aesthetic, teleological, and so on, to the end of finding a common structure pervading all varieties of experience, and defining the judgments peculiar to each. In these terms, the three philosophical *Critiques* might be seen as efforts to explain the conditions for the application of classes of predicates: (1) The first *Critique* (*The Critique of Pure Reason*) addressed the problem, how is it possible meaningfully to apply the predicates ". . . is the cause of . . . ," is earlier than, later than . . . etc.," and the problem, *is* it possible to apply meaningfully predicates such as ". . . is eternal . . . ," ". . . has a beginning in time . . . ," ". . . is omnipotent . . . ," and so on. (2) The second *Critique* (*The Critique of Practical Reason*) addressed the problem, how can we meaningfully use predicates of a moral kind, ". . . is right . . . ," ". . . is wrong . . . ," ". . . is a duty . . . ," ". . . is an obligation . . . ," with a second assault on the use of puzzling metaphysical predicates discussed in the first *Critique*, that is, ". . . is eternal . . . ," ". . . is omnipotent . . . ," ". . . is ultimately just . . . ," and so on. (3) The third *Critique* (*The Critique of Judgment*) is an effort to answer the question, how can we meaningfully use predicates such as ". . . is beautiful . . . ," ". . . is sublime . . . ," ". . . is purposeful . . . ," and the like, these constituting the class of aesthetic and teleological predicates.

In each of the above cases a class of predicates is defined as meaningful in terms of a set of conditions: (1) an analysis of experience in which an a priori part is distinguished from a given or substantive part; (2) metaphysical predicates are shown to be meaningless in terms of the distinction drawn in (1); (3) a defense of meaning elaborated for those matters that are ultimate for human beings, that is, the unconditioned strivings of human reason, through the introduction of a special class of mental contents, the so-called ideas of reason. These contents of awareness are too large for classification and identification in the usual conceptual manner because they escape forms of intuition and categories of the understanding. In this way Kant at the same time put limits on meaningful experience understood as conceptual and extended the boundaries of possible human experience by suggesting that there are longings of reason to which we must grant some kind of validity. This analysis has its point for aesthetic experience.

Kant never thought, as some later philosophers have, that aesthetic experience might be the way to give an account of experience in general; and he certainly was dissatisfied with an effort to account for aesthetic experience as merely a case to be subsumed under a general theory. He recognized that every kind of predicate raised special problems of meaning, so that his attempt to found a unified theory of experience never was realized, even though he "pretended" it was by creating architectonic parallels in all three *Critiques*. In contrast, Hume was able to formulate a unified theory, even though we see that his analysis of aesthetic judgments is impoverished. The difference, I suppose, is that between Scots economy and German metaphysical complexity; the first achieves its frugality through discounting, and the second its plumpness through compounding. And though the monetary metaphor is not intended to be profound, it may explain a good deal.

Before drawing the implications of these theories, we ought to note why the question, "How is experience possible?" was particularly apt in the eighteenth century. To be sure, it is *the* philosophical question; it has its statements and restatements throughout the history of philosophy. At times it takes on peculiar point, as it does in Enlightenment theories of experience, because the question is raised as a defense against solipsism. The question as we examine it is asked because the fact *that* experience occurs at all seems odd given the conclusions about the world which natural philosophy had come to. These are, roughly, the conclusions of Newtonian physics. If the mechanical world of natural philosophy is correctly depicted, then the qualities of human experience seem alien to and disconnected from that world, so that the question "How is experience possible?" is a seeking after unity and coherence, in this context. Obviously this is a different question from the one Plato asks in the *Theaetetus*, although he too is inquiring into the foundations of experience. But Plato is not puzzled *that* it is at all possible; he is puzzled because we cannot readily explain what seems so obvious. In short, the question "How is experience possible?" can be asked with the implication, "Is it possible?" and with the implication, *"What* makes it possible?" Hume and Kant are asking both questions, but the need to answer at all comes from the pressure of the first question, "Is it possible?"

It is relevant to this discussion now to speculate on the presentation of literary art works: is there, we ought ask, any stylistic evidence or evidence in the content to suggest that works of literary art can be created with these two different questions in mind, such that the question about experience underlying the creation of the work is somehow part of the work? This is a difficult question, and I am not sure what would count as a satisfactory answer, either affirmative or negative, but I shall consider it in an exploratory way, concentrating on the question in the eighteenth-century sense. I shall argue that at least in a crude sense the concerns of philosophical epistemology do appear in literary art; the philosopher makes the problems explicit, while the novelist or poet may assume them, or may reveal indirectly that the same problems interest him.

In making these comparisons I do not intend to explore the causal impact of literature on philosophy or of philosophy on literature as one might were he writing what we today call a "history of ideas." Philosophy and literature, I believe, influence one another in subtle ways difficult to document; but they do concern themselves with similar problems, and there are historical moments when their ways of structuring experience are alike. The discussion in this chapter points out the similarities in conceptions of experience on the part of eighteenth-century philosophers and writers whose works appeared about the same time. Hume's *A Treatise of Human Nature* appeared in 1739; the little review he wrote, "An Abstract of a Treatise of Human Nature," in 1740. Sterne's *A Sentimental Journey Through France and Italy* was published in 1768. Kant's *Critique of Pure Reason* was written during 1769–1780, and appeared in its first edition in 1781. *The Critique of Judgment* was published in 1790. Goethe's *The Sorrows of Young Werther* appeared in 1774.

I propose to begin with the distinction Hume makes between the limitations of the human understanding and the vast extent of the passions—the difference he asserts when he writes, "Reason is and ever ought to be the slave of the passions." This is Hume's "skeptical philosophy," a shocking assault on our assumptions about the power of

57

human intelligence, for the purpose of skepticism, in Hume's view, is to demonstrate the imperfections and narrow limits of human understanding so that we become open to the coordinate view that experience is possible because of our rich endowment of sentiment and feeling. As reason is impoverished, so the passionate side is swelled, not to a radical skepticism, ultimately, but rather to a sentimental naturalism. Passions, Hume insists, "are the only ties of our thoughts, they are really *to us* the cement of the universe, and all the operations of the mind must, in a great manner, depend on them." [2] Hume, who surprisingly relates his views through a rich metaphorical language, seriously intends the Newtonian implication: as gravity is the cement of the Newtonian mechanical order, so sentiment ties together the elements of human experience. The world—*my* world—*the* human world, and the experience through which the human world takes shape, is not structured by reason, if by reason we mean the power to establish relationships of logical entailment.

Hume has given an account of how experience is possible by arguing that we misunderstand the potency and confinements of our various faculties. Considering this account in the literary environment to which it contributed so much leads to the recognition of similar analyses of experience in literary art. The most obvious and interesting is Laurence Sterne's *A Sentimental Journey Through France and Italy*, a treatise on the cement of sentiment, and one of the most profound analyses of human passion ever written. It puts philosophical efforts at a phenomen-

[2] All quotations are from David Hume, "An Abstract of a Treatise of Human Nature," reprinted in *An Inquiry Concerning the Human Understanding* (New York: The Liberal Arts Press, 1955), pp. 183–198.

ology of feeling to shame; but out interest in it is as a literary work which exhibits in its very form and content a universe structured as Hume's account says it must be structured.

Since my interest is to show that works of literary art may on occasion be understood as realizing possibilities of experience, explanatory accounts of which are offered by philosophy, I shall consider *A Sentimental Journey* in terms of its structure. Just as Hume argues that according to reason any order of events is possible, since there is no logical necessity in experience, so Sterne makes clear that in his work the order of events is structured by the unpredictability and waywardness of feeling. For there is no necessity, no inevitability, no absolute objective order of events demonstrable. This natural chaos is shown by a simple emblematic surprise: the Preface follows six short chapterlike statements on a variety of scenes. The order of events in the book—both in a gross structural sense and in a refined affective sense—is determined by the cement of sentiment; the world opening to us is one in which actions and sentences bend to the pressures of feeling. The order of chapters, of actions, of encounters, could have been quite other than it is, and this is signaled to the reader by orthographic originality, dashes being the common punctuation mark. A mélange of statements, not a coercive order of events, makes up the text.

It is amusing to speculate on whether or not Hume might have written philosophy in this way; indeed, one of the perplexing things about philosophy is its need to be logical, orderly, and set in a pattern of exposition, even when it describes a world so ordered that any other order would be possible. Does philosophy, as a written text, contradict itself, at least in a case such as this, where life, it is argued, is a sentimental journey? It seems that a philosopher, by the nature of his work, could never write, much less undertake to experience, a sentimental journey. But this is like the philosophical bravado of Plato, who believed philosophers to be the best tragedians. To be sure, a philosopher might write a tragedy of suffering—many have—but no philosopher yet has, or could, write a tragedy of reversal and recognition. The point of this aside is that the philosophical itinerary must be differently ordered from the novelistic; so Hume could never write philosophy as Sterne wrote novels, even though the world Sterne gives us is a world as Hume imagines it to be from his analysis of the limitations of the understanding and the powerful cementing force of the passions.

Beyond the chapter order and the orthography, both structural aspects in the most obvious sense, there is a special quality to the events in their juxtaposition. Anything can follow anything, to be sure, as a theoretical matter, but in the reality of the life of feeling connections are made as affect is aroused. The specific following of events is structured by the association of ideas, these adhering to one another because of negative and positive charges of feeling they accumulate as the actor moves along. This principle in terms of which ideas adhere to one another is typically Humean in design. One good example of this association can be seen in the relation of the two volumes of *A Sentimental Journey* to one another. The connection occurs through the transition from a scene in a theater to a scene in a bookseller's shop. The association that holds these different places together is the sentiment of love—or, as we would say, sex. The thoughts of the storyteller are preoccupied with the sex-

ual feelings aroused by the Parisian women, the oppor-
tunities for affairs in a foreign land, and the obvious re-
laxed attitude of Frenchwomen toward sex in comparison
with the more puritanical inhibitions of the English. Even
the French gentlemen in religious orders are caught
making indecent advances to girls in the theater, and this
arouses in our ministerial traveler the possibility and al-
lowability of his own advances toward strange young
women. He is further freed by the ease with which Madame de Rambouliet tells him of her need to piss, and
then he imagines himself as a priest serving at the "fountain" of the nymphs. I suggest a close look at the text to
see the pattern of associations.

. . . I honestly confess, that many a thing gave me pain, and
that I blushed at many a word the first month—which I
found inconsequent and perfectly innocent the second.

Madame de Rambouliet, after an acquaintance of about six
weeks with her, had done me the honour to take me in her
coach about two leagues out of town—Of all women, Madame de Rambouliet is the most correct; and I never wish to
see one of more virtues and purity of heart—In our return
back, Madame de Rambouliet desired me to pull the cord—I
asked her, if she wanted anything—*Rien que pisser*, said Madame de Rambouliet—

Grieve not, gentle traveller, to let Madame de Rambouliet
p—ss on— And ye fair mystic nymphs! go each one *pluck
your rose*, and scatter them in your path—for Madame de
Rambouliet did no more—I handed Madame de Rambouliet
out of the coach; and had I been the priest of the chaste Cas-
talia, I could not have served at her fountain with a more
respectful decorum.[3]

[3] Laurence Sterne, *A Sentimental Journey Through France and Italy*
(Baltimore: Penguin Books, 1967), pp. 84–85. All subsequent quotations
are from this edition.

61

Immediately following this, which concludes the first volume, the scene changes to a happy encounter with a young servant girl in a bookshop.

The bookseller made a bow, and was going to say something, when a young decent girl of about twenty, who by her air and dress seemed to be *fille de chambre* to some devout woman of fashion, came into the shop and asked for *Les Egarements du Cœur & de l'Esprit:* the bookseller gave her the book directly; she pulled out a little green sattin purse run round with a ribband of the same colour, and putting her finger and thumb into it, she took out the money, and paid for it. As I had nothing more to stay me in the shop, we both walked out at the door together.

—And what have you to do, my dear, said I, with *The Wanderings of the Heart,* who scarce know yet you have one? nor till love has first told you it, or some faithless shepherd has made it ache, can'st thou ever be sure it is so.—*Le Dieu m'en guard!* said the girl.—With reason, said I; for if it is a good one, 'tis pity it should be stolen; 'tis a little treasure to thee, and gives a better air to your face, than if it was dressed out with pearls.

The young girl listened with a submissive attention, holding her sattin purse by its ribband in her hand all the time—'Tis a very small one, said I, taking hold of the bottom of it—she held it towards me—and there is very little in it, my dear, said I; but be but as good as thou art handsome, and heaven will fill it. I had a parcel of crowns in my hand to pay for Shakespear; and as she had let go the purse entirely, I put a single one in; and tying up the ribband in a bow-knot, returned it to her.

The young girl made me more a humble curtsy than a low one—'twas one of those quiet, thankful sinkings, where the spirit bows itself down—the body does no more than tell it—I never gave a girl a crown in my life which gave me half the pleasure. [Pp. 89–90]

The sequence of Yorick's affections are plainly set out: from covert lust, to sexual jealousy ("—but I see innocence, my dear, in your face—and foul befal the man who ever lays a snare in its way"), to possession (" 'Tis sweet to feel by what fine-spun threads our affections are drawn together"), to paternal and ministerial relinquishing of sexual feeling for benevolent charity. The action is structured through feeling, and that indeed is the cement of the novel's universe.

The first encounter with the servant girl is followed by a rather long description of a trip to Versailles where Yorick's sexual interests are further stimulated. He spends a good bit of time thinking about the train of events leading to sexual fulfillment. What, he wonders, is the sequence of sentiments that might lead to the greatest of pleasures? How might Yorick so arrange his life that consummation be his lot? Rather than a sequence of events leading to the pleasure he seeks—as the sexual act has a compulsiveness about it that once begun it has its way to fulfillment—Yorick's life is a series of interruptions. The waywardness of sentiment seems incapable of direction toward desired goals, but wanders and responds to every stimulus. And though pleasure be the leadstring of conduct, yet sentiment allows no structuring of the sort reason demands. Yorick thinks man "cannot trust the issue of his commotions to reason only." Yorick's life is a journey whose hoped-for end is never realized. Is this human life too? A passport he has labored to obtain implies directed motion toward a goal, but even the gaining of the passport seems an impossible task. Once the passport is obtained, Yorick ought to be ready to live, that is, to move toward his constant hope, which we are not surprised to find is sexual fulfillment. No sooner has he the passport than he thinks, "But there is nothing unmixed in this world; and some of our divines have carried it so far as to affirm, that enjoyment itself, was attended even with a sigh—and that the greatest *they knew of* terminated *in a general way,* in little better than a convulsion." Then there follows an interesting aside:

I remember the grave and learned Bevoriskius, in his commentary upon the generations from Adam, very naturally breaks off in the middle of a note, to give an account to the world of a couple of sparrows upon the out-edge of his window, which had incommoded him all the time he wrote, and at last had entirely taken him off from his genealogy.

—'Tis strange! writes Bevoriskius; but the facts are certain, for I have had the curiosity to mark them down one by one with my pen—but the cock-sparrow during the little time that I could have finished the other half this note, has actually interrupted me with the reiteration of his caresses three and twenty times and a half.

How merciful, adds Bevoriskius, is heaven to his creatures!

Ill fated Yorick! that the gravest of thy brethren should be able to write that to the world, which stains thy face with crimson, to copy in even thy study.

But this is nothing to my travels—So I twice—twice beg pardon for it. [Pp. 112–113]

Yorick is condemned by his own shame to beg pardon for mentioning the sparrow's lechery, whose sexual potency is such that he can have intercourse twenty-three and one-half times in the space of a sentence, while Yorick can in the same space of time only beg pardon (twice) for his preoccupation.

Then the traveler encounters the *fille de chambre* for the second time. Again in her presence he takes up his pen. It seems that sex and writing have become closely linked; indeed they are, for as sex is the unfulfilled, so Yorick's writing in its sequential organization and style, in its grammatical and syntactical niceties, is the unfulfilled, the incomplete, the accidental, the wayward in the sense that the feelings which drive his pen are actors on a stage, coming and going. As Hume said, the mind is a theater in which ideas come and go. Yorick's awareness is such a theater, one in which public view is given to the habitual parade of feeling; his world is structured of impressions and ideas lacking altogether the drive and purpose of rational argument which he longs for both physically and linguistically. Would that he could be consummate in art and in love. Human nature will not permit it.

The purse of the *fille de chambre* calls up their previous encounter.

When I alighted at the hotel, the porter told me a young woman with a band-box had been that moment inquiring for me.—I do not know, said the porter, whether she is gone or no. I took the key of my chamber of him, and went upstairs; and when I got within ten steps of the top of the landing before my door, I met her coming easily down.

It was the fair *fille de chambre* I had walked along the Quai de Conti with: Madame de R°°°° had sent her upon some commissions to a *merchande de modes* within a step or two of the hotel de Modene; and as I had failed in waiting upon her, had bid her inquire if I had left Paris; and if so, whether I had not left a letter addressed to her.

As the fair *fille de chambre* was so near my door she turned back, and went into the room with me for a moment or two whilst I wrote a card.

It was a fine still evening, in the latter end of the month of May—the crimson window-curtains (which were of the same colour of those of the bed) were drawn close—the sun was setting, and reflected through them so warm a tint into the fair *fille de chambre*'s face—I thought she blushed—the idea of it made me blush myself—we were quite alone; and that superinduced a second blush before the first could get off.

There is a sort of a pleasing half-guilty blush, where the blood is more in fault than the man—'tis sent impetuous from the heart, and virtue flies after it—not to call it back, but to make the sensation of it more delicious to the nerves—'tis associated.—

But I'll not describe it.—I felt something at first within me which was not in strict unison with the lesson of virtue I had given her the night before—I sought five minutes for a card—I knew I had not one—I took up a pen—I laid it down again—my hand trembled—the devil was in me.

I know as well as anyone he is an adversary whom if we resist he will fly from us—but I seldom resist him at all; from a terror, that though I may conquer, I may still get a hurt in the combat—so I give up the triumph for security; and instead of thinking to make him fly, I generally fly myself.

The fair *fille de chambre* came close up to the bureau where I was looking for a card—took up first the pen I cast down, then offered to hold me the ink: she offered it so sweetly, I was going to accept it—but I durst not—I have nothing, my dear, said I, to write upon.—Write it, said she, simply, upon any thing.—

I was just going to cry out, Then I will write it, fair girl! upon thy lips.—

—If I do, said I, I shall perish—so I took her by the hand,

and led her to the door, and begged she would not forget the lesson I had given her—She said, indeed she would not—and as she uttered it with some earnestness, she turned about, and gave me both her hands, closed together, into mine—it was impossible not to compress them in that situation—I wished to let them go; and all the time I held them, I kept arguing within myself against it—and still I held them on.—In two minutes I found I had all the battle to fight over again—and I felt my legs and every limb about me tremble at the idea.

The foot of the bed was within a yard and a half of the place where we were standing—I had still hold of her hands—and how it happened I can give no account, but I neither asked her—nor drew her—nor did I think of the bed—but so it did happen, we both sat down.

I'll just shew you, said the fair *fille de chambre*, the little purse I have been making to-day to hold your crown. So she put her hand into her right pocket, which was next me, and felt for it for some time—then into the left—"She had lost it." —I never bore expectation more quietly—it was in her right pocket at last—she pulled it out; it was of green taffeta, lined with a little bit of white quilted sattin, and just big enough to hold the crown—she put it into my hand—it was pretty; and I held it ten minutes with the back of my hand resting upon her lap—looking sometimes at the purse, sometimes on one side of it.

A stitch or two had broke out in the gathers of my stock—the fair *fille de chambre*, without saying a word, took out her little hussive, threaded a small needle, and sewed it up—I foresaw it would hazard the glory of the day; and as she passed her hand in silence across and across my neck in the manœuvre, I felt the laurels shake which fancy had wreathed about my head.

A strap had given way in her walk, and the buckle of her shoe was just falling off—See, said the *fille de chambre*, hold-

F

ing up her foot—I could not for my soul but fasten the buckle in return, and putting in the strap—and lifting up the other foot with it, when I had done, to see both were right—in doing it too suddenly—it unavoidably threw the fair *fille de chambre* off her center—and then—[Pp. 115–118]

The laurel, crown of poetry, is disturbed by the girl's presence. Of course, as we would expect, in the end Yorick finds the hand of the *fille de chambre,* but accidentally, and only when he expects the hand of another woman in the bed across from him. And we never know if even at the last there was a consummation. Surely not. For experience, like art, lacks fulfillments. Rather, both life and its representations in literary art are bits held together by the waywardness of feeling. The world, insofar as it has a structure, is a sentimental structure.

III

A much more grandiose, indeed sublime effort to reveal the world as a function of passion is presented in Goethe's novel *The Sorrows of Young Werther.* The narrative structure is not the first-person, journalistic, personally impressionistic method of Sterne, but the omniscient method of the author as creator of a fictional world. Within that world the protagonist, Werther, tries to capture and come to terms with the reality of physical nature whose surface appearance he draws and paints. But his artistic efforts are everywhere frustrated, for reasons that we cannot at first discern. The denouement of the book is a revelation of why artistic frustration leads to suicide. Like Yorick, Werther suffers the pangs of frustrated sexual longing, but he has not the comfort of hand-holding and displays of affection; rather, his is an experience of metaphysical denial, for the love he seeks is a part of a reality he desperately tries to break through to and possess, but it is a reality that eludes him. He is bound in a phenomenal realm behind which he senses a noumenal reality that ought to reveal itself but never does. The denial of this ultimate revelation is connected in his beliefs and sentiments with this love-longing.

In an obvious sense, this is a novelistic presentation of a theme which has had philosophical treatment, most relevantly in Kant's critical philosophy. Werther is a "Kantian" character in the sense that his aspirations are to the unconditioned, as Kant would say, and his feelings centered on himself flow from beliefs about the nature of reality.

For Werther, and presumably for the reader of the book, coherent experience is possible only if certain conditions are realized: first, clarity of the natural order, second, fulfillment in love. The first is denied him in ordinary daily experience because of the sense Werther has of a hidden reality to which he aspires. It is revealed, momentarily, in an experience of the sublime, but that is ruinous to human aspiration because it betrays human finitude.

Must it ever be thus—that the source of our happiness must also be the fountain of our misery? The rich and ardent feeling which filled my heart with a love of Nature, overwhelmed me with a torrent of delight, and brought all paradise before me, has now become an insupportable torment—a demon which perpetually pursues me. When I used to gaze from these rocks upon the mountains across the river and upon the green valley before me, and saw everything around budding and bursting; the hills clothed from foot to peak with tall, thick trees; the valleys in all their variety, shaded with the loveliest woods; and the river gently gliding along among the whispering reeds, mirroring the clouds which the soft evening breeze wafted across the sky—when I heard the groves about me melodious with the music of birds, and saw the million swarms of insects dancing in the last golden beams of the sun, whose setting rays awoke the humming beetles from their grassy beds, while the subdued tumult around me drew my attention to the ground, and I there observed the hard rock giving nourishment to the dry moss, while the heather flourished upon the arid sands below me—all this conveyed to me the holy fire which animates all Nature, and filled and glowed within my heart. I felt myself exalted by this over-flowing fullness to the perception of the Godhead, and the glorious forms of an infinite universe stirred within my soul! Stupendous mountains encompassed me, abysses yawned at my feet, and cataracts fell headlong down before me; rivers rolled through the plains below, and rocks and mountains resounded from afar. In the depths of the earth I saw the mysterious powers at work; on its surface, and beneath the heavens there teemed ten thousand living creatures. Everything is alive with an infinite variety of forms; mankind safeguards itself in little houses and settles and rules in its own way over the wide universe. Poor fool! in whose petty estimation all things are little. From the inaccessible mountains, across the wilderness which no mortal foot has trod, far as the confines of the unknown ocean, breathes the spirit of the eternal Creator; and every speck of dust which He has made finds favor in His sight—Ah, how often at that time has the flight of a crane, soaring above my head, inspired me with the desire to be transported to the shores of the immeasurable ocean, there to quaff the pleasures of life from the foaming goblet of the Infinite, and to realize, if but for a moment with the confined powers of my soul, the bliss of that Creator Who accomplishes all things in Himself, and through Himself!

My dear friend, the mere recollection of those hours consoles me. Even the effort to recall those ineffable emotions, and give them utterance, exalts my soul above itself, and makes me feel doubly the intensity of my present anguish.

It is as if a curtain had been drawn from before my eyes, and, instead of prospects of eternal life, the abyss of an ever-open grave yawned before me. Can we say of anything that it *is* when all passes away—when time, with the speed of a storm, carries all things onward—and our transitory existence, hurried along by the torrent, is swallowed up by the waves or dashed against the rocks? There is not a moment but consumes you and yours—not a moment in which you do not yourself destroy something. The most innocent walk costs thousands of poor insects their lives; one step destroys the delicate structures of the ant and turns a little world into chaos. No; it is not the great and rare catastrophes of the world, the floods which sweep away villages, the earthquakes that swallow up our towns, that affect me. My heart is wasted by the thought of that destructive power which lies latent in every part of universal Nature. Nature has formed nothing that does not destroy itself, and everything near it. And so, surrounded by earth and air and all the active forces, I stagger on with anguished heart; the universe to me is an ever devouring, ever ruminating monster.[4]

---

[4] Goethe, *The Sorrows of Young Werther,* trans. Victor Lange (New York: Holt, Rinehart & Winston, 1949), pp. 53–55. All subsequent quotations are from this edition.

. . . Dear Wilhelm, I am reduced to the state of mind of those unfortunate creatures who believe they are pursued by an evil spirit. Sometimes I am oppressed, not by apprehension or fear, but by an inexpressible inner fury which seems to tear up my heart and choke me. Then I wander about amid the horrors of the night, at this dreadful time of year.

Yesterday evening it drove me outside. A rapid thaw had suddenly set in: I had been told that the river had risen, that the brooks had all overflowed their banks, and that the whole valley of Wahlheim was under water! I rushed out after eleven o'clock. I beheld a terrible sight. The furious torrents rolled from the mountains in the moonlight—fields, trees, and hedges were torn up, and the entire valley was one deep lake, agitated by the roaring wind! And when the moon shone forth, and tinged the black clouds, and the wild torrent at my feet foamed and resounded with awful and grand impetuosity, I was overcome by feelings of fear and delight at once. With arms extended, I looked down into the yawning abyss, and cried, "Down! Down!" For a moment I was lost in the intense delight of ending my sorrows and my sufferings by a plunge into that gulf! But then I felt as if rooted to the earth, and incapable of ending my woes! My hour is not yet come: I feel it is not. Oh, Wilhelm, how willingly would I have given up my human existence to merge with the wind, or to embrace the torrent! Will not some day this imprisoned soul be released for such bliss?

I turned with sadness toward a favorite spot beneath a willow where I used to sit with Charlotte after a long walk. It, too, was submerged and I could hardly make out the willow tree. Wilhelm! And her meadows, I thought, the country near her lodge, the arbor devastated by the floods. . . . And a ray of past happiness fell upon me, as the mind of a prisoner is cheered by a dream of flocks, and fields and bygone honors. But I stood firm!—I have the courage to die! Perhaps I should have—but here I now sit, like an old woman who gathers her own firewood and begs her bread from door to door to ease her joyless, waning life, and lengthen it by a few moments. [Pp. 111–112]

Charlotte denies Werther, as she must, for her sense of filial and marital obligation is strong. Her virtue itself prompts Werther's love for her, yet, at the same time, her sexual domination of Werther oppresses and limits him so much that he can look nowhere else. Therefore, the story exhibits murkiness of affect because of Werther's own confusion: every scene is overlaid, as it were, with the viscosity of passion's distortion. The impotence of reason and the swell of passion make one giddy; and no doubt this is why the book has had such an impact on its readers through the years. But we no longer yield to the metaphysical longings of Werther, and sublimity cannot be found for us in an experience of nature. If we respond at all to the sublime, it is to the "sublime" in the guise of human violence and the power of the engineered.

Werther's love of beauty and fear of the sublime generate in him ambivalent feelings of such intensity that he eventually takes his own life. No easy, free association of sentiments, such as Sterne's Yorick enjoys, can sweeten Werther's existence. Rather, his whole being vacillates, as if subjected to cosmic forces of attraction and repulsion emanating from the beautiful and the sublime. This presentation of experience is close to the philosophical analysis presented in Kant's "Critique of Aesthetical Judgment," which constitutes the first part of *The Critique of Judgment*. *Werther* stands to Kant's thought about the life of feeling somewhat in the way that *Sentimental Jour-*

73

ney stands to Hume's analysis of the grounds of experience.

The point of Kant's third *Critique* is that the life of feeling is a contribution to experience, and if we ask, "How is experience possible?" we must analyze not only the understanding and the reason, but the feelings as well. And in doing this we come up against a curious set of predicates, ". . . is beautiful . . . ," ". . . is sublime . . . ," ". . . is purposeful . . ." to which a special analysis must be given because they refer to feelings and are predicated on the basis of sentiments, such as feelings of pleasure and of fear. They are therefore subjective, yet function as part of judgments in which we attribute characteristics to events. These are self-referential judgments in one important sense: they tell us something about the nature of human experience and how it is possible. Through an analysis of these judgments we find a way to suggest that theoretical and practical judgments are ultimately united, for attributions of beauty affirm a continuity and compatibility between what is and what ought to be. Attributions of sublimity, on the other hand, suggest natural antagonism to human aspiration. Out of this experience is forged a precarious possibility of human freedom in the midst of compulsion and destruction. The possibility for human experience now takes a new and ominous turn in Kant's thought, though he never fully developed the implications of what he discovered. A novel such as *Werther* does develop it fully and in so doing establishes a mode of experience we today find somewhat trying.

What Kant discovered is that human experience in its humanness, distinguishing it from experience in general for all rational beings and experience in general for all moral beings, becomes possible through a delicate balance of human choice in accepting or rejecting pleasure, and in affirming its creative potential. That is to say, as *human* beings we define ourselves in art. Logically speaking, this means we define ourselves as human when we can use the predicates "is beautiful," "is sublime," "is purposeful." Outside that accomplishment, in making theoretical and moral judgments, we are not affirming our uniqueness as humans, but what we have in common with other rational beings within the realm of the rational. So we see that what gives human experience its human dimension is the beautiful, and what makes this possible is a nonrational endowment of feeling and sentiment. We are what we are as feeling beings.

But this leads to an unhappy conclusion: the human is, of all that we participate in, the most precarious and possibly the most unfulfilled aspect of our condition. The likelihood that we can complete ourselves as human is slight, and should we succeed in accomplishing this growth, we may suffer a self-diminution because of a contradiction within experience itself. If we could succeed as artists and as appreciators of the beautiful we might escape this contradiction; but the experience of the beautiful and the sublime is not unconnected with our experience as rational beings making theoretical and moral judgments. As rational beings we harbor metaphysical longings which drive us to seek answers to ultimate questions, which, because of the nature of human experience, we are logically and ontologically forever incapable of answering. This longing Kant refers to as the drive toward the unconditioned, the desire to pose and solve ultimate problems of a theological and cosmological nature.

The deficiency we recognize in ourselves when we learn that we cannot answer them is compensated for to some extent by our experience of beauty. The beautiful in nature and in art can be the bridge between our theoretical limitations as scientists and our practical longings as moralists. Yet when we turn to the experience of the beautiful we discover a contradiction which the experience of Werther makes clear.

Both Werther the character and *Werther* the book show us this contradiction which arises because of our experience of beauty and our experience of sublimity. The book shows us a case in which it is not possible to make these two kinds of experience consistent; this split in experience is an expression of a deep flaw in the philosophical assumption of experiential coherence, for when we try to show, as Kant did, that art can make a world consonant with human longing, what in fact results is an inadequacy of experience due to the inadequacy of art itself which follows from the nature of reality insofar as humans can know it. We recognize this in the incompatibility of our different responses to the beautiful and to the sublime.

The beautiful somehow enlarges our feelings, expands our sense of kinship with other modes of existence; the sublime diminishes and denies us. Thus art and the activity of making art assume beauty as the object of the artistic quest, but in the quest something is encountered which denies the power and sufficiency of art. The consequence is a shocking recognition of an unbridgeable chasm within the very activity—art—in which we thought to find our nature made whole. For we see a radical separation in our theoretical and moral judgments, the first analyzing what *is* in terms of verifiable statements (crudely, science), and the second analyzing what ought to be in terms of aspiration toward moral rightness and individual perfection (crudely, ethics). Accepting this difficulty of is-ought separation, we look toward our experience of the beautiful and our power as artistic creators to find a wholeness in what we make, a wholeness denied in what we find. But our belief that this is possible is shown to be an expression of innocence, since as the effort to work out the artistic proceeds, it too comes up against an incompatibility, that presented by the experience of the sublime.

What exactly is this experience? Kant defines it first as an encounter with that which is of infinite magnitude, and then defines it as an encounter with that which is of infinite power. In both cases, no concepts can contain what we intuit, and the resulting affect is fear. But our fear is counterbalanced by a retreat to the assertion of moral being in the face of natural indifference to moral being. The dread, awe, fear that sublimity engenders make us anxious about ourselves because of our fragility and finitude, but at the same time arouse in us an appreciation of our special moral stance, our value as moral beings even in the face of overwhelming natural force. Supposedly, then, as Kant describes the situation, we begin with a negative affect (we feel our freedom abridged) but respond by asserting, in a dialectic of self-preservation through feeling, a positive defense of what is indestructible in us, our moral being. On the other hand, the experience of the beautiful is positive from the start and guides us to an assertion of and defense of ourselves as members of a civilized community. Kant tried to believe that the beautiful and the sublime were ultimately compatible counterparts that made human life possible and explained how experience as such was possible, that is, structured and meaningful. But this bridges the chasm between beauty and sublimity by philosophic hope; in fact, as I believe *Werther* shows, the philosophic gambit is unacceptable.

It is not acceptable because in experience these two kinds of encounters are separate and antagonistic, as Kant first recognized, though he never faced the consequence of this fact. Experience of the sublime is far more destructive to the self than Kant is willing to admit. Kant sees the destructiveness but cannot accept that as the ultimate condition of human life, whereas Goethe builds his whole novel around the ambivalence and inconsistency which the efforts of art are unable to reconcile. And since the novel *Werther* is mimetic to the extent that it represents these conflicts, it leaves us feeling uncomfortable with an awareness that rather than healing a breach, art which grows out of and mirrors that duality is condemned to reassert it in a form that proves finally its ineradicability. The novel itself is testimony to the plight of the protagonist.

The presentment of a natural bifurcation and a threatening natural power which animates Kant's thought about nature and obsesses the hero of *Werther* is denied in subsequent idealism, but that overcoming of the antagonism between beauty and sublimity (which Hegel attempted) is yet another effort to give an account of experience. Insofar as the poetic treatment of nature goes, the distinction between beauty and sublimity lasts well into the nineteenth century, as will be evident when we consider Wordsworth's *Prelude*. But by that time the dualism of reason and feeling which was fundamental to Hume and Kant, and which provides a subject for Sterne and Goethe, has been largely transcended. A rather different, more unified conception of human nature and experience can be defended.

IV

The philosophical contradictions encountered in the effort to account for the beautiful as a bridge between the theoretical and the practical is matched by a similar difficulty in literature. It is hard for most of us to feel sympathy for the eighteenth-century manner of presenting the consequences of artistic frustration in pursuing the sublime. In *Werther*, human striving for the unconditioned as something dimly sensed in experience is described as follows:

To lift the curtain, to step behind it—that is all! And why all these doubts and delays? Because we know not what it is like behind—because there is no return—and because our mind suspects that all is darkness and confusion, where we have no certainty. [P. 113]

Goethe has no difficulty assuming that the contradiction between beauty and sublimity can drive an artist out of his mind, and can lead, as in Werther's case, to suicide. The response to the sense of something lying beyond the phenomenal is to attempt a bridge through art, but the

79

effort, if it succeeds, forces the artist to step through the veil of appearance into madness or death. This seems to us an artificial resolution.

The philosophical resolution is no better; impatience with it led to a different account of the grounds of experience in philosophical idealism. This position, which I shall consider in the next chapter, developed out of dissatisfaction with the eighteenth-century efforts to answer the question, "How is experience possible?" For Hume and for Kant experience, in one important respect, is not realizable. A coherent whole experience of nature is never possible because of the limitations of the human endowment. One aspect of this limitation can be explored through the incompatibility of beauty and sublimity. Art, which imitates nature, is equally inconsistent and flawed, for as we cannot make our experience whole in nature, so we cannot make it whole in art. Kant, trying to overcome this limitation, thought that he could use art as the bridge between the theoretical and the moral, but his analysis led him into a contradiction which he never satisfactorily resolved.

The philosophical and literary examples presented in this chapter offer an essentially dualistic analysis of experience. It is the great achievement of idealistic attacks upon eighteenth-century empiricism to articulate a monism of consciousness. Idealism brought into accounts of experience another important, unifying concept, that of dynamic growth and change. Persons and cultural products are seen to be part of a growth process. I think it is correct to affirm philosophical explanations of consciousness as accounts of how human beings "grow up." We seek in philosophy and in literature explanations of how awareness gets the shape it has, what the shape means, what determines it, and what it commits us to. The question, "How is experience possible?" is an effort to focus our interest on what matters most to us as human beings. It is the philosopher's way of inquiring into individual awareness and social development. Taking philosophical accounts together with literary art allows us to entertain different approaches to the same kinds of experience. Philosophy argues its possibility; literary art offers it whole. In this sense literary art is the dream of philosophy.

Chapter 3

Art as a Phenomenology of the Imagination

I

The philosophical and literary exploration of experience in terms of a circumscribed, deductive reason, and a pervasive, powerful sentiment was subsequently rejected by the philosophical and literary outlook referred to as "idealism." Idealism grows out of exasperation with the engineering needed to maintain theoretical and practical reason as separate domains, mediated by an assumed but undemonstrable purposiveness, and out of impatience with empiricistic impoverishment of experience. The richness of experience, the preservation of essential human values can be achieved, idealism promises, if we eradicate the dualisms of empiricism and recognize that reality is one. We need no bridge where there is no chasm. And furthermore, the cultural stuff of art, taken by Kant to be the bridge between human aspiration and mechanical nature, can itself provide the evidence we need to build a monistic idealism of reality, for art, when taken seriously as an object of thought, ceases to be a set of formal principles enlivened by charm; rather, art comes into its fulfillment when it is *interpreted* in accord with a self-conscious method. This method Hegel somewhat misleadingly referred to as a "science" (*Wissenschaft*) of art.

We must understand that when Hegel called for a "science of art" as the urgent necessity of his day, he had in mind the uses to which art could be put in constructing cultural history, and by the term *Wissenschaft* he intended something more inclusive than we do by "science." We might refer to his term as "learning" or "cultural inquiry," but for simplicity I shall use the common English term for translation, that is, "science." Hegel argued that just as human actions, historically considered, could be used as keys to the progress of spirit through time, so products of human creativity could be used to establish an objective set of facts that would, if properly interpreted, verify philosophy's interpretation of the historical process. But Hegel's interest in art goes far beyond that, for he believed, as many thinkers do today, that art does not receive its fullest exploitation as an object of appearance; rather, art is most fully realized when it becomes the object of thought. When mind subjects art to scientific contemplation, mind satisfies its essential nature, and in so doing raises art up to its highest possibility.

The determination of art's essential nature means for Hegel the discovery of the truth embodied in art, for he assumes that the purpose of art is to embody truth in sensuous or material configuration. Regarding art this way, he believed, leads us to see that art exhibits an "ideal or inward necessity." This notion of art as exhibiting necessity—progress and evolution that could not be other than it is—provides the central justification for a sci-

G

ence of art as a broad cultural inquiry. If art exhibits a necessary order, it, like nature (and history as a whole), will be amenable to systematic inquiry; and we ought to be able to formulate precise laws describing art's evolution in terms of style progression, just as we can formulate laws of natural events. *Kunstwissenschaft*, a science of art, then constitutes Hegel's philosophic method, for a science of art is an interpretation of art and its history according to the principles of a peculiar hermeneutic in whose labyrinths we are still wandering.

The science of art envisaged by Hegel and elaborated by his followers would use art as a symptom of a general historical development, and at the same time explain the content of art, that is, its truth, in terms of a general theory of cultural progress. Hence a science of art would have to explain a number of difficult problems: (1) why specific materials were used at certain times in the development of art; (2) why forms evolved in the sequence art history records; (3) what each art meant in the total cultural complex of a specific period. There are, however, other interesting questions it would not answer: (1) why a specific artist produced what he did in individual terms; (2) why the consciousness of artists was moulded by forces outside individual awareness. In short, looking at art as Hegel did, the creative will of individual artists ceased to be significant. It is this blindness in Hegelian theory that led Arnold Hauser to call Hegelian philosophy of art "art history without names." [1]

If Hegel's generalizations about cultural development are correct, there is no reason why art cannot be used as

[1] Arnold Hauser, *Philosophy of Art History* (New York: Knopf, 1959), Ch. IV.

he wished to use it, provided it is possible to find in art the data he claims are available there. This is the question Hegelian "science of art" poses for us: can we find in art all that Hegel says is to be found there?

Two issues determine whether or not a science of art in Hegel's sense is possible. The first is the claim that the development of art exhibits a necessary sequence of events; the second is the claim that the work of art communicates a *Weltanschauung*.

The discovery of a necessary sequence of events can be considered, in an oversimplification, the primary aim of science. However, no interpretation of the concept of lawful relationship, except on Leibnizian grounds, will allow that a causal relationship is a necessary relationship. This, the necessity of logical entailment, is not the necessity that Hegel has in mind. Rather, the necessity that a science of art would lay bare and explain would be the necessity of the progressive stages of the development of spirit through time. Thus the "laws" Hegel would seek must give an account of necessary relationships holding between successive art forms. These in turn would be logically derivable from general theoretical statements having to do with self-consciousness as such, one manifestation of which is art. Can Hegel rightly claim that the statements about the development of spirit exhibit a set of necessarily related events?

Hegel cannot accept the criticism that statements about spirit are at best only possible; for to argue that there is contingency here is to reintroduce the distinctions between possibility and necessity which his whole ontology labors to overcome. They are the distinctions which in his eyes vitiated the work of Hume and Kant, since they argued that cause and effect are contingently related, as Hume claims, or at best are related by means of an a priori principle, as Kant claimed. But Hume and Kant agree, as against Hegel, that by "causal relationship" we mean an empirical sequence of events made up of discernibly different elements. Hegel, on the other hand, claims that the seeming opposites of the causal relationship are in reality identical. The concrete universal," as he calls it, is a category within which cause and effect become identical. Thus when mind reaches the point where it overcomes the distinction between mere appearance and the inner nature of an event, experience ceases to be divided into compartments of individual events and becomes a whole. In Hegel's language, the dialectic becomes for itself what it is in itself. All distinctions, therefore, which externally considered appear contingent, now are grasped in their inner necessity, and we understand the real as the rational, that is, that which cannot be otherwise than it is.

This is a puzzling, difficult conception of science which unfortunately does not seem to be supported by the few truths we have won in our observation of nature and human life. That it is a possible ideal, a vision of knowledge in its most exalted perfection cannot be denied; it seems singularly inapplicable to the realm of natural science and to the domain of art. The necessity which Hegel claims for art applies to it as it moves progressively through the "symbolic," "classical," and "romantic" phases he carefully distinguishes in his *Lectures on the Philosophy of the Fine Arts*. In the first phase, the symbolic, there is no concrete union of meaning and form; in the second, there is a union, and in the third, the outer form becomes an inadequate expression of an inner spiritual meaning now raised above sensuous presentation.

Are these distinctions ones that we would want a science of art, should one be possible, to tell us? I think not, because distinctions of that sort evade just the questions which a science, as we think of it, ought to answer. The goal Hegel set himself is really beyond that which we can reasonably set for any science; we would be satisfied with much less, would welcome answers to much more limited questions, before moving on to the largest, most abstruse issues. If Hegel were successful, he would answer questions of the following sort: why the art of a particular people took the form it did; why the exploration, development, decline of a style took place; is there a most likely sequence of stylistic organization in a given art and why that sequence is most likely; and, finally, do all the arts in fact exhibit similarity of developmental forms. Indeed, it may be possible to find answers to these questions, but not in the language of necessary logical sequences and relationships. Probabilities, trends, correlations, likelihoods are the relationships we have to be content with. If we ask more of a science of art, we pretend to greater precision than in our science of nature. I conclude, therefore, that on the first count, Hegel's science of art must be incapable of realization. What of the second, that a science of art is a discipline devoted to the discovery of a *Weltanschauung?*

The justification for this kind of art history is to be found in a defense of the art object. The problem is this: can we justify, through the inspection of art works, a *Weltanschauung?* Hegel, when he claims a science of art is possible, assumes that art works can be used in this way. It has often been argued, in an effort to deny Hegel's assumption, that there is no parallel for this kind of interpretation in the natural sciences, that there is no such object of knowledge, and that therefore the search for *Weltanschauungen* is pointless. On the other side, it has been argued that there is a different mode of knowing involved in cultural products, and that therefore a different kind of analysis is due them as compared with the kind of analysis appropriate to natural events. A science of art, this defense says, must be different from a science of nature, yet both are, properly, sciences in being systematic and intersubjective, the latter with certain important reservations.

The first difficulty with the idea of a *Weltanschauung* is that, as Dilthey made clear, *Weltanschauungen* lie outside the domain of theory. We do not create the lineaments of a *Weltanschauung* in the same way that we create a scientific theory. The products of reason, which include theories, as well as cultural products such as art, are themselves manifestations of a *Weltanschauung*. Hence the grasp and articulation of a *Weltanschauung* require an activity of mind which is essentially different from the mental activities required for science, history, and the like. The question then is, how, if at all, can a *Weltanschauung* be grasped?

It was Mannheim who tried to cope with this problem by introducing the distinction between objective, expressive, and documentary meaning. I think Mannheim has made clear a crucial aspect of Hegel's theoretical thought by bringing into our awareness distinctions Hegel did not clearly formulate.

The facts that every art historian—the Hegelian as well

as others—has to work with are the objects made by men at various times in the past. A close attention to these, Mannheim points out, reveals three distinct presentations which, while given simultaneously, can be distinguished through careful analysis. The first is called by Mannheim "objective meaning." That is simply what is self-contained in the object, and requires no more for its comprehension than an identification of the elements in the object. Within the objective meaning is to be found what Mannheim refers to as the "expressive meaning." That is to say, within the sensuous presentation there are not only a set of identifiable objects, but also a "psychic content," an *expression*, which is a reflection of, indeed the expression of, attitudes, presuppositions, beliefs, and the outlook of the artist and the society responsible for the work. It is given just as much as objective meaning, but to be fully understood it requires an analysis of the historical background of the work. The art historian can make himself thoroughly at home in the climate of the period when the work was produced, and thereby come to grasp the expressive meaning. There is, furthermore, a third meaning, named by Mannheim "documentary." Documentary meaning is what, in the words of Panofsky, a work "betrays" but does not explicitly "parade." Documentary meaning is not intention, requires no conscious effort on the part of the artist, but is the "ethos" breathed by the work. It may, unlike expressive meaning, be found in a fragment of a work. The documentary meaning is itself interpreted through unconscious assumptions, so that it must be determined anew for every generation. The greatest intellectual toleration is required to see that in grasping the *Weltanschauung* of a past age, one is in subtle and unrealized ways influenced by the *Weltan-schauung* of his own. Hence the history of the interpretations of documentary meanings is itself a history of *Weltanschauungen* which gives an insight (necessarily from a limited point of view) into the time when the interpretation was made.

What account can we give of the status of documentary meanings, and what account can we give of the method by which such meanings are apprehended? The first reply to a view such as Mannheim's is that by his own insistence, the articulation of the apprehension of a *Weltanschauung* is of necessity an atheoretical, nonscientific procedure. Only in part is it amenable to ordinary scientific methods, for the theory of *Weltanschauung* is an *interpretation,* not an *explanation.* By explanation Mannheim means causal analysis. The only place where causal explanation becomes relevant is in the establishment of the fact that a *Weltanschauung* did give rise to a particular manifestation. There is, by the theory itself, no causal relationship to be found between one documentary meaning and another; hence, in the terms of a Hegelian theory of art, there is a necessary discontinuity, not a necessary relationship of entailment, between one and another phase of art's progress. The discovery of documentary meanings is to be compared to tracing various actions of one person back to a personality. When and if we can show that both acts, or both manifestations, are part of one and the same totality, then to some extent we can find causal relationships. We must show that the personality, or the culture, is capable of giving rise to both events. Mannheim sums it up this way: "Interpretation serves for the deeper understanding of meanings; causal explanation shows the condition for the actualization or realization of a given meaning." [2]

Interpretation calls for a giving up of the "mechanical, atomistic methods" of science and the development of new methods which must be directed to the distillation of the *Weltanschauung* of an epoch from the various objectifications of the epoch. The difficult problem is to describe the unity we feel in all the works that belong to the same period in terms precise enough to permit verification and agreement. This depends upon new concepts which await the work of the cultural historian. Mannheim suggests choosing the domain of art as the most likely starting point for this undertaking.

If such an atheoretical inquiry into art is possible, it has not yet been realized. No independent means of verifying the nature of a supposed *Weltanschauung* seems possible unless the sphere of the directly given *Weltanschauung* in question can be evaluated by reference to facts of a totally different kind. While there can well be a method appropriate to the discovery of documentary meaning, no science of documentary meaning is definable. If we take seriously the problem confronting a science of art in its effort to re-create a *Weltanschauung*, we must look for the means of testing our results. It appears that only the intuitive faculty by means of which the *Weltanschauung* is grasped can be appealed to; hence competing claims cannot be tested. The conclusion must be that the notion of "correctness" here is ambiguous, and though we may freely construct interpretations, we

[2] Karl Mannheim, "On the Interpretation of Weltanschauungen," in Paul Kecskemeti, ed., *Essays on the Sociology of Knowledge* (London: Routledge & Kegan Paul, 1959), p. 81.

must be willing to allow other interpretations, both antecedent and subsequent to ours, a legitimate place. This
would deny the possibility of founding a science of art
upon the claim of objectivity and certainty.

But this failure in no way diminishes the profound and
fruitful insights which Hegel brought into our thought
about art. The historical revolution he effected expanded
art structures in several important ways, introducing new
sets of values to the traditional artistic variables. It is as if
he discovered a whole new geometry, so revolutionary is
his impact upon the way we construe the domain of art.
Two definite consequences of this revolution are: (1) the
reorganization and reopening to new interpretations of
the art of the past; (2) the production of new kinds of art
structures unknown and indeed impossible before. Thus
old structures are seen anew, and new kinds of structures
are introduced.

Changes of this sort are the bases for style changes in
art, as well as for changes in the methods and goals of
criticism. To my mind the historical revolution effected
by Hegel is the most profound in all the philosophical
thought of the West. Its impact on art was to change our
notion of the art symbol more radically than the change
wrought by Augustine, for after Hegel art became endowed with the power of *expression*, a conception of art
that makes *imitation* in its classical and medieval forms
no longer satisfactory. With Hegel, style becomes the
clue to the inwardness of art, to values that before were
ignored. This conception of artistic meaning is dependent
upon a new notion of beauty as a key to the correspondence between the ideal content of art (something recognized by thought), and the sensuous configuration of art

(the outer aspect recognized by sense). The arts thus become symbols of great complexity telling the story of the unfolding of unlimited dimensions of human awareness. For Hegel this is expressed by saying that art can be seen as the idea realizing self-consciousness in one of its aspects. For us this means that the interpretation of art, like the interpretation of all cultural objects, is never at an end. Vast landscapes of historical art studies now reveal themselves to eyes which to be sure are at times weary of the vistas; but also animated with the continuous opening up of unexpected meanings.

Of course this meant that one of the consequences of the historical revolution was the use of art on behalf of extra-artistic theories, a kind of glorious historicism much disparaged today. But more important is what the historical revolution did to art itself. It brought all art—of whatever cultural origin, of whatever original purpose—into a discourse of universal predication. Attributes of one object became meaningful as they were applied to or compared with the attributes of others; every critical assertion about one work of art was seen to have unexpected relevance to other works, often lying at a great temporal distance from it. Far-reaching comparisons can be entered into: Sappho with Yeats; Rembrandt with cave painting; Palestrina with Cage. A new simultaneity has been granted to objects and to our experience of them. We have not yet exhausted the implications of this exercise of thought upon art.

So far I have stressed the method Hegel elaborated to cope with cultural objects, particularly art works, and I have only alluded to the account of experience that philosophic idealism provides. Idealism, as a philosophic account of experience, asks how it is that the world and the self are related, for it is obvious both for the person and for the species that awareness of self and objects grows, deepens, and evolves. Since human reality is established by human awareness, it is justified in a philosophy of experience to begin with the self or ego, and ask what the stages of ego development are. This was the task undertaken by Friedrich Schelling, from whom Hegel learned so much; indeed Schelling's account of experience constitutes the foundation for both poetic and philosophic developments of nineteenth-century idealism. Although Wordsworth, whose presentation of experience I shall consider next, did not know Schelling's thought directly, he had ample doses of idealistic philosophy—a sure antidote to the native empiricism he grew to loath—administered by Coleridge. So it is appropriate to say that idealism as a philosophic outlook helped shape Wordsworth's conception of experience, even though he arrived at his views through intense self-examination.

Idealism, as formulated by Schelling, suggests that there are two ways to give an account of experience: we may begin with an objective factor, such as nature, and ask how the subjective factor, the self, comes to agree with and be joined to nature. Or we can begin with the subjective factor, the self, and ask how the objective comes into articulation and is joined with the subjective. Schelling's so-called transcendental philosophy begins with the subjective factor, and asks how the world grows out of the ego. Philosophy traces the steps to full awareness, and documents the kinds of activities which each stage of awareness finds to be its satisfactory means of expression. Ultimately, the status of human beings in the world and the reciprocal interdependency of self and nature are best expressed in art. In the aesthetic stages of transcendental idealism, the wholly comprehensive work of art comes into being, and presents to awareness the satisfactory joining of subject and object. Philosophy not only charts the course leading to this harmony, but also illustrates its consummation, indeed *is* its success.

In this sense the art of the poet Wordsworth realizes the consummation described by philosophical idealism, and although Wordsworth came to his construction of experience by ways quite different from Hegel, there is a fascinating likeness between the account of experience in Hegel's restructuing of art and that in Wordsworth's *The Prelude, Or Growth of a Poet's Mind.*[3]

II

At the time idealistic philosophy of art was coming into its interpretive power, several important works of art were being structured in terms of idealistic assumptions.[4] And just as the experience described by Hume and Kant found its literary counterpart in the art of Sterne and Goethe respectively, so the experience described by Hegel found its complement in *The Prelude* of Wordsworth.

[3] Full texts of the idealistic position on art can be found in A. Hofstadter and R. Kuhns, *Philosophies of Art and Beauty* (New York: Random House, 1964), pp. 277–576.

[4] Hegel, *Phenomenology of Mind*, published in 1807; Wordsworth, *The Prelude*, written 1799–1805, published 1850.

The Prelude carries the reader through a dialectical examination of the poet's thought and life by means of a history of his imagination. The first stage is childhood, within which there are two forces contraposed to one another: beauty and fear ("I grew up/Fostered alike by beauty and by fear").[5] But the root experience is that of beauty within which there lies a contradiction, for experience of the beautiful ("The bond of union between life and joy" [I, 558]) contains within it the experience of sublimity from which fear and awe grow. The dialectic of the beautiful and the sublime is taken by Wordsworth and presented as a reality more surely and more convincingly than anything described by Burke or Kant. Nature is capable of arousing within the child feelings both of the wholeness of beauty and the threatening dread of overpowering force ("My brain worked with a dim and undetermined sense of unknown modes of being" [I, 390]). He describes the beautiful as if before a painting:

> I held unconscious intercourse with beauty
> Old as creation, drinking in a pure
> Organic pleasure from the silver wreaths
> Of curling mist, or from the level plain
> Of waters coloured by impending clouds.
>
> [I, 562]

But this initial dialectic, the tension of beauty and sublimity, forces a synthesis at a new, and to the poet less adequate, level of response.

---

[5] Wordsworth, *The Prelude*, ed. Ernest de Selincourt (Oxford: Clarendon Press, 1959), I, 301–302. All subsequent quotations are from this edition.

96

> Such, verily, is the first
> Poetic spirit of our human life,
> By uniform control of after years,
> In most, abated or suppressed; in some,
> Through every change of growth and of decay,
> Pre-eminent till death.
>
> [II, 260]

The growth of intellect is enforced through the pressure of society and the child's need to cope with powers he as yet can little understand. Beauty, that avenue to the "Sentiment of Being" (II, 400) conflicts with intellect,

> . . . that false secondary power
> By which we multiply distinctions, then
> Deem that our puny boundaries are things
> That we perceive, and not that we have made.
>
> [II, 216]

So misled, we replace imagination in its early manifestations by intellect. It is marvelously described poetically by Wordsworth:
   Compare

> An auxiliar light
> Came from my mind, which on the setting sun
> Bestowed new splendour; the melodious birds,
> The fluttering breezes, fountains that run on . . .
>
> [II, 368]

with

> Mine eyes were crossed by butterflies, ears vexed
> By chattering popinjays; the inner heart

97

Seemed trivial, and the impresses without
Of a too gaudy region.

[III, 446]

The mode of statement as well as the images are carefully
chosen to set the strain of conflict within the epistemological context of philosophic talk. Wordsworth is responding with imagination to the denial of imagination he encountered as a young man forced to attend Cambridge,
forced to "grow up," that is to cover over the natural pre-
sentments of intuitive imagination by the rigid classifica-
tions of intellect. The conflict, described phenomenologically, is between a light coming from the mind,
enlightening all that is perceived, and light coming to the
mind from without in a flutter of butterflies and a chatter
of foolish talkers. A too gaudy exterior denies and suffo-
cates the inner light. The contrast between birds and butterflies, sun and "gaudy region," mind and eyes–ears describes the puzzle of perception as it has fascinated
philosophers. Wordsworth suggests that the reality we
find is a function of the mode of perception. At each stage
of our development there is a dialectic of poetic-work-
ing-through, beginning in crude imagination, denial
through intellect, reaffirmation of imagination. And at
each stage along the way to poetic liberation there is a
reality to which we grant validity, though only in the dialectic itself can we come to see the poverty of the earlier
stages. Although this is a thoroughly "Hegelian" treatment of the growth of awareness, Wordsworth came to
his vision of poetry as the phenomenology of the imagination from a rejection of crude empiricism and a preoccupation with the origin and power of imaginative poetic
discourse. He is like Hegel in his reaction to empiricism,

quite individual in his own artistic development. Wordsworth, as the next step in his argument shows, came to
the view that there is a creative power of imagination far
beyond that of intellect, and he would utterly reject Hegel's demand that intellect dominate art.

At the second stage of development, in which the intellect has suffused imagination, a new tension is felt, a tension appropriate to a mature and thoughtful person. Now
it is the conflict between nature and art, an inevitable
conflict given the empiricistic demands of intellect.
Wordsworth works this out on a sophisticated level by
means of the dream of the Arab (V, 80). The controlling
images are still, as before, images of external objects perceived. While previously he compared birds and butterflies, now he compares a stone and a shell. He begins
with the lament:

> Oh! why hath not the Mind
> Some element to stamp her image on
> In nature somewhat nearer to her own?
>
> [V, 45]

The dream of the Arab explains why this deficiency
plagues us. The question to be answered is, "How is the
intelligible structure of the universe [stone] related to the
beautiful appearance of the natural [shell]?" There is a
parallel here to Spinoza's distinction between *natura na-
turata* and *natura naturans,* a distinction between the
solid, unchanging structure of all that is and the process of
nature whose change goes on within the intelligible
framework. For the poet, imagination is the power to en-
liven nature (symbolized by the shell), and the intellect is
the power to discover nature's intelligible structure (sym-

H

bolized by the stone). The mind can stamp her image on nature through imagination. Poetry is just that creative exercise, and grows out of an early exposure to the stuff of self-effacement:

> Oh! give us once again the wishing cap
> Of Fortunatus, and the invisible coat
> Of Jack the Giant-Killer, Robin Hood,
> And Sabra in the forest with St. George!
> The child, whose love is here, at least, doth reap
> One precious gain, that he forgets himself.
>
> [V, 341]

Strangely, to our sensibility, this early exposure prepares the imagination to cope with the beautiful and the sublime. While initially these two forces as they manifest themselves in the child's experience are antithetical, driving the person to an overcoming in a flight to intellect, there is, with the passing of intellectual resolutions over into imagination at a higher level, a way to resolve the antithesis of beauty and sublimity in a positive affirmation of the imagination without losing the ontological significance of the joy of beauty and the dread of sublimity. The poet describes the recovery of a drowned man from Esthwaite's Lake:

> At last, the dead man, 'mid that beauteous scene
> Of trees and hills and water, bolt upright
> Rose, with his ghastly face, a spectre shape
> Of terror; yet no soul-debasing fear,
> Young as I was, a child not nine years old,
> Possessed me, for my inner eye had seen
> Such sights before, among the shining streams
> Of faery land, the forest of romance.

Their spirit hallowed the sad spectacle
With decoration of ideal grace;
A dignity, a smoothness, like the works
Of Grecian art, and purest poesy.

[V, 448]

At last the poet succeeds in joining beauty and sublimity, but the way to his self-overcoming is through the knitting into imagination of the intellectual power as an energy put to the creation of art. His dream has shown him the way, which then is reaffirmed through the reinterpretation of his most ghastly childhood experience. The power of his art is the power of transformation that occurs within *The Prelude* as it unfolds before us. The successful integration of the powers of thought and imagination is demonstrated through the poem.

And in this poem the rising up of the dead man is transformed into a tale of romance. It is unlikely that the nine-year-old child experienced this as romance, but the shock of childhood memory was so great that Wordsworth was compelled to come to terms with it, and he did so by integrating the memory with his adult imaginative vision, known to us as the poem we read. In this way the dialectic of imagination transforms memory from dreadful recollection to poetic recognition since, within the poem itself, imagination realizes its mature power to transform the past into romance.

How this process of imaginative growth comes about is one of the wonders of *The Prelude,* for every aspect of the poem contributes to it. The structure of the language, use of sentences, stanzas, word order, images, formal patterning elements, the way the ideas move—often awkwardly—enable us, the readers, to have the experience the poem as a whole is concerned to reveal. That experience, which is the substance of the poem itself, I refer to as a phenomenology of imagination.

The poet tries to convey to the reader his conviction that the power of art depends upon a sensitivity to nature.

> . . . he, who in his youth
> A daily wanderer among woods and fields
> With living Nature hath been intimate,
> Not only in that raw unpractised time
> Is stirred to ecstasy, as others are,
> By glittering verse; but further, doth receive,
> In measure only dealt out to himself,
> Knowledge and increase of enduring joy
> From the great Nature that exists in works
> Of mighty Poets. Visionary power
> Attends the motion of the viewless winds,
> Embodied in the mystery of words:
> There, darkness makes abode, and all the host
> Of shadowy things work endless changes . . .
>
> [V, 586]

It is the task of the fifth book to make this evolution real for us by carrying us, as readers, through the movement of this same development. Once that transformation is effected, the rest of the poem can move to its imaginative work without need to educate the reader. Of course, this first large step of the dialectic of imagination does not complete the evolution, but it is the achievement of art, from which the higher achievements, described later in the poem, can come. If we make comparison with Hegel's phenomenology of mind, with his conception of the stages of dialectical self-awareness, there is a close parallel. For Hegel too sees art as the first step to full human self-consciousness, beginning with the early stages of nature interpretation, moving to the preoccupation with the human figure, and finally to the expressive mode of imagery in Romantic poetry. Wordsworth sees this, too, as the human preparation for the highest achievements, although for Wordsworth the statement of higher poetic and imaginative awareness is reached through poetry and the writing of poetry. Though they agree that art is moving toward a religious mode of awareness, for Wordsworth the great heights are essentially a kind of poetry, for Hegel a kind of philosophy (see *The Prelude,* XIV, 63 ff., V, 500 ff.). Wordsworth has written a phenomenology of the imagination, a celebration of that divine power, as Hegel has written a defense of mind through tracing its evolution in a phenomenology whose inclusiveness would swallow *The Prelude* as but a morsel.

Yet *the Prelude* establishes its independence as a work of artistic validity through an original dialectic of the imagination. *The Prelude* gives an account of experience in fundamental respects like that offered by Hegel in *The Phenomenology of Mind.* The poet compacts within himself stages of development which idealism claims occur through large reaches of cultural time. Wordsworth folds up history into the self. I think of this as a psychologizing of the dialectic, analogous to another assault from a different side, namely the political deformation of the dialectic in the work of Marx. Wordsworth's deformation of the idealistic stages of consciousness is closer to the development of idealism late in the century, one that had a revolutionary impact on the way we think about art, on the way art is produced, and upon the possibilities for artistic experience. I refer of course to the work of Freud, and to psychoanalytic theory. Wordsworth's structuring of the poetic life as a dialectic of imagination is prophetic; but that is simply another way of indicating its richness.

III

Wordsworth conceives the growth of poetic power to be an overcoming of the duality of beauty and sublimity, proof of which is found in the exercise of the imagination at a higher level than is possible for awareness in childhood. In poetry joy and dread are brought together, tolerated, and explored. Poetically less mature states are those in which joy and dread are denied in the overbearing exercise of intellect. In rejecting philosophy as he does, in finding philosophical analyses of experience destructive to the deepest human values, Wordsworth fails, as poets generally do, to see the affinity between philosophical accounts of experience and poetic presentations of experience. Since philosophical modes of presentation are *arguments*, and poetic modes of presentation are *performances*, it is difficult for philosophy and poetry to inhabit the same consciousness. Certainly Hegel's effort to subordinate poetry to philosophy and Wordsworth's effort to denigrate philosophy as destructive of poetry express antagonistic conceptions of consciousness. Although each explores the growing awareness of the person, each uses distinctly original ways of making that sensible process known.

I characterize the two methods of making known the movement toward self-consciousness as argument and performance. Something needs to be said about the aspects of experience each seizes upon, and about their complementary possibilities, for I believe philosophical and literary modes of statement do enlarge one another in the sense that they take for exploration different aspects of our awareness of ourselves.

I have already described Hegel's "science of art" as an exploration of growing self-consciousness. His conception of philosophical argument explores the relationship between cultural products as modes of expression and an ontological reality which is, at least in its logical structure, expressed. His analysis seeks to exhibit the past as an accumulation of cultural acts to which his method of interpretation gives philosophical sense; and through this exercise of thought we come to understand ourselves as an eminence raised upon the past. From the vantage point of our present we can survey the progress of thought, subordinating human performance to philosophical argument, and replacing the expressive relationship of feeling with the logical relationship of dialectic. In this move Hegel continues the philosophical domination of poetry begun long ago by Plato.

In contrast, Wordsworth rejects the logical connections and the historical stuff of idealistic philosophy. In their place he puts the connections of synaesthesia and the stuff of memory. This substitution compactly asserts the difference between argument and performance, for the latter is a bodying forth in poetic language of a realm to which the poet and only the poet has access, but to which all of us wish to be admitted through the poet's power. Just as the philosopher assumes that all can share his views because of the power of logic—all intellects fundamentally work the same way and are molded by and directed by reason—so the poet assumes that all can come to participate in what is initially private through the sharing of memory, and in sensory capacities which may be stimulated by the power of language.

What is it that enables language in its poetic use to cope with the past as memory, and the present as a synaesthetic whole? In seeking to work out explicitly the power of memory and synaesthesia, I am stating what it is that distinguishes poetic performance from philosophical argument, comparing the use of the past as history and as memory, and comparing the use of the present as dialectical relationship and as synaesthesia. We might state the difference this way: what holds argument together is the cement of validity; what holds performance together is the interpenetration of sensory and conceptual capacities, the cement of synaesthesia. These differences are profound, and I do not claim that the kinds of experience offered by poetry and philosophy are the same; rather I am claiming that in both poetry and philosophy there is an effort to account for the relationship of past and present, and to account for the wholeness, integrity, and coherence of experience. I shall discuss both memory and synaesthesia in an effort to locate precisely the ways in which Wordsworth's poetic use of language creates experience in an artistic mode.

Memory, a natural mental power whose source and strength are mysterious, is the psychological ground which makes shared experience possible. Wordsworth's interest in memory, like most artists', is aroused by the fact that in memory an individual shares his life with others through participation in a common past from which stories can be drawn. The past, as the tellings have it, is a time we have all been through, a communal experience not unlike family sharing. As the feelings of a shared past grow with maturity, so the conviction of communal purpose bestows a meaning upon performances. Artistic performances increase in power and scope as the individual comes to participate more and more in the past. This way of seeing the past is not alien to Hegel's philosophic method, for as we become aware of the past we do participate with other minds in an enlarged awareness. The inquiry into history as Hegel carries it out and the poetic evocation of childhood as Wordsworth presents it in *The Prelude* have similar consequences, even though each depends upon different assumptions about reality.

The quality of a shared life to which I refer is stimulated by childhood experiences. Children learn about the past through family stories, photographs, heirlooms, and documents, and come to believe they have lived through more than their summable years can number.[6] In reflecting on this process, as we must when we read *The Prelude,* we can be helped by a detailed consideration of memory. I shall therefore consider the concept of memory from three aspects: recognition, recollection, and anamnesis.

---

[6] This aspect of growing up is well described by Natalia Ginzberg in her recollection, *Lessico Familiare* (Turin: Einaudi, 1963). In translation, *Family Sayings* (New York: E. P. Dutton, 1967).

Recognition.

We have a variety of terms to describe the processes of memory, though there is little agreement on their range of meaning. I begin with "recognition," the form of which, *re*-cognize, suggests an obvious applicability: recognition is a repetition of cognition, a seeing again, assuming a similarity to a prior occasion. For recognition to occur there must be a presentation to awareness, an objective manifestation requiring a response, or the recurrence within thought of something entertained before. *The Prelude* again and again uses recognition as the experiential form in which the poet's life takes on coherence.

The natural impulse of the young poet to make representations of his experiences is stirred by the recurrences in events: repetitions demand names, call forth symbolizing gestures, encourage anticipatory postures. Simply walking, or floating in a boat on a lake, or seeing recognizable flowers and trees create in the poetic awareness complicated orders of feeling, thought, physical movements which come to be stated through simple images. Any event may become the stuff of poetic representation because of repetitions, but of course there are those basic repetitions in the ebb and flow of lives and seasons which deeply move us. This is the realm of events to which performances are most often addressed. Thinking of them as they occur in *The Prelude*, we come to know how they differ in order of magnitude—though not in their importance for the poetic consciousness—from the realm of historical events, to which *The Prelude* also makes reference.

108

For the poet, and this is especially true for Wordsworth, the making of poetry is an answer to a felt need to reactivate powers inherent in natural things. He shares this with all primitive peoples for whom art making is in effect revivifying the virtues inherent in sacred places. So too, the repeated telling of tales, as in the recital of the *Iliad*, the singing of epic verse, annual ceremonial performances of drama and dance, are all reassurances that the community can benefit from spiritual resources. Recalling one's childhood, reanimation of a rock painting, recital of a traditional story, performance of a ritual dance—performance in all its varieties—bestow a benediction upon the participants. The ability to recognize the recurrences of natural events, which these performances actualize, rests as the source of a conviction that there is a steadfastness in nature from which the individual and the community can draw support.

Recollection.

Recollection refers to that function of memory which enables us to bring into awareness events most intimately part of our own history. Recollections have about them the quality of "me-ness." To be sure, recognitions may have that quality as well, but need not, because they come out of a variety of repetitions, of which only some gather about them the private quality of recollection. In one sense, of course, all memory is recollection since to remember is a function of individual awareness, but this sense of recollection as personal memory is tautological, since it is always *I* who remember. What we refer to in

recollection is that aspect of memory which is by definition unshareable. Obviously we possess individually a
store of recollections, the exploration of which is part of
the artist's work of making the assemblage of art. Beyond
that fund is a public domain of history, of theorem to
which all have access and from which the educated mind
draws its shareable recognitions as against private recollections. Something of this distinction resides in Wordsworth's use of the stone and the shell. And like all artists,
his poetic experience must be set against the external
world of knowledge, that suffocating subject of university
concern.

Philosophers have puzzled over this distinction as well.
Plato, eccentrically, thought the recollection of the Pythag-
orean theorem a shareable memory in a private yet common sense. The truths of mathematics he considered part
of a reality to which every mind had access prenatally.
He succeeded, in at least a poetic if not a philosophical
way, in crossing the ambiguous line between the private
and the public, but drew the ridicule of philosophers like
father Protagoras who saw man as the measure of all
things, of things that are, and of things that are not.

As Wordsworth tries to convince us, the self, in its
search for the integration of past and present, public and
private, is naturally sympathetic to the Platonic assumption since so much of our experience is seemingly shared
recollection. But Wordsworth realized that one's own recollections take shape in a social matrix, so that the life of
poetry is in inescapable essentials a communal life. It is
one of the powers of art—Plato saw this too—to transform
the synthetic propositions about the past, as they would
be formulated by historians, into analytical propositions

of recollection, so that the past revealed by the poet is more akin to the realm of mathematical propositions than it is to history. Art makes recollections into a commonly available cosmos, much as the contemplation described by Plato opens up the eternal realm of forms to the individual mind. Plato was the first to state this power of art: it is an instrument of reconciliation, uniting the individual in his privacy with communal reality. Seeing art endowed with this power, both Plato and Wordsworth attempt to create those poetic-philosophical statements which will reconcile argument and performance.

Considered in this way, art establishes the reality of the past by enabling the individual to internalize and discover as his own all that other persons have undergone and witnessed. The work of art is the embodiment of the awareness of others, once but private recollections, now public legacy. The shareability of art works establishes a set of public entities, a related order of events for everyone to encounter and to know. A poem like *The Prelude* is one such entity, referring in many of its details to other such entities, and altogether making up a cosmos of performances. To these performances the philosopher, like Hegel, comes with his transmuting wand of argument.

Anamnesis

Plato falls back upon myth to describe anamnesis, so difficult is it to know when the total awareness to which anamnesis refers is achieved. The term has a special significance for the conception of awareness that Plato wants to develop in his dialogues, and it will help us to complete our discussion of memory in the context of idealism. Like so many of the ideal psychic states described in the dialogues, anamnesis is a state toward which a life points, but at which it never fully arrives until, perhaps, it has escaped earthly existence. This conception of memory expresses the idealistic hope that the awareness of the individual can be enlarged to share in all awarenesses simultaneously, for anamnesis refers to a power of memory which, were it realized, would raise the mind above and outside time. When the individual feels himself caught up in an enlarged awareness of this kind, he has a recognition of events as contemporaneous, independent of a specific historical source, and exhibiting a coherence in comparison to which private sense perceptions are so many detached and irrelevant tokens. Neither Plato nor Wordsworth can explain how the awareness of the individual becomes so enlarged, nor just where the feeling that anamnesis is achieved begins, but they agree that the condition named by the word is a special enlargement of recollection in which memory space is furnished spatially, rather than merely ordered sequentially.

The sense one has of being lifted out of time, and therefore freed from the coercive power of death, is quickened by artistic performance. Here, both Plato and Wordsworth agree, an attitude can be developed which defines the highest possibility for human nature, bringing us as human beings close to the divine. This attitude resides as an unrealized disposition in all of us, and is brought to consciousness by the artistic concern for a medium such as that of language. Following Plato, I shall call this developed disposition "care."

By the term "care" I do not have in mind the sense of the concept which Heidegger plays with in his consideration of *Sorge* and *Besorge*, but rather the sense Plato gets at in his use of the term *epimeleton*, as it occurs in the *Phaedrus* and the *Laws*. Socrates introduces the concept when he relates the myth to Phaedrus. "Soul," says Socrates, "considered collectively, has the care (epimeleitai) of all that which is soulless (apsuxou), and it traverses the whole heaven, appearing sometimes in one form and sometimes in another; and when it is perfect and fully winged, it mounts upward and governs the whole world." [7]

In the *Laws* the disposition of care is assigned to the overseer of the cosmic order in the very name he bears: "He who cares for the World-all," the *Epimeloumenos*. He is the great administrator of all cosmic order in whom the good of the totality of what is is preserved. [8] Although Plato argues that only the philosopher exercises care, the artist expresses care in his work through his dedication and his love of the medium. It is this aspect of art as care to which Wordsworth draws our attention in *The Prelude*, for although the artist is the most narcissistic of persons, his care is for the bodying forth of his recollections so that participation in something larger than the self is possible. In caring absolutely for his performance, the artist cares for the consequences of his art; the excellently wrought performance objectifies, makes communally available what otherwise would remain private. In this particular sense of dedication to performance, the art life of the artist is analogous to the life described by Plato as the life of the *Epimeloumenos* who cares for what he has created. The artist creates his world, as the *Epimeloume-*

---

[7] Plato, *Phaedrus*, trans. H. N. Fowler (Cambridge: Harvard University Press, 1914), 246 b-c.

[8] Plato, *Laws*, 903 ff.; 904.

nos creates *the* world, and in so doing expends infinite love on his creation, and above all seeks its good. The consequence for the artist, since he explores and creates himself, is the availability of that self as a structured object. Once that is accomplished, as it is when a structured object such as *The Prelude* comes into existence, the private aspects of memory are made public, and are joined to the already existing public domain of performances. The poet then joins his awareness to that of others, and contributes to the furnishing of that realm of memory to which Plato gave the name anamnesis.

But memory, so briefly discussed here, is itself a complex capacity whose reality, as it comes to be witnessed in anamnesis, is dependent upon immediate and primitive sensitivities. These sensitivities are essential to art, and are the givens which enable the artist to make out of his private awareness something greater in which others, who possess like sensitivities, can participate. The capacity to which I shall refer has been given the name synaesthesia by psychologists, and although it is too complex to be dealt with thoroughly here, I shall discuss it as it bears upon the poetic power.

Synaesthesia, the psychological condition of sensory interpenetration, has been called by Erich von Hornbostel "a sensuous [experience] which is not limited to one single sense." His romantic description, in the spirit of Bauhaus aesthetics, explains the concept:

Lyonel Feininger, when fifty years old and at the height of his powers, sat down one day and wrote organ fugues. Until then he had only painted fugues. Now the blind can see his pictures. Even in art the sense-sphere is largely indifferent; transposition from one sphere to another is possible, though not always as completely as here, where (I speak of the pictures) strong linear tensions are pulled tightly together by the clear austerity of the laws of counterpoint.[9]

Sensory interpenetration and amplitude are the conditions Wordsworth defends as an essential gift to the poetic mind. His academic years, when he felt obligated to listen to philosophy, imposed a cognitive restraint upon his senses, in the narrow belief that avenues to awareness are defined by a tradition hostile to artistic modes of perception. Wordsworth presses us with all his poetic might to see that our synaesthetic powers have been overlaid by sensory repression, the consequence of schooling in sensory inhibition. Eyes are for seeing, ears for hearing; each sense modality, we have been taught, owns its limited slice of the sensory spectrum. Our infatuation with *evidence* in a scientific sense has led to restricted use of natural receptivities. Consequently, a sensuously impoverished audience unable to respond to poetic thought has been created. Philosophy, Wordsworth concluded, generates a destructive prejudice toward poetry: under the influence of empiricistic epistemology we have come to treat experience as fragmentary, consisting of "data" or "qualities" fed singly into the mind, then bound together by habit to make "experience." The qualitative wholeness of poetic language and the experience it creates are lost; and most impoverishing in this loss is an inability to respond to the natural metaphors of artistic media, for we tend to translate poetry into "thought." Unable to per-

[9] Erich M. von Hornbostel, "The Unity of the Senses," in Willis D. Ellis, ed., *A Source Book of Gestalt Psychology* (New York: Humanities Press, 1950), p. 215.

I

ceive the artistic, we translate it by an unconscious process into something inert.

Wordsworth's defense of poetry, therefore, is to be found in his poetic effort to make the natural metaphors of nature and art available to his repressed readers. When history and argument have overwhelmed the mind, human beings lose touch with the most vital part of themselves, memory and the large sensory endowment with which life is begun. Philosophy and science have together almost killed performance.

Performance, a defense of poetry such as *The Prelude* asserts, remains the mode of action essential to the preservation of the self, of awareness of one's individuality as a person. In performance, as contrasted with argument and experiment, the recollections of the individual are made into the recognitions of the community. To be sure, performance does not yield "knowledge" in the way argument and experiment do, but it does culminate in a showing, revealing reiteration of the past in which the whole person participates. The rightness of performance, then, is to be found in its own order, and not in a method external to the order. In poetry the doubt and skepticism of science is vanquished.

One of the most destructive consequences of scientific skepticism to which poetry is the necessary antidote follows from its indifference to a fundamental aspect of human life, its dependence upon powers, realities, natures that are not human. One of the goals of poetic art is to make known the dependencies and deficiencies of human life, and to suggest ways in which they can be repaired through making the natural order outside the human congenial with and satisfying to human needs. When science and philosophy, as Wordsworth knew them, tend to alienate human experience from the rest of the natural order, poetry shows its continuities with nature. In "explaining" this to the reader, *The Prelude* shows the way to perseverance and salvation.

This sounds a religious theme, yet idealistic art, such as Wordsworth's poetry, is not religious in any simple sense. It is religious in a complicated sense, because it assumes a basic religious metaphor as its structuring principle. It is the idea of *imago dei*: what exists is patterned after a divine exemplar, the thought and will of a divine being. Yet Wordsworth knows that the notion of "made in the image of" derives from an observation of *human* making, and it is then subsequently extended to cosmic being. Our awareness of dependency derives metaphorical power from this direction of our thought, from our interest first of all in our own creative work, and then, by analogy, to the universe. For that we possess such powers must imply that the universe as a whole grows out of the exercise of like powers on the part of a supremely gifted artisan.

The consequences of this analogy are radical, for in extending to the cosmic forces a power of making similar to the human, the human itself is transformed. Human life, its sources, energies, and purposes can now be placed in external reality. A guarantee of human worth, establishment of natural privilege, flows from a mysterious source outside the human. Where self-inspection never can discover a justifying account of human experience for the poet, analogy allows him to use performance, a human action, as the characteristic of deity, and thereby win for his needs an account of his dependency which humanizes the cosmos. He sees the order of nature and man's place in it as from a universal perspective of deity.

The belief thereby generated of a sustaining from without endows nature with purpose, and by renewed application of the analogy, human making becomes the image of divine creation. This recognition of purposiveness in human making is taken to be a replication or imitation of natural order, for it is a re-enactment of divine efficacies. The artistic imitation then takes into itself an urgency and power it otherwise would lack; what the poet reveals, what he sees and hears, comes as a *truth*, because it is authoritative. What the poet says becomes human making endowed with *necessity*. This is not, however, the necessity of causal relationship (the object of experiment), and this is not the necessity of logical entailment (the object of argument). Rather, this is synaesthetic necessity, a rightness in the structure of experience itself, a rightness in the order of sensory immediacy. Here at last the validity of immediate experience, without the need for a mediating method, has been achieved. In this way the poetic can be said to be right and necessary; in this way the poetic recovers the values which were lost to philosophy and science in the revolution of the centuries preceding Wordsworth's life. But Wordsworth's poetry has been infected by the cultural attitudes he hopes to overcome, and the magnitude of his task, the force he must expend to bring poetry up to the claims of argument and experiment, affects the form of what he writes.

IV

The Prelude is a poetically most unpoetic work, if by "poetic" we think of language made beautiful and compelling in its formal originality. Wordsworth occasionally hits a markedly interesting conjunction of words, but more often than not there is an awkwardness and sometimes an embarrassing crudeness in the way he puts words together. The poem itself is often not beautiful; more often it has a craggy ruggedness and rudeness that seems something like the landscape Wordsworth imagines he inhabited as a youth. But more striking than any of these characteristics is the strange way the thought moves, the kinds of events, powers, possibilities, affects, judgments which to Wordsworth make poetry. Most of us would never have considered his ordering of elements possible as a poetic mode of statement, yet Wordsworth carries it off, partly through his sense of his own gifts and his conviction that he is a poet.

Consider the opening lines of Book V. "Contemplation" is described as spreading through the universe, and as a consequence penetrates the soul of all, but most importantly of the poet, whose reaction is to feel grief for man. The cause of the grief is not human suffering, great as that is, but the rewards achieved by dint of exercise and thought: "there, there, it is / That sadness finds its fuel." The word "fuel" is one of the slightly gauche, ugly words out of which Wordsworth makes his poetry. The poet then describes, in a passage of high abstraction, the thoughts he has had while writing this poem (which he calls Verse—with a capital V). The upshot of this long and gnarled passage is that the poet is stricken when he thinks man may pass away, that the earth and all man's work thereon are possibly to be obliterated; yet should this occur, "the living Presence" would still "subsist"—yet where would be all human thought and passion? And the stanza concludes with the lament mentioned at the beginning of this analysis.

> When Contemplation, like the night-calm felt
> Through earth and sky, spreads widely, and sends deep
> Into the soul its tranquillizing power,
> Even then I sometimes grieve for thee, O Man,
> Earth's paramount Creature! not so much for woes
> That thou endurest; heavy though that weight be,
> Cloud-like it mounts, or touched with light divine
> Doth melt away; but for those palms achieved,
> Through length of time, by patient exercise
> Of study and hard thought; there, there, it is
> That sadness finds its fuel. Hitherto,
> In progress through this Verse, my mind hath looked
> Upon the speaking face of earth and heaven
> As her prime teacher, intercourse with man
> Established by the sovereign Intellect,
> Who through that bodily image hath diffused,
> As might appear to the eye of fleeting time,
> A deathless spirit. Thou also, man! hast wrought,
> For commerce of thy nature with herself,
> Things that aspire to unconquerable life;
> And yet we feel—we cannot choose but feel—
> That they must perish. Tremblings of the heart
> It gives, to think that our immortal being
> No more shall need such garments; and yet man,
> As long as he shall be the child of earth,

Might almost "weep to have" what he may lose,
Nor be himself extinguished, but survive,
Abject, depressed, forlorn, disconsolate.
A thought is with me sometimes, and I say,—
Should the whole frame of earth by inward throes
Be wrenched, or fire come down from far to scorch
Her pleasant habitations, and dry up
Old Ocean, in his bed left singed and bare,
Yet would the living Presence still subsist
Victorious, and composure would ensue,
And kindlings like the morning—presage sure
Of day returning and of life revived.
But all the meditations of mankind,
Yea, all the adamantine holds of truth
By reason built, or passion, which itself
Is highest reason in a soul sublime;
The consecrated works of Bard and Sage,
Sensuous or intellectual, wrought by men,
Twin labourers and heirs of the same hopes;
Where would they be? Oh! why hath not the Mind
Some element to stamp her image on
In nature somewhat nearer to her own?

[V, 1]

It has taken Wordsworth a long time to say something simple; he has given himself the liberty of a verse form as open and free as possible, and he has used language as clumsy as the thought permits. Consider the string of adjectives modifying the imagined condition of man: abject, depressed, forlorn, disconsolate (l. 28). The juxtaposition of these words in terms of both their traditional employment and their characterizing power works to the peculiar Wordsworthian tone. Thought and poetic structure are all of a piece here, exemplifying the trite observation of Pope. That this may be a poetic fact in no way concludes our evaluation, for unity of form and content, as it is sometimes called, may be of the banal and trivial, as well as of the profound. Wordsworth falls into neither one nor the other; like all great poets his work eludes simple-mindedness on the one hand and philosophical depth on the other. It is, as Kant would have said, like nature in its unself-consciousness, yet unlike nature in its rules. But because it is the product of genius, it is as though nature gave the rules to art. This is as good a description as any, though still quite inadequate.

Because nature is frequently ugly, to assert that art is like nature is not to evaluate, but simply to observe that an underlying coherence characterizes a work. Wordsworth's poem is coherent; it is clumsy and awkward and full of the disjunctions which flow from a mind somewhat unclear about itself and its thoughts. It struggles more than it succeeds, but then that is the subject of the poem itself: the exhausting effort to let imagination triumph. It does, in the end, but then as it succeeds, so intellect and conceptual clarity which are the mark of intellect must yield. Displacement of this sort is Wordsworth's goal, for he believes it is what makes a poet, what makes art. Can we therefore assign this to all poetry? Hardly, for many poets never could accept the consequences. Imagine Marvell so disposed, or Eliot, or Wallace Stevens. It is a question of what aspect of the self shall guide the hand. Wordsworth happily lets the recollections of his early life come back to haunt us; it is *they* that shall be given poetic place. His aim is to give us, the readers, this experience, to so contrive his verse that we too shall put imaginative wholeness ahead of thought. To read *The Prelude*, then, on its own terms and according to its own demands, we must allow the same rich, suggestive, sloppy course of affective states, moods, and images to entertain us. We can do this, despite our training in clarity and rigor, if we but succumb to that power within us, the power of memory, whose many faces Wordsworth allows to be seen: recognition, recollection, and Platonic anamnesis; all three play about in the first stanza of Book V.

Examining the first forty-nine lines of Book V reveals no more than other passages would; it is paradigmatic. The poet yields to recollections, which in turn provide the recognitions of an educated mind, and these two courses finally are combined into the sense of a divine presence whose company once was enjoyed. Wordsworth has made the fullest exploitation of memory. That this should be the case is peculiar to Wordsworth and to some other artists; no doubt it has a place in the artistic and philosophical idealism of the time. However it originates, such commitment to memory creates artistic problems of a special kind, for memory does not issue forth in composed and syntactically routine sentences. Memory is chaotic; yet poetry must be, at least on the primitive linguistic level, clear and coherent. How can memory be given form by poetry? The answer Wordsworth found was one he inherited from a debased Platonism which, however philosophically unsatisfactory, worked well enough for *The Prelude* because he was able to join to the Platonic theory of anamnesis a miniature dialectic of memory. First in the process is recollection, the private, personally meaningful connection with the past. His relationship to his own childhood and all that he holds dear as *his* experience must have a public life if it is to be the stuff of art. The second, externalizing function of memory is recognition, through which separate awarenesses share a common order in the present and the past. The poet tries to give public form to recollection but he cannot give it over to the public since in its publicness it loses the quality of "me-ness," and the person is deprived of what is most securely his. Poetry, in short, is a threat to recollection.

Thus when the poet describes the spread of contemplation in the opening of Book V, he gives an account of the condition of his poetic reflections. He sinks into himself, and there finds worlds which must be externalized and shared. The means for this process of externalization is poetry, whose composition must be such to rouse in the reader recognition: "Yes, it is thus; I too know this function of memory." But now the poet has given over, as it were, his own most precious and indefinable self to the examination of others. He cannot save his privacy except through a call to the reader to join with him in a higher synthesis of memory, the common realm of anamnesis whose reality and accessibility are made certain by a divine power. Lines 11–22 in the long passage from *The Prelude* quoted above are not simply a description of the lot of mortal man, but most especially of the poet, who having given over all he possesses to another is in danger of perishing. All creations of the spirit, and that includes poetic utterance, are lost unless a way can be found to join what is created to the reality entered into by anamnesis. The lament that the mind has not an element to stamp her image on in nature is answered by the dream. There is no stamping upon, but only a joining with. The human memory is a fragment of that divine reality to which all fragmentary consciousnesses must return. Poetry and geometric truth are then in fundamental reality the same.

Wordsworth denies, therefore, that the poetic impress is what counts, for no mind can do more than create an evanescence. Should I be impressed by his poetry, I am only reacting to the most momentary externalization of the inner reality. Art can be successful only when it leads the reader to join himself, in an aspiration of anamnesis, to the reality of imagination. Art fails when it demands that attention be centered on its separated, momentary, essentially private manifestations as the poetry of *this* or *that* one poet. A phenomenology of the imagination, like the phenomenology of mind in the Hegelian sense, is an account of how the awareness moves to fullest self-consciousness in the merging of the one recollection with the anamnesis available to all finite memories. Wordsworth's poem, in this sense, can then be seen as a call to an exercise of the imagination analogous with Hegel's call to an exercise of mind. The work of art is truly a *working toward*, a freeing oneself from the boundaries of private recollection and joining it to the common memory in the one reality to which Wordsworth gives the names "Presence" and "Divine."

Why is the poem, after all this is said, so clumsy? One answer is that it is clumsy, rather bumptious thinking, and the ideas are, after all, unwieldy because of their traditional accretions. Wordsworth is falling back upon old encrusted thoughts, dredging them out of a common poetic slime from which they have been pulled and into which they have been thrown back for thousands of years. Like the dead body rising up out of the lake, the poetic analysis of experience Wordsworth offers is out of the depths of our literary past. They are drowned thoughts in a wet season; but for all that, they are also, like the drowned man, reminiscent of the reality to which we aspire. Old Platonism may be, in the world of ideas, the symbol of that ultimate reality, the noumenal or the spiritual, call it what you will, which other literary statements have symbolized in different ways. Platonism is Wordsworth's white whale. But it works, after all. Limping, lurching, crashing along as it does, *The Prelude* is an impressive poem, perhaps because it is made up of such old relics. It is a reconstructed Fort Dearborn of the soul, offering protection for all of us who thought Plato had something to say. And for those who did not and do not . . . ? Well, the fort is constantly under attack.

The poem from Book V to the end is a description of how imagination, under the guidance of poetry, can overcome the limits of a private vision. To be sure, theoretical reason is overcome by story, but there remains the claim of practical or moral reason, a powerful force to which the poet is expected to respond. He describes his outmaneuvering of practical reason in Books XI and XII.

> So I fared,
> Dragging all precepts, judgments, maxims, creeds,
> Like culprits to the bar; calling the mind,
> Suspiciously, to establish in plain day
> Her titles and her honours; now believing,
> Now disbelieving; endlessly perplexed
> With impulse, motive, right and wrong, the ground
> Of obligation, what the rule and whence
> The sanction; till, demanding formal *proof*,
> And seeking it in everything, I lost

> All feeling of conviction, and, in fine,
> Sick, wearied out with contrarieties,
> Yielded up moral questions in despair.
>
> [XI, 293]

Such a tale is bound to find sympathetic hearers, for it describes the perplexities of philosophic training in the desiccated classroom of moral philosophy. The poet turns from philosophy to make his statement in another mode. The curious outcome is the extent to which *The Prelude* shares the philosophic assumptions and in part realizes the philosophic goals of Wordsworth's day.

> I had known
> Too forcibly, too early in my life,
> Visitings of imaginative power
> For this to last: I shook the habit off
> Entirely and for ever, and again
> In Nature's presence stood, as now I stand,
> A sensitive being, a *creative* soul.
>
> [XII, 201]

The self is free at last, imagination given precedence over the understanding. Now poetry can claim its triumph in the liberation of imagination enlightened by the force of love (Book IV, 208). The mind, whose limitation seemed to be its impotence to impress itself on nature, is now given a power equal to that of nature; empiricism of the understanding is shown to be wrong. The correct epistemology is found in crediting imagination with the same reality we grant nature:

> A balance, an ennobling interchange
> Of action from without and from within
>
> [XIII, 375]

Mind does impress itself, through the exercise of imagination whose source is all of memory: recognition, recollection, and ultimately anamnesis. For man this faculty is every bit as "real" as anything "objective," for the outer world is nothing if not focused by the creative imagination. All that has come to us, in our private lives as well as in the history of human experience, can be meaningful only through imagination. The shell and the stone are the two sources of reality, insofar as "reality" means to us the content of awareness. For in the end that is the human realm, what awareness possesses, but it does not even know the full extent of its awareness until it gives imagination its full exercise in art.

Idealism asserts this as a fundamental tenet of its theory of human self-consciousness: the very exercise of faculties such as intellect, will, affect, the states of mind aroused in imaginative constructions such as poetry are steps along the way to liberation from lower levels of consciousness. Sensitivity to nature is identified as a capacity to feel, no longer an ability to give rules. The idealistic theory of genius differs markedly from that of its generating theory, the sort of epistemological dualisms I have discussed in the previous chapter. While genius for Kant was the ability to give rules as nature might, yet to give rules whose descriptions could never be used as directives for making, for Wordsworth genius is a sensibility of feeling.

> From Nature doth emotion come, and moods
> Of calmness equally are Nature's gift:
> This is her glory; these two attributes
> Are sister horns that constitute her strength.
> Hence Genius, born to thrive by interchange

Of peace and excitation, finds in her
His best and purest friend; from her receives
That energy by which he seeks the truth,
From her that happy stillness of the mind
Which fits him to receive it when unsought.

[XIII, 1]

This receptivity implies a movement upward and outward, to larger, more encompassing states of awareness
and higher states of awareness that carry the genius close
to the divine. Idealism, in expressing this optimistic possibility, introduces a conception of art that has created
great controversy. Not only does the individual move to
higher and larger conditions of awareness, but art as a
whole does too. Coleridge, in commenting on his friend's
work, expressed this possibility: "*The Prelude* was to infer
and reveal the proof of, and necessity for, the whole state
of man and society being subject to and illustrative of a
redemptive process in operation, showing how this idea
reconciled all the anomalies and promised future glory
and restoration."

Wordsworth takes up the same idea:

That Poets, even as Prophets, each with each
Connected in a mighty scheme of truth

[XIII, 301]

and

I seemed about this time to gain clear sight
Of a new world—a world, too, that was fit
To be transmitted, and to other eyes
Made visible . . .

[XIII, 369]

Wordsworth believes he has discovered his own voice, in part as an overcoming of philosophy; but his conscious rejection of philosophical analyses of experience accompanies an unconscious agreement with an idealistic philosophy of experience. Were this to be pointed out to him, one can imagine his welcoming it as a confirmation of the Divine realizing itself in separate consciousness. Indeed, for all we know, Wordsworth might be correct, were he to have believed this. The purpose of the exploration undertaken here is to show that as a matter of historical fact strong consistencies are to be found in the philosophy and the poetry of two great minds. *The Prelude* gives an account of experience in several basic respects like that offered by the speculations of Hegel and his idealistic tradition. I cannot give an explanation of this beyond the banal theory of intellectual coherence in terms of which we find the past manifesting styles and periods; the kinds of experience afforded by art are in some cases complementary to the possibilities of experience analyzed and defended in philosophic inquiry.

For early philosophical idealism in the thought of Schelling, and for the phenomenology of imagination worked out in *The Prelude*, artistic consciousness provided philosophy with the reality of a unified self and world. Thus, in a specific sense the philosopher and the poet required one another, and the product of art realized a value which was not reducible to the logical, the moral, or the aesthetic. The analysis of values according to an atomistic empiricism had been overcome, it was believed, by a realization of values in an expanded and inclusive sense fit for the modern consciousness. In this way idealism regarded itself as a step into modernity, not according to the model of a mechanistic science, but according to a model of the expanded self. Idealistic modes of awareness, in both philosophy and poetry, were believed to be definite advances into a higher consciousness. This has had marked theoretical consequences, as I remarked earlier, in both political theory and psychology.

To many writers, however, the kinds of values defended by idealistic accounts of experience are far removed from the simple spiritual values of the past. To them, the threat of an empiricistic aestheticizing of art has been overcome by a return to values of a more obvious religious kind. One such writer who tried to establish more traditional solutions to the problems of modernity was Tolstoy, whose reaffirmation of the power of literary art took a quite different form from Wordsworth's idealism.

K

Chapter 4

Art as a Defense of Moral Values

Modernity, defined as a shift in the purposes of art from moral to aesthetic values, has always been under attack; but those who decry the aestheticizing of art have been, more than not, poor artists. Their contentious works, written under polemical impulses, were tracts for their times, aged manifestoes in ours. Telling criticism as a part of successful artistry is extremely rare. One case we all know well, and admire, though we may find it overly intense in its insistence on the moral basis of art, is Tolstoy's *Resurrection.* I shall consider the demand he makes for a return to the moral values that, in his view, informed the great art of the past. Although Tolstoy would not regard himself as attacking modernity, since his world was not artistically sophisticated and self-conscious in that sense, he did think of his work as propagandistic, gospel-like in a specific sense, aimed against the degeneracy, the decadence of his society. He saw himself fighting a society decayed, not an art that had become aesthetic. The aestheticism he recognized could be accounted for, he argued, in terms of the selfish, auto-stimulating needs of a degenerate audience. Aestheticism is a response to a moral lack. Therefore the intent of art must be moral.

The aesthetic will either take care of itself or become irrelevant. Just what he thought about the artistry of his later work it is difficult to say, but the path he cleared through the tangled aesthetic of his time is clearly blazed. He saw, as we do, that only occasionally do literary works concern themselves with moral values. For every work concerned with moral values there are countless ones whose sense is other than moral. I have already discussed the aestheticizing tendency within some of the greatest writing of the eighteenth and nineteenth centuries, work which reflected and reinforced philosophical accounts of experience. Tolstoy was sensitive to these developments and tried to move literary art back to moral involvement.

It is worth noting that Tolstoy's concern with the possible moral concern of art is not unlike our own, for in both British and American literary studies at the present time we see demands that literature be committed to moral values and be judged on that basis. Yet ambivalence toward the call to moral literature is natural since it is widely believed that as judicious philosophy ought to avoid the fervor of literature, so poetry ought to reject systematic conceptual thought.

Tolstoy has been pointed out as one who gives weight to this generalization; he is a poor philosopher, to be sure. And few philosophers, if any, could be poets. But I think we must avoid a confrontation between philosopher and poet as such, and ask why each may try the other's tasks. I am led to carry out this experiment by my own disappointment in philosophic efforts to deal with pressing moral issues. At the same time, I have never been able to accept Tolstoy's didactic works, and to a lesser extent his novel *Resurrection*, as morally enlightening. One reason for this, I suppose, is his religious solutions to issues that require much more. The essential ingredient in Tolstoy's later writing is moral concern. I am willing, therefore, to join literary to philosophical inquiry in the hope that each may reinforce and enlighten the other. Following Tolstoy's lead, I shall take up the problems of rules and coercion, for it is in action according to rules, and in the application of force by one group upon another, that he sees the source of much of our moral confusion.

I

Resurrection was once much admired; now it has suffered the fate of many monumental creations whose silhouettes forever stand at the horizon but whose details are never seen for the great distances at which they are viewed. Looking closely at the novel, we see its central question: "By what right does one person within a society coerce another member of that society?" Subsidiary to this question are the following: "Can we explain the means by which individuals come to believe that they have the right to coerce others?" "What enables individuals to act so that there ceases to be human regard between them?" By human regard, Tolstoy means feelings of love. Finally, "How does it come about that individuals are able to replace duty toward others with duties to an office or role?" In Tolstoy's words: "He [Nekhlyudov] asked a very simple question: 'Why, and by what right, do some people lock up, torment, exile, flog, and kill others, while they are themselves just like those whom they torment, flog, and kill?' " [1]

These questions embarrass us because they are so basic and because they immediately bring to mind countless violations of the principles they suggest. And they embarrass us because we know so many silly, wrong-headed, witless efforts to give answers. Tolstoy himself gives easy answers: as if one could act always out of love; or as if adherence to one religion or one religious teacher could make men behave humanely toward one another. I suppose this simplicity has made readers reject the moral content of *Resurrection* and look for whatever "artistic" merit it may have. This derives in part from our own feelings of helplessness; how can we go on giving simpleminded answers when we have so much evidence of human depravity?

We must stop ourselves here; this response is not the appropriate one, for Tolstoy is not asking simply, "How can we win out against evil?" though to be sure he wonders about this. He is asking, more specifically, "By what *right* does one person coerce another?" And that is a different, a meaningful, a responsible question. But we fail to respond to it because we have come to accept the fact and we take it as a basic assumption that there is no issue of right here at all, only an issue of power. I shall argue that Tolstoy is quite correct in saying that the issue is an issue of right, no matter what the power exercised may be. When Tolstoy asks if the person who exercises power

---

[1] Leo Tolstoy, *Resurrection,* trans. Louise and Aylmer Maude (New York: W. W. Norton, 1966), p. 349. All subsequent quotations are from this edition.

has the "right" to do so, his implied answer is negative, for he believes that any exercise of power is evil. Our first reply to him, naturally, is that there are a variety of power situations, and there can be the exercise of power in situations in which persons freely accept the authority of a few over the many. But that is to give oneself over to the forms of human organization guided by fallible human thought. It would be far better, Tolstoy argues, if we could dispense altogether with such social structures. Where there are rules there are grounds for right in the legal sense; where there are rules power is legitimized. This is the kind of social structure Tolstoy examines in *Resurrection*, for he never makes the naïve mistake of assuming, as we often do, that people who prevail over others are acting out of selfish interest alone.

Does one who condemns "inferior" persons to the gas chamber consider that an issue of right is involved? Do repressive judges, acting out of their own selfish impulses, really believe or bother to consider whether rights are involved in their decisions? No, we tell ourselves; we are too sophisticated for that kind of question, since we *know* that coercive action springs from aggression whose aim is benefit for the self. However, such cynical answers are not in accord with the facts, for where we find coercion and unfairness the interesting and important fact, as Tolstoy saw, is that we do find all kinds of rules under whose sanction coercion is justified. So there is a giving of rules, both to guide and justify our behavior. That we work within a rule framework is obvious; Tolstoy carefully constructs just such a rule framework in the novel. Even when the action is bestial, behavior is defended by rules. We know this from many, many instances in our own political past and present.

Furthermore, coercion itself is always rule justified, whether it be coercion according to just principles or coercion by individuals for their own selfish ends. Philosophers have long recognized this. A contemporary philosopher of law, H. L. A. Hart, has defined "coercion" as "compelled actions *where there is an existing system or rules* conferring authority on persons to prohibit behavior and to visit breaches of the prohibition with appropriate coercive, repressive, or punitory techniques of the system." [2]

In general, then, coercion is thought justified when provision is made to set forth a demand in a specific situation, and punishment imposed if the demand is not responded to appropriately. An example is imprisonment following a soldier's failure to keep his watch. Military law spells out in detail what is demanded in the situation and what follows nonperformance. Military law provides a simple example of a coercive system.

A looser, less exacting system is that of civil life in which there are varieties of rule systems governing behavior and imposing punishments for failure to perform in specified ways. While there is far more flexibility in civil life, the important point here too is that coercion requires rules, for no matter how readily we jump to coercion, we find it hard to exercise coercion unless we have rules to go by, unless we have ready at hand a penalty spelled out to be imposed in case of delinquency. Without these conditions we are ill at ease; let them be met and we joyfully find it easy to be coercive. Give the rule, no matter how absurd, and there are persons who will work it into a context of justifying propositions. Insinuate

[2] H. L. A. Hart, *The Concept of Law* (Oxford: Clarendon Press, 1961), Ch. II. My emphasis.

that there is no rule, and the same persons are thrown into confusion and doubt.

One of the penetrating observations in *Resurrection* is how these rules function and what their source is. Rules of coercion grow out of human need, the political system, demands of the state, the will of the sovereign, ancestral tradition, and, insofar as limited rules are needed to solve immediate problems, arbitrary ad hoc decisions of those in places of power. There are many rule sources; we find it easy to accept them all. We find it hardest to give them up and convince ourselves that rules should originate within the self. Given the many rule sources, we can ask the fundamental questions: (1) What makes rules just, aside from their source? (2) By what right does one person impose rules upon another? Pressing as these questions are, the answer to them is usually sought in careful argument about ends and means. We all know the utilitarian, Kantian, and intuitionistic answers. We do not, however, fit these answers into a psychological framework, and this Tolstoy tries to do. In doing so, he is consciously rejecting that defense of rules which he thought of as "science." One of the tasks enumerated by the writer for his protagonist, Nekhlyudov, is an inquiry into "the reasons why all these very different persons were in prison, while others just like them were going about free, and even judging them" (p. 348). When the expert books are marshaled, they yield no answers, but only "deliberations as to whether human beings had free will or not; whether or not signs of criminality could be detected by measuring the skull; what part heredity played in crime; whether immorality could be inherited; what madness is, what degeneration is, and what temperament is; how climate, food, ignorance, imitativeness, hypnotism, or passion affect crime; what society is; what its duties are—and so on" (p. 349). The underlying crucial question, "By what right do some people punish others?" is never answered.

In anticipation of our argument, we can say that Tolstoy is going to take the position that rules are bad even if freely chosen, whereas the political tradition out of which he writes—a tradition including utilitarianism, Kantian ethics, and a certain kind of idealistic intuitionism—defends rules on a variety of grounds. *Resurrection*, therefore, is a radical book. It truthfully represents the uncertainty out of which rules are sought and defended, but it cannot find any rule system that would do away with the evils of coercion. *Resurrection* is a far more self-conscious, self-referential novel than is *Anna Karenina*. And it is this in two senses: first it undertakes to expose the rule-formulating and rule-applying procedures of plot structure—that is, it is an "honest" novel in a way Tolstoy believed his earlier works were not. In this respect he regards it as standing in judgment upon his earlier work, and as such is consistent with his rejection of "aestheticized art" as argued in *What Is Art?* Second, it is a reversion to his own beginnings as a writer in a curious artistic regression, for the hero, Nekhlyudov, is taken from the first autobiographical writing Tolstoy did, *Childhood, Boyhood and Youth*. In the second of these sketches we meet the boyhood friend Nekhlyudov, "an enthusiast," and one who exhibited "ecstatic adoration of the ideal of virtue, and a conviction that the purpose of man's life is continually to perfect himself." [3] In choosing

[3] Leo Tolstoy, *Childhood, Boyhood and Youth*, trans. Louise and Aylmer Maude (London: Oxford University Press, 1930), Chs. XXV, XXVII.

Nekhlyudov as his hero for *Resurrection,* Tolstoy rejoins his older artistic self with his first, his new sense of conduct with that which he regarded as his true moral foundation. Both as a moral and an artistic self, Tolstoy represents himself in *Resurrection.* In daring to do this, Tolstoy is certain to repel us, for artistry ought not deny its own development. Consonant with his dedication to "honesty," a quality that the autobiographical writings claimed marked the relationship between the "I" and Nekhlyudov, Tolstoy allows himself to begin a novel with a strong negative affect. In radical distinction from *War and Peace* and *Anna Karenina, Resurrection* begins in discomfort, dissatisfaction, and unease.

Regressions of this kind are unusual in art, but not unknown, nor are they unlikely as preoccupations of artists who, advanced in life, look back to their early work. Psychologically, Tolstoy is a regressed or regressive person in his later years, and his art bears this out. We know from his diaries that he longed for his mother, wished to be reunited with her, and that his last thoughts were of his infancy, his need to be suckled, and his deep feeling of loss. Perhaps, again speaking psychologically, there is a basis for his stylistic and moral position in his need to be reunited with his mother, whose loss he felt all his life. His religious solutions to the deep moral and political questions he posed in *Resurrection* take on new point in this context, for to be once again as little children under divine guidance is, in a form that has social sanction, the regression to infancy.

In saying this I do not want to offer a "solution" to the limitations of *Resurrection,* but to point out that it poses special artistic problems to the analysis I am making. It may be that the moralizing of art which Tolstoy defends against the aestheticizing tendencies of his day has several sources, and we ought to explore each one of them. I therefore suggest a psychological aspect of his last work which brings it into connection with the first writing he did.

Let us turn now to the climate of affect which we enter upon opening the book.

Unease pervades the opening of the novel. The hero of *Resurrection*, Nekhlyudov, is characterized by insecurity; what he *ought* to do, how he *ought* to behave, how he *ought* to respond to others are debilitating preoccupations for him. He acts most readily and easily under commands. His first positive action, taken amid the consideration of overwhelming uncertainties in his private life, is to answer the summons to jury duty; at least, this is clear, indifference would be followed by prescribed punishment, by the forfeiture of 300 rubles. It is noted that he denied himself a horse that cost the same, so he regards a fine of 300 rubles as a meaningful sanction. Our first acquaintance with Nekhlyudov, then, is in a specific circumstance in which rules and judging are the grounds of action. He is compelled by an external authority to sit in judgment on another person. This is the basic condition for all rule application, whatever its origin and purpose. However, and this is Tolstoy's novelistic purpose, the contexts of rule abiding and rule making are many; we shall follow Nekhlyudov from this situation through several others, and finally shall see him coerced by self-imposed moral sanctions of a different sort.

The general affective tone of Nekhlyudov's life is *unpleasantness,* a quality repeatedly inserted by Tolstoy into the reflections of the hero. We the readers find the novel somewhat unpleasant; the antagonist finds his life pervaded by the same feeling. Indeed, the novel, like Nekhyludov's life, is repellent. Did Tolstoy intend this? I think that may be unanswerable, but I suspect that there is a concern with the revolting in *Resurrection* in order to generate the feeling of unease, and in the extreme case, revulsion. We are helped to this by the repeated statement that every aspect of Nekhyludov's life is "unpleasant to him": his love affairs, estates, social obligations, efforts at art, future prospects, living conditions in his parents' house, the recollection of past incidents—all is tinged with faint disgust, every emotion like a bad taste. In this condition the character can be concerned with only one thing, escape from unpleasantness. Life so constituted cannot be concerned with anything as abstract and impersonal as justice; it can only be compelled by a desire to deaden present feelings or transform them to more pleasant feelings. One cannot be concerned with questions of right or wrong until one has found some comfort. Despite the fact that Nekhlyudov's life is one of scruple, his scruple derives from inhibition and fear of unpleasantness. Rule acceptance, conformity, "being good," derives really from the hope that by making further sacrifices of himself he will enjoy something pleasant. But the more he imposes scrupulosity, the more he suffers. This condition is not peculiar to the hero; it is a condition of social life. The distinguishing mark in him is his unwillingness, ultimately, to efface the unease through acceptance of a destructive imposition of rules upon others. He is in the right condition to do that, but he never becomes a routine functionary, a mere subsumption under a set of rules.

It is worthwhile discovering how he avoids the fate of most of his contemporaries.

We learn, through recollections of his earlier life, that Nekhlyudov has occasionally acted coercively toward others, but on the whole his life has been one of rule obeying, and of a detachment from those rules that would compel him to coerce others, because of a condition we would call "depression." Suffering depression, he is seeking a justification for the pervasive unpleasantness he feels, and the jury summons solves the problem for that day: he is given seemingly harmless rules under which he can act. His actions are given sanctions, at least for the moment. But the situation he accepts turns out to be far more complicated than anything he is prepared to face, since the juridical coercion of jury duty, trial, law, penalty before the law, imprisonment, and all the other possible penalties require from the one who judges a clarity, a perspicacity about the grounds and ends of action which Nekhlyudov lacks entirely. Of course he is not alone in this: everyone involved, from judge to attorneys to priest to courtroom functionaries are all thoroughly incompetent; and all of them are thrust into the rule system carrying with them the feelings, needs, impulses, petty gratifications which are totally irrelevant to the deliberations they are compelled, again by the rule system, to undertake. Yet they all subject themselves to this system—as each of us does to his own—because only by accepting the system of rules can actions be given meaning, or so we tell ourselves. Tolstoy wanted to challenge that assumption, but he did not realize that such a challenge is so fundamental, so thoroughly dissolving of the whole legal structure that his charge requires him to offer a thoughtful reconstruction of behavior according to rule. I shall return to this problem later.

What we recognize in Nekhlyudov is the sense of propriety he feels when he discovers that jury duty has a sanction; indeed, the whole juridical system constitutes the sanction, and therefore he has, for a moment, a return of ease. Thus comforted, he hopes to perform his duty. But once again duty is confronted with feelings of anxiety; even here the rule system under which he had hoped to act with comfort, fails him, for the person he must judge is a woman he seduced and made pregnant: he must judge one he has ruined. Now this seems extreme to us, and although Tolstoy found the germ for his story in a "real" event, we dislike the neat tying up of juror with defendant; it strikes us as artificial. To say it "really happened thus" is no answer. The only justifying answer I can give is that by choosing this situation Tolstoy gets to the nub of the rule-imposing, rule-accepting conditions of human life. Nekhlyudov sitting in judgment upon Katusha, the innocent one, now living a life under a "different" set of rules, confronts himself, and us, with the ultimate challenge to the feeling of specialness and superiority he carries with him (see pp. 19–20). "Had he been asked why he considered himself superior to the majority of people he could not have given an answer; the life he had been living of late was not particularly meritorious . . . he did claim superiority, accepted as his due the respect paid him, and was hurt if he did not get it." What can he fall back on in this case? Were he sitting in judgment on a prostitute he could find the two rule systems grounds for indifference; but here he is himself a participant in both systems, personally attached to the

144

defendant, and therefore unable to keep separate through anaesthesia what becomes connected inevitably through affect. Thus he is forced to traverse the great space between defendant and juror and can no longer be, in our phrase, "objective." This is precisely the point Tolstoy wants us to see; we cannot give sense to the notion of "objective judgment" because it denies all that morality seeks. Rule systems are designed to separate people, to stifle feeling, to put action under rule and remove it from feeling. Therefore, a hero must be found who cannot rely upon such social defenses; he must be one who responds with immediate feeling, a sympathy which annihilates rules.

It is necessary, if we are to understand this curious and somewhat disappointing plot structure, to raise the question of rules explicitly, and to examine Tolstoy's beliefs about rules as a guide to conduct. I have already said that Tolstoy rejects both the utilitarian and Kantian conceptions of morality. He rejects all rules, whether they be based on a greatest happiness principle or upon a conception of moral duty as a universalizable imperative. In order to convince us that we too must rethink our unreflective acceptance of rule systems, he presents the conflict of this seemingly bizarre trial.

The rule system underlying the trial is the Russian penal system, whose functioning and whose deliberate social structuring we are shown in detail. Scenes of prison life, official decision making, transportation of so-called criminals, Siberia as a prison and land of exile—all of these social structures present themselves to us. We think this is Tolstoy's "realism." But it is much more than that: it is a realism whose purpose is to show us a way of coping with an essentially *religious* problem, namely, the problem of bringing order and meaning into human life. The Russian penal system is a substitute for religion; it *is* the religion of the society Tolstoy presents. This shocking revelation tears the social fabric so carefully woven in the aristocratic world which we came to know in his earlier novels. Something inhuman has come to take the place of religion in the ordinary traditional sense: bureaucratic officialdom and its related system of punishments. Rule systems of this sort create a break or division in society between those who enforce the rules and those who, it is assumed, violate them. This division is usually taken as neutral, that is, a logical consequence of rules, but not in any case itself a value to be considered. Tolstoy, with his sensitivity to religious goals and needs, does see the social chasms which rules maintain as values of the society. Socially, the rule system with its enforcing mechanism—law courts, prisons, exile—is a fundamental value of the society answering to a deep and pervasive need. It is not merely an expression of aggression, or selfishness, or economic exploitation. It is something which expresses one of the deepest human concerns, that is, the effort to create social order in an alien and hostile world. In this respect *Resurrection* is a novel which takes social problems seriously in an effort to say something profoundly remedial.

That Tolstoy's solution is religious has significance beyond his commitment merely to a spiritual regeneration in society. He proposes a *religious* solution to what is *essentially* a religious issue: namely, what is the *right* (in an ultimate cosmological sense) order of society?—a religious issue dealt with in the nineteenth century by a repressive, rule-dominated order of an enforcing aristocracy and

146

preyed-upon commoners. Tolstoy's conception of political life is thoroughly religious, and therefore he is allowed to see the rule system of bureaucratic Russia in a somewhat different way from sociologists and philosophers. Indeed, his reading of utilitarian tracts and his listening to social welfare preachers had given him a strong sense of revulsion; their insensitivity was shocking. Contrary to their theses was the one he set out to confirm in *Resurrection*, namely, that the deep chasm in society caused by the whole penal system was an expression of an essentially perverted religious longing. The division between the "good" and the "evil," the legal "untouchables" and the "punishables" was itself an expression of a need to establish order here on earth that somehow mirrored and reaffirmed the order of cosmic justice. The need was genuine, human, implacable; the expression perverse, devilish, and corrigible.

The whole system of imprisonment and servitude that the novel carefully lays bare provides Russia with an order, like a scene from an eschatological drama or painting. We sense that there is within the society a pollution whose presence must first be acknowledged, and then isolated. Bureaucratic rule making is an effort at a cathartic separating out of evil from good in an insane effort to save the society; there is a fanatical compulsiveness about the way all officials bend to their tasks. But to themselves their motivation is one of preferment: as Tolstoy states it,

they thought not of men and their duty towards them but only of the office they themselves filled and considered the obligations of that office to be above human relations. . . . It is only necessary that these people should be governors,

L

inspectors, policemen; that they should be fully convinced
that there is a kind of business, called Government service,
which allows men to treat other men as things without having human brotherly relations with them; and that they
should be so linked together by this Government service that
the responsibility for the results of their deeds should not fall
on any one of them individually. [Pp. 391, 393]

Their success dependent upon promotion and favor, they
structure their actions by rules condoning injury to others. It is not merely a case of hostile impulse, but rather
of self-interest. If self-interest demands hurt, then hurt is
done. But justification of hurt remains a condition, and
that is realized through rules. Once the rules are formulated, it is easy to believe that congruence of rules with
justice is assured, for the rules are said to be utilitarian,
for the common good. Their existence is proof of social
stability; and so it is, for stability does follow upon order,
and order upon specific routines. But the rules are misleading because they can be variously interpreted. Given
a rule, that such and such is to be realized because such
and such is a part of the social good, a variety of actions
can be taken toward the desired end. One of the difficulties with a utilitarian position, as we all know, is that the
way to the common good is not intuitively and certainly
known; hence the need for agencies of interpretation
such as the courts, the legislature, or a powerful executive. But all utilitarian systems have argued that there is a
condition against which rebellion and disobedience are
justified, that is, in which life is endangered. Tolstoy is
aware that the crucial situation is that in which a life or
lives are exchanged for rule obedience. In *Resurrection*,
application of the rules, abiding by the rules, entails the
sacrifice of life or personal freedom. Of course the func-

148

tionaries are quite willing to make this exchange, because through rules petty officials are able to unburden themselves of the guilt normally attaching to actions destructive of life and freedom.

One social purpose of rules is distancing decisions from the one who acts so that he escapes the guilt that normally would follow upon an attack against another person. All the ghastly suffering imposed upon prisoners, the absolutely loony limitations put upon others through prescriptions, follow from rules formulated "up there," on official heights where the petty functionaries need never tread. If they should gain the posts of rule making, they will have been prepared to see the need of the system as such. A reiterated chorus in *Resurrection* is this: "We cannot allow that; it is against the rules." Wildly idiosyncratic instances are provided by the rules concerning punishment and marriage.

Nekhlyudov told him that the person he was interested in was a woman, that she was wrongfully convicted, and that a petition had been sent to the Emperor on her behalf.

"Yes, well?" said the General.

"I was promised in Petersburg that the news concerning her fate would be sent to me not later than this month, and to this place—"

The General stretched his hand with its stumpy fingers towards the table and rang a bell, still looking at Nekhlyudov, puffing at his cigarette, and coughing very loudly.

"So I would like to ask that this woman might be allowed to remain here until the answer to her petition comes."

The footman, an orderly in uniform, came in.

"Ask if Anna Vasilyevna is up," said the General to the orderly, "and bring some more tea." Then, turning to Nekhlyudov, "Yes, and what else?"

"My other request concerns a political prisoner who is with the same gang."

"Is that so?" said the General, with a significant shake of the head.

"He is seriously ill—dying—and he will probably be left here in the hospital. So one of the political women prisoners would like to stay behind with him."

"She is no relation of his?"

"No, but she is willing to marry him if that will enable her to remain."

The General, looking fixedly with twinkling eyes at his interlocutor, and with an evident wish to discomfit him, listened in silence, smoking all the time.

When Nekhlyudov had finished, the General took a book from the table, and wetting his finger quickly turned over the pages and found the statute relating to marriages, and read it.

"What is she sentenced to?" he asked, looking up from the book.

"She? To hard labour."

"Well then, the position of one sentenced to that cannot be bettered by marriage."

"Yes, but—"

"Excuse me. Even if a free man should marry her, she would have to serve her term. The question in such cases is, whose is the heavier punishment, hers or his?"

"They are both sentenced to hard labour."

"Very well; so they are quits," said the General, with a laugh. "She's got the same that he has, but as he is sick he may be left behind, and of course what can be done to lighten his fate shall be done. But as for her, even if she did marry him, she could not remain behind—"

"Her Excellency is having coffee," the footman announced. The General nodded and continued:—

"However, I will think about it. What are their names? Put them down here."

Nekhlyudov wrote down their names.

Nekhlyudov's request to be allowed to see the dying man the General answered by saying:—

"Neither can I do that. Of course I do not suspect you; but you take an interest in him and in the others, and you have money, and here with us anything can be done with money. They tell me: 'Put down bribery.' But how can I put down bribery when everybody takes bribes? And the lower the rank the more ready they are to be bribed. How can one find it out across more than three thousand miles? Out there any official is a little Tsar, just as I am here," and he laughed. "You have probably been to see the political prisoners: you gave money and got permission, eh?" he said with a smile. "Is is not so?"

"Yes, it is."

"I quite understand that you had to do it. You pity a political prisoner and wish to see him. And the inspector or the convoy soldier accepts because he has a salary of a shilling a day, and a family, and he can't help accepting it. In his place and in yours I should act in the same way as you and he did. But in my position I do not permit myself to swerve an inch from the letter of the law, just because I am a man and might be influenced by pity. I am a member of the executive and I have been placed in a position of trust on certain conditions, and those conditions I must carry out. . . . Well, so that business is finished. And now let us hear what is going on in the metropolis"; and the General began questioning and relating, with an evident desire both to hear the news and to show off his own knowledge and humanity. [Pp. 474–476]

Tolstoy underlines another aspect of rule-directed actions: the one who enforces rules needs to believe that he aligns himself with cultural values that are positive, enlightened, humane. Rules provide the cement of our cultural universe; one can hardly defend them if they are not designed for someone's welfare; yet most rule systems limit and cause suffering to some. It is important that we be made aware of "the social world" against which the rules appear to be impotent, but on whose behalf the rules can be justified. Thus Tolstoy is correct in taking Nekhlyudov as the hero, for he belongs to the socially unimpeachable world of riches and power but becomes entangled in the rule-dominated world of the poor. He is therefore at once above and subject to rules; but since he invoked rules only when his own insecurity demanded it, he now sees that for some their whole life is determined by rules he need know nothing of.

Beneath the rule system as a means of preferment is the deeper, cosmological implication to which I alluded above. Now that we have seen how rules function in allaying guilt on the level of manifest behavior, we should consider the latent feelings and wishes underlying coercion. Tolstoy sees the issue as essentially a religious one, and therefore he is on the right track in attacking the perverseness of the bureaucratic penal system in religious terms. He is right both in his revulsion and in his counter-suggestion insofar as it *is* a religious issue. But just how it is a religious issue originally he does not see; rather he sees it as an expression of indifference which puts preferment above compassion.

As an attempt to answer the question, "By what right does one person coerce another," Tolstoy's novel is philosophically superficial, but there is a novelistic presentation of great power which possesses us and which Tolstoy created almost, as it were, despite his philosophical

preoccupation. The social order in *Resurrection* is a coherent, meaningful order that provides the inhabitants
with a sense of rightness and purpose. But the rightness
and purpose derive from a belief in the fundamental
dualism of good and evil, and the belief that evil, when
discovered, can be rooted out. The novel, consistent with
Russian intellectual ideals of the nineteenth century,
deals with this dualism in terms of a religious paradigm,
that of society as a family of little children. In the family,
evil, it was assumed, could be controlled. The Russian answer to a social ethic of division in which there was pollution and isolation was *childlikeness*. Among little children
aggression is reduced, dependency and cooperation
heightened, for life is organized under the family and the
father, rather than the state and the ruler. Tolstoy clearly
states this preference and believes it offers a solution to
the problem that led him to write *Resurrection*. How can
we overcome coercion? Let us be as little children under
God.

I I

The force of this resolution cannot be appraised without a
consideration of the concept of justice, for Tolstoy has
created a novelistic conflict of great complexity. And the
place of justice in the society he sees is not easy to determine. I hope to clarify the concept as Tolstoy deals with
it by devoting some attention to the idea of the "just society" as it takes shape during the course of *Resurrection*.
I shall begin with the community of prisoners.

We might think every community in the book is unjust. But it is evident that when a community comes into being outside everyday Russian urban and country life, it takes on a new quality. Thus, the Siberian community of the damned is the prisoners' regeneration of the unjust society out of which they have come. Once outcast and rejected, human beings can begin to make a just society. Tolstoy suggests in this way that justice is realizable only in a community that is separated from and set over against the ordinary community; that is, a basic requirement for the just community is a schism in terms of which the outcast and morally unacceptable establish the justice in the name of which they were cast out in the first place.

This has some interesting corollaries: (1) Within a homogeneous, unified community there is no justice in the sense we are interested in. For example, we would not look to primitive communities, as we call them, to discover what constitutes a just community. (2) We cannot realize justice in our more complicated communities unless a radical process of alienation occurs out of which a community emerges, separates, and splits off from the community at large. (3) The just community requires its moral counterpart: that which in the eyes of the just community is the unjust community.

Interesting theoretical consequences follow from these corollaries: (1) The concept Tolstoy has of *the* unified just community under God is by his own analysis impossible. (2) Any just community is doomed to falter and either become unjust, or spawn in its turn an alienated community which will then, momentarily, be the just community.

I have stated the moral and political issues in *Resurrection* as formal propositions in order to show more clearly how a novel with unusually ambitious conceptual intentions gets into difficulty. But since it is a *novel*, not a treatise in ethics or political theory, another set of values is involved, namely, literary values. The relationship of conceptual content and literary values is one of the most impressive problems Tolstoy confronts; he believed he could let the conceptual content direct the literary shapes of the novel. But as we shall see, that was a naïve belief. The literary statement as such makes demands of a kind that fundamentally determine the conceptual outcomes; and they, of course, in their own way, affect the novel.

The novel takes human action, thought, and belief as its substance, and presents it to us as an interpretable set of complex events. All performances within the novel, and the novel itself as one mode of artistic performance, rest upon the possibility of what we loosely call "interpretation." That is, within the novel, as conceived in the nineteenth century, interpretation of action was assumed to be a part of reading the novel, and the author himself helped the reader in the interpretation of his characters' conduct, beliefs, intentions, and purposes. But so too the reader was expected to interpret the novel as a whole. That is, the novel had a "message." The novel, artistically considered, had its counterpart in everyday life, and its reality, its principles, its meaning were to be established by setting it against and within everyday life. So the novel is analogous to an alienated community—like the prisoner society in Siberia—in the sense that it exists and has meaning in terms of an idealized set of principles, never to be realized in the everyday world, as the prison community exhibits principles never to be realized in the unjust society. Tolstoy's novel, *Resurrection*, exists in terms of a double analogy: the prison life is to the city life as the novel is to the everyday world. A relationship is presented in the novel which is understood when we see that it is an analogue to a relationship holding between the novel and the world.

This conception of the novel, which flourished in the nineteenth century, was not the only conception of the novel and of literature; another conception rejects the moral message—or the possibility and sufficiency of a moral message—on behalf of an aesthetic construction. In this case Tolstoy set out to create a novel which would self-consciously overturn and annihilate the aestheticizing of art by showing the reader that through aestheticizing art the novel could only be a pastime of little worth, whereas in taking back to itself the moralizing of action it could once again be a force for reconstructive good. The fact of social life that most appalled him and led him to "moralize" his art was the coercion exercised by one group upon another. But this was possible, he thought, because of a duality of consciousness in men that enabled them to isolate what they said and what they thought, what they did and what they believed. Somehow the re- alization of justice demanded an integration of the per- son, so that he could no longer tolerate saying and think- ing, doing and believing as isolated from one another. But then, the integration of the person was possible only if it were possible to integrate art, so that what the artist presented in, say, a novel, could not be isolated from real life. Integration of saying and thinking, doing and believ- ing in the novelistic world was a condition for integration within the actual lived world, because then there would no longer be possible the "escape" into art. What obtained in art and what obtained in life had to be the same. But this assumes that what obtains in art is interpretable in some kind of direct, obvious, nonconfusing manner. Because if interpretation of art is ambiguous, confused, liable to antagonisms of different readings, then the moral imperatives of conduct would be suffused by aesthetic puzzles. Morally clear, persuasive art means understandable art by simple interpretive steps, whereas the aestheticizing of art meant the introduction of interpretive puzzles or ambiguities to 'which the reader must give his attention at the expense of truth.

We know from Tolstoy's own comments about his art that he was early initiated into the simplicity of a "sentimental" mode of presentation derived from Laurence Sterne, Xavier de Maistre, and R. Toepffer. The reality presented by these books has been described in the previous chapter, for Sterne's "Humean" world is essentially that of de Maistre and Toepffer—a somewhat cynical, yet deeply felt "self-realizing" portrait of the excesses of romanticism. *The* world is not remade by human effort, but *a* world can be created by the withdrawal into one's room, or library, or fantasies about women. Tolstoy does not reproduce this genre of literary retreat, but he learns from it that a writer must distinguish the world of public events from human interpretations of events. However, here an interesting puzzle appears: the literary work as narrative using language is open to misunderstanding and interpretation. When there is interpretation, disagreements about meaning can arise, and the simple *truth* to which literature aspires may be dimmed or denied. If the purpose of art is to cement human beings together in a community of goodness (the purpose Tolstoy defines in

What Is Art?) then its meaning must be unambiguous. This in turn requires the simplest most direct mode of writing, something he attempted in *Resurrection*.

And yet the novel is not life. To return to the analogy I made earlier, the novel as an art form is as remote from experience as prison life in Siberia is remote from the everyday life of Moscow or St. Petersburg. Both art and its created ideal community, the prison community of Siberia, depend upon being removed from the reality to which they make reference. Within the novel then, in two respects, there is the creation of a redeemed realm that we are to appreciate in its comparison to the fallen realm. The novel is reality redeemed; the prison community is the community of everyday life redeemed. Tolstoy has assumed the traditional ideology and iconography of Christianity to make his novel work. He believed that as his art overcame the dualism between art and life, so it would overcome the dualism of good and evil within life. But this renovation is to be achieved only if there can be an overcoming of a fundamental dualism in human awareness.

Coercion is possible, Tolstoy thought, because of a duality in awareness that allowed persons to say one thing and think another, act one way and believe another. If we could collapse that duality of awareness we might find brotherhood and justice. But the very feat of presenting that duality in the novel form makes it dependent on the dualism of awareness in the way the novel as art form itself functions. So the means Tolstoy sought to overcome the problem was in itself an exhibition and confirmation of the insoluability of the problem. I think that accounts for the essential sadness which per-

vades *Resurrection,* and the way Nekhlyudov's depression
is repeated. Tolstoy himself seems depressed, saddened
and made almost desperate, by the impossibility of the
solution he seeks. He has posed a problem he cannot
solve. And he cannot solve it because he is locked into
the dualities of consciousness which the solution of the
problem would have to reduce to one. Art cannot remove
the dualism, and, on the other hand, the successful reduc-
tion of these dualities by philosophical argument is also
open to doubt.

What we in fact inhabit is not the just kingdom, and
we wonder why, given the ideals so amply argued by
philosophers, the Gospels, and religious seers, we are unable to realize the just society. And we wonder why it is,
though we are endowed with the capacity to feel guilt,
do often feel guilty, and do respond to those feelings,
that we remain outside the just kingdom. This is the
question that so troubled Tolstoy and led him to write
Resurrection. Man inhabits a world of political reality and
gospel longing: the two are wildly incommensurate.

We see that the just kingdom, whether pictured as a
novelistic reality, or argued as a set of ethical norms, remains outside our capacity, because in the first case the
very mode of presentation makes a single reality impossible: once the novel as such is accepted, so too is the
duality of the "real world" and the "art world" or the
"novel's world." On the other hand, once the philosophic
argument is accepted as the postulation of norms, the inadequacy of human capacity to include all of itself in one
community is evident. In both cases justice seems the un-
realizable, yet still the absolutely best and only condition
for man if he is to be human. Under the pressure of that

seeming impossibility, Tolstoy takes the only way out, a way that satisfies neither art nor philosophy. It is to urge that the Kingdom of God is within us, and to say that only if we subject the self to the commandments of an inspired religious leader can we be just. Justice then means giving up an essential part of our humanity. It means this in the two senses of "human" that I have taken as central to a resolution of the problem of justice: first, the artistic way, and second, the philosophic way. The novel *Resurrection* cannot provide an answer because as a work of art it requires two worlds, the real world of everyday life, and the novelistic world it creates. So too the prison community cannot work because it requires the larger community outside itself in order to exist. The created prison community, in which justice is realized, requires the special condition of a smaller community within a larger one from which it splits off.

Tolstoy began his intellectual life as a rational reformer who believed a whole, just society might be forged. Like Nekhlyudov, who proposes rational reform of the tax laws and selfless distribution of his land to peasants, Tolstoy seeks social means to improve an unjust order. All his reading, however, convinced Tolstoy that the philosophers, many of whom proposed specific remedies, were unable to cope with coercion and destructive aggression. His failure to find satisfactory solutions among rationalistic and utilitarian theories made all the more obvious and appealing the idea that the way to the resolution of conflict lay in art. Tolstoy, as an artist, tries to discover techniques—more efficacious than those of economic idealists—to make art the instrument of reform. In his writing on the purpose of art, he articulates how the unified community might be achieved:

Many conditions must be fulfilled to enable a man to produce a real work of art. It is necessary that he should stand on the level of the highest life conception of his time, that he should experience feeling and have the desire and capacity to transmit it, and that he should, moreover, have a talent for some of the forms of art. It is very seldom that all these conditions necessary to the production of true art are combined.

If a work be good as art, then the feeling expressed by the artist—be it moral or immoral—transmits itself to other people. If transmitted to others, then they feel it, and all interpretations are superfluous. . . . An artist's work cannot be interpreted. Had it been possible to explain in words what he wished to convey, the artist would have expressed himself in words. He expressed it by his art, only because the feeling he experienced could not be otherwise transmitted. The interpretation of works of art by words only indicates that the interpreter is himself incapable of feeling the infection of art . . .[4]

Universal art has a definite and indubitable internal criterion—religious perception. . . .[5]

There is one indubitable indication distinguishing real art from its counterfeit, namely the infectiousness of art. If a man, without exercising effort and without altering his standpoint, on reading, hearing, or seeing another man's work, experiences a mental condition which unites him with that man and with other people who also partake of that work of art, then the object evoking that condition is a work of art.[6]

Reading *Resurrection* with Tolstoy's art theory in mind suggests an uncertainty in his vision of reform: the novel solves the problem of justice through depicting the prison community in conflict with the larger community, but the novel as an affective instrument should solve the

[4] Leo Tolstoy, *What Is Art?* trans. Aylmer Maude (New York: Thomas Y. Crowell, n.d.), p. 114.
[5] *Ibid.*, p. 119.
[6] *Ibid.*, p. 152.

problem of communal unity without creating a duality of the sort it depicts. The novel works against the intention of the artist for two reasons: its form, which is seductively aesthetic; its content, which shows us a moral society achieved as an alienated subgroup within a larger, evil society. But Tolstoy believed that, properly created, art can realize the community of affectively cohesive, homogeneously constrained individuals. The community of an audience is like the community of persons under religious restraint, subordinating themselves to a central object from which emanates a qualitatively definite, coercively binding feeling. Could it not be the case that art casts an affective net over the crabbed disputes and aggressive differences of intellect? Art becomes the terrestrial instrument of supreme harmony. Tolstoy's "theory" of art is in fact a theocratic aestheticism.

III

Tolstoy's philosophical and literary purposes are not consonant with one another. The literary tradition he accepts and hopes to exploit is that of the sentimental man, defined by Sterne, Rousseau, and Hume. The philosophical tradition he accepts and hopes to deny is that of Kantian rationalism and English utilitarianism, both of which are profoundly areligious, non-Christian in the dogmatic sense, and community centered in a political realism that Tolstoy hoped to understand but came to distrust. But we see an essential contradiction in writing a novel out of these two sources: on the one hand, the sentimental novel must explore the affective life with a dedication to its essential primacy in human conduct; on the other, philosophically, rationalistic-utilitarian ethics must place the emphasis and raise to first eminence human reason. Tolstoy cannot find a guide to life in either, and therefore he creates a novel resting on an incomplete and insufficient theory of human nature and individual conduct. So considered, *Resurrection* appears to me to be a quest—in the end unsuccessful—but a quest for a solution to the paradoxes generated by theories which take these twin sources of human nature as ultimate. Tolstoy cannot opt for either; and therefore resolves them by an unsatisfactory theocratic aestheticism, as I have termed it.

Coercion remains the critical issue, for coercion is the unavoidable consequence of rule-dominated, rule-defined action. Tolstoy cannot answer his questions about coercion because he cannot reconcile his views of a development in feeling and a rational self-insight that would enable one to act toward others within the boundaries of selflessness as he believed it to be defined by Christian ideals. The lack in both the literary and philosophical traditions that Tolstoy saw and wanted to reimburse was an attitude toward others which they countenanced, namely, the attitude that there are some persons wholly incapable of being just or acting justly and therefore to them no just action and no just conduct is due. If we assume, as John Rawls has suggested,[7] that we owe justice to those with a sense of justice, then we must find a ground for attributing to all persons the capacity for a sense of justice. Nei-

[7] See John Rawls' interesting essay, "The Sense of Justice," *Philosophical Review*, 72 (July 1963): 227–240.

M

ther sentimentalism nor utilitarianism will do this. Kantianism does, but only if we act as if we are members of a kingdom of ends. Tolstoy goes on to assert that by divine coercion we are in fact and must behave as members of a community in which all have the capacity for justice. Thus the coercion he sees exercised in society, he suggests, can only be controlled by a countercoercion, that of a religious domination under a coercive spirit. Tolstoy's solution is essentially antirational and anti-affective. Not that he denies these powers to human beings; he merely distrusts them. What tender, self-insightful propensities there are need to be nurtured and ultimately commanded.

Coercion can be wielded on behalf of justice, to be sure, but in fact it is most usually applied on behalf of discriminatory beliefs that are not at all beliefs about equality of sensitivity and capacity, but beliefs about radical differences of moral sensitivity and moral worth. Thus in most cases, as Tolstoy shows us in *Resurrection,* coercion wielded on behalf of "justice" is in fact an unjustifiable abuse of force on grounds that some persons are allegedly inferior. What it means to say a person is "inferior" constitutes a large part of the content of *Resurrection,* for Tolstoy knows, with the insight into his own class gained in the course of his rich and privileged life, inferiority includes not simply the notion of less deserving, less moral worth, less capacity as a communal participant, but also the assumption that one's inferiors are totally without a sense of justice and without the capacity to develop a sense of justice. That is the point of Tolstoy's emphasis on the ideal prison community in which persons, left to their natural selves, develop understanding, forbearance, and the will to treat one another as ends, not simply as means. *Resurrection* shows us the evils of prison life under the surveillance of "the system" and the warm humaneness of prison life in Siberia, where the uncoerced self expresses itself in love. Of course, we know this is not the way persons behave under those conditions, yet we are capable of hoping that they might, and there is every moral reason to entertain the ideal of the just prison community as the best kingdom for moral beings. Tolstoy has taken an artificial society within an evil community and structured it according to his vision. This is naïve, but, like much fantasy, its naïveté expresses a central insight.

Tolstoy makes us see that once we assume that a person cannot have a sense of justice, we feel all the more right in abusing him. He is degraded to the less than human. Tolstoy's question, then, but in a revised form, is this: "By what posture and by what self-deception do some persons believe that others are incapable of having a sense of justice?" This is really a question more fundamental than the question, "By what right do some persons coerce others?" because coercion is simply a consequence of the underlying belief about the inability of persons to be just and to participate in a just community. It appears to me that Tolstoy's answer is naïve because he simply creates a just community within the unjust community—a device upon which religious and moral reformers frequently depend. But persons living inside and outside the "just community" are not that different and distinct in kind from one another. Just as Brook Farm, Oneida, and Rousseau's fantasies of communal tranquillity are unrealistic, so the belief in the humaneness of the prison community is unrealistic. There cannot be such a community, especially one erected on the foundation of assumed transgression and guilt. But we cannot deny Tolstoy's insight: that outcasts initially share a common bond. In the prison community all have been declared guilty, and there is, psychologically, a foundation of guilt upon which a community might be built. That is, all are equal, and, in Tolstoy's view, equality is the primary precondition for justice. Just as *all* must be as little children to enter into the kingdom of heaven, so *all* must be outcasts if they are to enter into a just community. In this way, the prisoners exhibit that quality without which social justice cannot be realized: they are all admittedly "other" than the society of rule and law.

The position taken in *Resurrection* is in effect this: let us substitute for all punishment and coercive systems in modern societies the simple exhortation, "love one another." Let us live as the Gospels tell us to live; let our authority be the teachings of an inspired man of God. What this asks is that family guilt, or "authority guilt" be the *only* kind of guilt; that participation in the family be extended to the whole of humanity. We shall be as little children. In psychological terms this means cutting off the maturation process at an early stage: arresting development, as we say. In Freudian terms this means channeling the early stages of psychosexual development into the whole moral behavior system, so that we achieve what might be called "polymorphous perverse morality." That is, just as the early stages of sexual growth exhibit a stage of generalized sexual sensitivity, so the early stages of moral maturation (an integral part of the growth of the person as sexual being) exhibit a sensitivity to all issues as dependent upon and as reactions to the wishes, moods, commandments, and evaluations of the parents. We in fact know that such a stage exists, when all issues are appraised in reference to the authoritarian parental system of values. It is the immediate judgment of the omnipresent parent that controls behavior. Godly people like Tolstoy have that attitude too; but the parent is the Divine Presence in each of us. Somehow the parental voice is internalized, and the pronouncements continue. How this happens is difficult to explain, but Freud attempted to give an account of it in "The Future of an Illusion." This is an interesting view of morality, and we ought to explore it.

Persons who can appraise the rightness and wrongness of conduct only through the presence of authority are morally undeveloped, for they are then subservient to the will of another, and one of the goals of moral maturation is the self-sufficiency of the deciding actor. Of course the mature person cannot judge each situation in itself totally afresh, and he therefore works out general rules of conduct to govern his daily life. Rules are important, among other reasons, because they depersonalize the norms of conduct, and therefore make appraisal of their sufficiency or insufficiency far easier.

Of course, having the presence of the Divine Teacher within still raises all the problems of capricious and ambiguous commandments which clear rules are supposed to overcome. And there is a further difficulty attendant upon this stage of moral development: positive contributions to the family or to the society as family are not articulated. If we should all be as little children, then I suppose no one can be expected to reprimand another; if we are to love one another, then it is unlikely we will impose painful or possibly destructive tasks upon one another. And surely the recalcitrant and the naughty will be lovingly tolerated. In asking the question, "By what right does one person or group coerce another person or group?" Tolstoy directs our attention to the system of punishments and to the brutalities which follow from rules, because, in accepting punishment, individuals are allowed to prey upon one another in the name of rules that are accepted at a late stage of moral maturation. If we could induce arrested moral development, then we could enjoy the simplicities of familial morality.

To answer Tolstoy, and still retain a strong sense of the merit of his views, we must take the next step to consider *what we gain—and what we lose—by growing up morally.* It may turn out that his objections to rules will allow us to consider ways of controlling and modifying them as we impose them in our communities.

The familial moral pattern lacks an aspect of moral life that I should call hortatory: as children we are expected to be compliant; we are not expected to urge one another to feats of social constructiveness. Yet the rule system that we develop is so structured that punishments are of two sorts; there are first the punishments of a retributory kind: if you do X, then suffer Y. This has the advantage of making clear where we stand when we perform in specified ways. Second, there are the punishments which attend nonperformance. They are of a different sort and raise many difficult problems because the society is always somewhat unclear about the extent and the need to penalize. The issues that I want to concentrate on are those which animate *Resurrection*, namely, issues having to do with rule formulations stating what will happen if a person refuses to take an action considered beneficial or necessary to the society, or if he refuses to impose upon others penalties for their rule-breaking activity. Rules of this sort have to do with contributions to the social good. The developed stages of morality then introduce a new set of rules of a peculiar kind: these are rules in which you may be required to do hurt to others on behalf of social goals considered good or necessary. If you fail to perform these actions, you suffer penalties. It is in regard to the second sort of rules that coercion becomes interesting, for the situation is definitely nonfamilial. The parents will not ask a child to injure another child on behalf of the family good, but a society will demand that some persons do injury to others on behalf of a wide variety of supposed goods.

In order to make demands of this sort, there must be an assumption of moral indifference, that is, that those against whom action of an injurious kind is to be taken are not themselves possessors of a sense of justice, or an assumption that they have behaved in such a way that we no longer are obliged to treat them justly. But what could place them in that category? Sometimes it is enough that they be declared "enemies." There is no limit to the forms of natural paranoia to which we are all subject, and which will lead us readily to abrogate obligations toward others. Any community can create a threat, either from within or without, and in terms of that threat call upon rules that enjoin persons to do hurt and to suffer hurt. For our discussion it does not matter whether the threat be real or imagined; the issue for us is simply, "By what right do we institute those rules which enjoin persons to injure and be injured?" This issue is what troubles Tolstoy. In resolving the issue, he offers a corollary to rationalistic ethics: "The obligation of justice is owed to those who have a sense of justice." This entails "I am obliged to obey coercive demands only when the coercer gives evidence that he freely and willingly accepts the same coercive force directed against himself."

This has interesting implications for the position of rules in society. As long as there are rules which justify the coercive action of one person or group against another, there will be injustice. Every rule then must be formulated in such a way that when a demand is made that the individual give up something—even his life—for the welfare of the group, the person exercising the coercion shall be himself subject to that coercion. This realizes the condition Tolstoy wanted, by regressing to the family stage of morality, without being infantile and simpleminded about the source of social rules. By postulating this as the will of a divine being, Tolstoy believed we could justify an ideal moral condition of adult life: namely, what we require of others in self-abnegation we must also require of ourselves. Of course this position can be argued without the religious superstructure.

But how can we deal with the maniac who cannot differentiate the destruction of the whole world from the scratching of his finger? I must fight against him, to be sure, but he at least has the necessary logical consistency of madness, and that consistency must be introduced into all moral discourse. We can readily imagine, especially today, a wild, indiscriminate self-destruction in which a person would gladly suffer death for a rule. This ultimate perversion comes close to all who replace moral emotions with rules. But this is once again another of those human perversions that follows from the capacity to be just, as other perversions follow from other capacities. To be human is to be capable of growth toward self-enlargement or self-extinction. To be just, that is, to assume that there is a capacity for justice, can lead to outrageous perversions, such as those we see in our own communities where, for example, the test for a capacity for justice is imposed upon the young, who must be willing to destroy themselves to pass the test.

Tolstoy believes that the moral perversions he saw in *his* society were the result of overrefined moral development: that a moral regression to the familial community was the only corrective. Yet is Tolstoy's essential infantilism to be rejected? Here we confront the crucial paradox: if we insist on developing orthogenic ideals, which I believe is the position I must defend, then how can we avoid the moral perversions of justice as coercion under the guise of communal welfare? Tolstoy has a powerful conception to place against the Kantian ideal of justice as the liberal tradition conceives it: the conception we might call "minimal moral demands." While the just society must postulate a sense of justice, and that we owe just conduct to those with such a sense, there must be as well a limitation upon the coercive demands which such a system allows. The limitation can only come from a moral ideal quite different from that in the Kantian tradition; a moral ideal somehow based upon the family. This is the ideal Tolstoy would have us hold before us, and he can give concrete reality to the ideal only in a picture of prison life. But once we see it that way we see also the inadequacy of Tolstoy's moral infantilism. The condition of human life, morally, must be that of the exiles in Siberia; to break out of that confinement, and its moral insurance against coercion, is to step into the wider world of mature justice and its possible perversions. Tolstoy's success, morally, is in showing us a defect in a widely held conception of justice, but his failure is in a willingness to sacrifice the development of all our capacities to child-like harmony. Among those sacrificed capacities I would place the artistic as well, for Tolstoy's confusions are exhibited in his literary as well as his philosophic practices.

Tolstoy's artistic vision is a function of his moral infantilism, for the curious "arrest" in his development as a person became a subject of his art. He early realized—the young autobiographical writings make this clear—that imagination is the source of his deepest gratifications. Certainly in his younger years, and covertly in his later life, he would rather live in the "prison" of his imagination than risk the world's coercion. The world is death, from whose assault art, like the mother, offers protective embraces. Prison life in Siberia, by an obvious transformation of imaginative power, becomes the place where artistic creativity flourishes: there, imagination is free to realize consoling fantasies. This association of prison with art was not original: the association is a nineteenth-century theme, but more specifically it found expression in a book Tolstoy loved. Just as Tolstoy reached old age, his imagination returned not only to memories of infancy, but also to the earliest artistic stimulation in romantic fantasy. Xavier de Maistre's *Voyage autour de ma chambre* creates the prison room where-in the artist creates his "real" world. Its last words, a fitting epitaph to Tolstoy's artistic life, are these:

Charmant pays de l'imagination, toi que l'Être bienfaisant par excellence a livré aux hommes pour les consoler de la réalité, il faut que je te quitte.—C'est aujourd'hui que certaines personnes dont je dépends prétendent me rendre ma liberté. Comme s'ils me l'avaient enlevée! comme s'il était en leur pouvoir de me la ravir un seul instant, et de m'empêcher de parcourir à mon gré le vaste espace toujours ouvert devant moi!—Ils m'ont défendu de parcourir une ville, un point; mais ils m'ont laissé l'univers entier: l'immensité et l'éternité sont à mes ordres.

C'est aujourd'hui donc que je suis libre, ou plutôt que je vais rentrer dans les fers. Le joug des affaires va de nouveau peser sur moi; je ne ferai plus un pas qui ne soit mesuré par la bienséance et le devoir.—Heureux encore si quelque déesse capricieuse ne me fait pas oublier l'un et l'autre, et si j'échappe à cette nouvelle et dangereuse captivité!

Eh! que ne me laisse-t-on achever mon voyage! Était-ce donc pour me punir qu'on m'avait relégué dans ma chambre, —dans cette contrée délicieuse qui renferme tous les biens et toutes les richesses du monde? Autant vaudrait exiler une souris dans un grenier.

Cependant jamais je ne me suis aperçu plus clairement que je suis *double*.—Pendant que je regrette mes jouissances imaginaires, je me sens consolé par force; une puissance secrète m'entraîne;—elle me dit que j'ai besoin de l'air du ciel, et que la· solitude ressemble à la mort.—Me voilà paré; —ma porte s'ouvre;—j'erre sous les spacieux portiques de la rue du Pô;—mille fantômes agréables voltigent devant mes yeux.—Oui, voilà bien cet hôtel,—cette porte, cet escalier; —je tressaille d'avance!

C'est ainsi qu'on éprouve un avant-goût acide lorsqu'on coupe un citron pour le manger.

O ma bête, ma pauvre bête, prends garde à toi! [8]

[8] Xavier de Maistre, *Voyage autour de ma chambre* (Paris: Alphonse Lemerre, 1876), pp. 79–80.

[Delightful realm of imagination, which the benevolent Being has bestowed upon man to console him for the realities of life, I must quit thee.

Today, certain persons on whom I am dependent, affect to restore me to liberty. As if they ever had deprived me of it! As if it were in their power to snatch it from me for a single instant, and to prevent me from traversing, at my will, the vast space ever open before me! They have forbidden me to go into one city, one given point, and they have left me the whole universe, immensity, and eternity at command. Today, then, I am free, or rather I must return into bondage. The yoke of business is again to weigh me down; and every step I take must conform with politeness and duty. Fortunate shall I be if some capricious goddess does not make me forget both, and if I escape from this new and dangerous captivity!

Oh, why did they not allow me to finish my journey! Was it as a punishment that I was exiled to my chamber, to that delightful country which contains all the riches and blessings of the world? As well might they exile a mouse to a granary. Still, never did I more clearly perceive that I am double than I do now. Whilst I regret my imaginary joys, I feel myself consoled involuntarily: an unseen power carries me along, and tells me I need the air of heaven, and that solitude resembles death. I am ready; my door opens; I wander under the spacious porticos of the Rue du Po! A thousand agreeable visions float before my eyes. Yes! there is that mansion! that door! that staircase! I thrill with expectation.

In like manner, slicing a lemon gives one a foretaste, and makes the mouth water.

Ah! *Bestia!* my poor *Bestia!* Beware! [9]]

[9] Xavier de Maistre, *A Journey Round My Room,* trans. Edmund Goldsmid (Edinburgh: privately printed, 1885), pp. 92—93.

I V

A moral and an aesthetic paradox inform Tolstoy's last novel. Morally the work suggests that an answer to nineteenth-century utilitarian and rationalistic ethics can be found in creating a society in which minimal moral demands are made. The ideal of an orthogenic restructuring of the social order by means of philosophical thought is rejected for theocratic coercion. Tolstoy believed that the need to be destructively coercive is so great in human beings that it can be suppressed only by suprahuman restraint. Since we cannot help ourselves, we seek help in a force whose source is mysterious but which we have seen in some few examples of the Christian life. Since our adult conduct involves us in evil, we must be as little children.

Although we find Tolstoy's solution to the problem of social coercion naïve, we certainly do not have a moral answer to put in the place of his. The problem *Resurrection* poses remains as troublesome for us as for its author.

Aesthetically, the novel exists for us as a work of art in which the moral paradox becomes an object of fascination, the complexities of which we admire, the solution to which we do not require. Merely confronting the issue enlarges our consciousness of human life; moral paradoxes, when they are the stuff of art, transcend their implacability. And indeed art may be the means to find tolerable, though not necessarily acceptable, what philosophy must reject. If this is so, then a defense somewhat different from that raised in *What Is Art?* can be made for literary art. We cannot accept Tolstoy's effort to exchange moral and religious for aesthetic values, but we can see the purpose of an art which takes moral values as its subject matter. Tolstoy's last novel, rather than illustrating and confirming the truth of *What Is Art?* demonstrates another artistic possibility.

Tolstoy's failure to confirm his doctrine of art, and to reverse the values of modernity, leads to the aesthetic paradox. Tolstoy could not see that the aesthetic presentation of a moral problem could itself be a contribution to our understanding of the problem. While attempting to refute modernity in its aestheticizing aspect, he yet wrote a good novel whose values are aesthetic. The moral issue he sought to resolve remains. From his point of view, in terms of his philosophical concerns, I think it is fair to say the novel is a failure; and it is a failure not only because it fails to solve the moral problem of coercion, creating in its place a moral paradox, but also because it made a moral subject the stuff of *art*. This is precisely the outcome Tolstoy wanted to avoid. It must be said immediately thereafter that by virtue of its failure insofar as Tolstoy's intention was concerned, it succeeds as a novel.

Chapter 5

Modernity and Death

There [in literature] *we still find
people who know how to die.*

FREUD

Despite our literary preoccupation with violence and
death, it is extraordinary in this day to find a novel about
dying. Art, or what passes as art, can readily depict the
contortions of death; it can only through much greater effort and with a more delicate hand present the living of
life as a preparation for death—to present death not as a
terminal event, the sudden, unexpected ending of a life,
but the dominant theme lived throughout a life. Indeed,
the problem of writing about dying is made the more difficult by our fear, which compels us to prefer to read
about death rather than about dying; yet alongside that is
our need to come to an understanding of death which
makes dying one of the great subjects of art. Death demands but a rhetoric; dying an aesthetic and a philosophy.

Contemporary literature, dwelling on the fact of death
with stupid morbidity, assumes that the tragic is to be
found in the violent interruption death effects, annihilating a promising future and transforming the past into an

apparent refuge. Death is seen to separate the hero from his unrealized future and his happier past. This treatment of death is the opposite of the traditional philosophical one in which life is lived in full awareness of death, and one central concern of life is to embrace death as a natural culmination rather than a violent interruption. Perhaps preoccupation with death rather than with dying is a function of a change that has come about in the way we regard the past. This change is part of what we mean when we use the terms *the modern* and *modernity*.

We no longer look back to a past with longing in the belief that there was a golden age when men were happy, at peace with one another; but we do believe now, partly as a disillusionment about the possibility of a happier future, that each individual has the possibility of a happy time in his childhood. The dialectic of beliefs about the past is curious, for it moves from the postulation of a golden age to the rejection of that in favor of a commitment to progress and the better time to come, to the rejection of both in favor of—all that is left to us—the possibility of a carefree childhood. However, substantiation that there ever was such a time for any person requires private recollection, the truth of which is dubious since we all know what tricks our wishes play with memory. Each one of us, then, by assumptions of modernity, suffers a private and privileged "golden age," or at least the belief that one *might* have been happy once.

The present is therefore isolated; neither a future of expectation nor a past of comforting recollection has any reality and as such any real causal relationship to the present. In that isolation one cannot "prepare" for death, since the sense of life continuity is denied. Death must come as a violent, unexpected, and annihilating intrusion.

Another consequence of the modern attitude toward the past is that the dialetic of beliefs and doubts about the past subjects narrative art—such as that we find in the historical novel—to an odd limitation: the past it conjures up cannot be believed to be a golden age, nor can it be grounded in any sort of private recollection. All storytelling then, is the storyteller's lie about the past; we have come to regard historical fiction as a kind of fantasy.

Stating the issue this way, one recognizes an old thesis: Plato first suggested this to be the necessary condition of story, and his willingness to belabor the thesis derived from his conviction that philosophers, not poets, are the only true knowers. His motive was self-seeking, for he wanted to subordinate story to philosophy where, he was convinced, lay the truth, if truth were possible for man. One of philosophy's possessions was the stern willingness to inquire into, and possibly to gain knowledge of, dying well. In contrast to this sober, argumentative exploration of dying, the poets depicted dying as horrible and death as fearful; their example could only induce an unhealthy and nonphilosophic anxiety.

We have created a literature today based on Plato's aesthetic of poetic untruth without having as a concern the subject of dying, for it is, as Plato predicted, too painful for most to contemplate seriously. But why could not literature now take up dying as a serious theme? If it should do so, it would then fall into that rare genre, philosophical literature, of which, despite Plato's denial, we have had some examples in the past, though fewer in the present.

When we do encounter philosophical novels in our

N

time, they are usually "novels of ideas" in a didactic sense; but the work I discuss here is, I believe, a philosophical novel concerned principally with the theme of death, yet it is *not* a novel of ideas in the didactic sense. Rather, it assumes as a foundation, without being explicit about this, the political vision of Plato and the psychological insight of Freud. The mind that produced *The Leopard* [1] was aware of the dangers within historical narration due to the change modernity has wrought in the power of narrative art. Modernity suspects all portrayals of the past as mere expressive discharges of the present, rooted in private and cultural psychic needs. Questions of truth in art are considered irrelevant largely because we have come to accept, unquestioningly, an expressive theory of art in the place of the imitative or mimetic theory of art, within the logic of which truth could be defended as an artistic value.

But, given our assumption of the expressive theory of art, what are we to make of a novel in which the hero himself exhibits the complexities of a man accepting the changes of modernity, yet perpetuating in his private concerns the traditional attitudes of the past toward death? The writer in this case is clearly taking the problem of modernity and death as a subject for reflection, and even dares to suggest in this setting that truth may be an object of his story.

Here the question of truth is posed in the context of a theory first fully articulated by Freud who, in his contribution to art theory, was as revolutionary as Augustine

---

[1] G. T. di Lampedusa, *The Leopard*, trans. Archibald Colquhoun (New York: Pantheon, 1960). All quotations are from this edition. See also Lampedusa's *Opere* (Milan: Feltrinelli, 1965).

and Hegel. Like them, he developed a method of interpretation which depended upon a general theory of meaning. Freud turned idealism toward the self, adjusting the Hegelian method of interpretation to the demands of understanding psychic life. According to psychoanalytic theory, art can be interpreted to yield up its inner truths just as dreams, fantasies, slips of the tongue, jokes, and all the characteristic actions of everyday life can. When the psychoanalytic way of looking at human action is assumed by an artist, as it is by Lampedusa, we are solicited to read the story with a sensitivity to details of conduct, gesture, verbal peculiarity which we might otherwise fail to notice. Once we know how to use the psychoanalytic method of interpretation, we are in a position to see the art of the past and to respond to the art of our own time in a new way, just as we learned to see ourselves and the past afresh from the insights of Hegel.

To understand in what terms *The Leopard* solicits careful reading, I shall say something about psychoanalytic theory as a method of interpretation. The two fundamental concepts of psychoanalytic theory most important to literary art are the unconscious and psychic conflict. "The unconscious" is a term introduced to provide a conceptual instrument for the hypothesis that mental processes are made available in two ways: through events evident in consciousness, and through events which, while not immediately available to consciousness, may on occasion become available, and at all times influence consciousness so that what an individual thinks, feels, and performs is in part at least determined by unconscious mental events. The artist, on this theory, can be understood to create in terms of both conscious and unconscious processes; his work is responded to with like complexity. Artistic creativity produces a work in close touch with the unconscious, and therefore our response to art is determined by material communicated by the work which is not ordinarily available in conscious experience. The reader will respond to the literary work in both its conscious and unconscious aspects, in both conscious and unconscious ways. To discover and bring into awareness the unconscious elements and that part of the reader's experience which is an unconscious response requires considerable training, yet the process of interpretation can be developed for art as it has been for the interpretation of dreams. Like dreams, art exhibits a latent and a manifest content; I shall return to this distinction shortly.

"Psychic conflict" refers to the fact that for any individual, wishes, needs, purposes, obligations will not be in accord with one another because basic instinctual demands will be frustrated by external social and moral demands, and also because, within the economy of psychic life, there are conflicts of a sort that cannot be resolved. There are, to be sure, means available to cope with such conflicts (social amelioration, self-insight, sublimation), but however conscious a person is of himself, there are inevitable conflicts within the self, and these are compounded by conflicts in the familial, communal, natural environment. Human products made in the urgencies of these conflicts will deal with them in a variety of ways. Artistic performance allows the deepest, most disturbing conflicts to find articulate though obscured form; and therefore art has an important private and public function. Yet to be acceptable in matters of such sensitivity, art must resort to a dual means of communication, as do dreams. Censorship by the ego and expressive urgencies from the id compel the artist both to obscure and to reveal the content of his art. Hence the distinction between latent and manifest content. The second is directly and obviously present: the remembered dream, the perceived and recognized art content; the first is partially obscured, implied, alluded to, masked, but capable of being known because of a symbolism in which it covertly points to itself.

The psychoanalytic method of interpretation makes available to us the latent content, those universal, deeply felt conflicts of psychic life which not only impel us to perform, but consume a great deal of our reflective waking life. Therefore, the recovery of the unconscious side of artistic performance, while not exhaustive of a work of art, and in many cases not even aesthetically central, is without doubt the recovery of the fundamental content for which, in Freud's view, art is produced and to which we turn for gratification and for truth. Freud never pretended that aesthetic aspects of art were amenable to the psychoanalytic method of inquiry, and permitted an interpretive schism to exist between content and form. Some of his followers, however, especially those influenced by Melanie Klein in England, hope to extend the competence of psychoanalytic method to the aesthetic.

The psychoanalytic revolution, like the allegorical and the historical revolutions of Augustine and Hegel, changed art radically. Not only do we read the art of the past differently, we create differently in the present. So with a novel like *The Leopard*, the reader is expected to develop sensitivities of a new kind, to attend to actions and thoughts in a new way, to read with a theory that is not the theory in terms of which other literary works are structured, even though they will also yield to this method. In the case of *The Leopard* there is a conscious use made of several ideas explored by Freud in his essays, so I shall try to read with the sense that everything counts, that one can "divine secret and concealed things from the despised and unnoticed features, from the rubbish-heap, as it were, of our observations." [2]

I

The protagonist of *The Leopard,* Don Fabrizio, Prince of Salina, is a Sicilian aristocrat, yet a man of revolutionary involvement, for he is born into the *ancien régime* and compelled to live through the Risorgimento of the nineteenth century. He is witness to the several kinds of government men frame for themselves and the many character types for whom they function poorly and well. In himself he sees the sorrowfully impotent man of passion and the joyously effective man of intellect. Yet neither aspect of himself can stay in the assurance of its proper place any more than the governments of decadent Bourbons and progressive Garibaldini can convince us of the right and better order. For both in the self and in the polity, these sides exist; now one, now the other has ascendency, which is to say overcomes the other only to be

[2] Sigmund Freud, "The Moses of Michelangelo," *Standard Edition* (London: Hogarth Press, 1955), 13:222.

overcome in its turn. So considered, this novel could be called a representation of the relativity of all patterns of self and state which we try, forever unsuccessfully, to coerce structurally with ideas and actions.

Although the story is told in the specific terms of Italy's consolidation under Garibaldini and King Victor Emmanuel, yet it is a universal—and therefore artful—presentation of interdependent realities: self and polity. In these terms, it is a novel which expresses an insight of the ancient world and the earliest literature we have from Greece. Because of the close dependence of self and polity in their ambivalences, the story must be told with an emphasis on shifting values. This is fictionally realized through the technique of shifting viewpoints, but without systematic perspective. Thus, it is not told with flashback, nor with chapters moving successively from one character to another—all this being far too artificial for the realities Lampedusa wishes to convey. Rather, it is told from an unusually omniscient present, *our* present of about 1959–1961, yet a present fully aware of the past both in its contemporaneous manifestation—how the past was in its presentness to those experiencing it—and in its pastness to ourselves who can only tell stories about it. The past is therefore permeated by a thoroughly twentieth-century mind, and events are never without their relevant towardness to the present, while the present (*our* present, that is, as readers now) is always shown to be reminiscent of a pattern or duplication in the past.

In this way a tale of Sicily in the nineteenth century can mention the names of Freud, Eisenstein, the year 1960, World War II, and can indulge in novelistic editorials such as this: "It should not be forgotten that romanticism was then at high noon" (p. 118). Events can be compared:

> put in modern terms, he could be said to be in the state of mind of someone today who thinks he has boarded one of the old planes which potter between Palermo and Naples, and suddenly finds himself shut inside a super Jet and realizes he will be at his destination almost before there will be time to make the sign of the Cross. [P. 119]

The impression achieved is of a reality in which there is no crucial past or present, but rather all events participate in a tenseless world made by art. And yet, we come into this possibility of timelessness through the temporal unfolding of a story.

Timelessness confronts the self, phenomenologically, in the expectation of death. The novel sounds this preoccupation, as if a perpetual tolling, in the opening words: *"Nunc et in hora mortis nostrae. Amen."* As if closing this parenthesis, the death of Don Fabrizio concludes the main action of the novel; yet the book does not end there, but continues with a brief account of the survivors. This simple coda, once a trite novelistic device to tie up all the loose ends, becomes a structural contribution to a central theme: just as the shifting temporal perspective of the omniscient narrator establishes the timelessness of life lived through generations, so the survivors' thoughts and actions give us a shocking realization of what an individual death means. We are forced to look upon the Prince's death ultimately in the way we regard the death of any individual, including the death of the reader himself. For an individual death is always survived by the awareness of others even though its suffocation cuts off all events for the one who dies. From one point of view, therefore, death is a finality; from another, it is but a succeeded event. This is as true in the world of literature as it is true in life. How this inevitable continuation of consciousness is handled in literature determines to a large extent the kind of work that is produced.

Lampedusa's treatment of time determines the kind of novel he writes; he has removed any possibility of tragedy in the traditional sense. That is to say, the tragedy of *reversal* and *recognition,* in which necessity is realized by means of a plot with a beginning, middle, and end, has been deemed inappropriate precisely because in this case the work is a *historical* novel in the sense explained above of a novel that takes the self and the polity as mutually interacting. For the tragedy of reversal and recognition, inevitability must be realized in the actions of the hero; in *The Leopard* it exists for the hero, to be sure, not in his actions, but rather in the principles of nature and of history. The Prince's expanding awareness of inevitable cosmic and historical processes constitutes a central theme of the novel. This, then, I suggest, is a tragedy, but not a tragedy of reversal and recognition; it is rather a tragedy of suffering.

Aristotle, with his usual thoroughness, was careful to distinguish this kind of tragedy from that of reversal and recognition, of character, and of the spectacular:

There are four types of tragedy, the same number as the elements we mentioned earlier: the complex tragedy, in which reversal and recognition are the whole drama; the tragedy of suffering . . . the tragedy of character . . . and fourth, the spectacular tragedy. . . .[3]

[3] Aristotle, *Poetics,* trans. G. M. A. Grube (New York: Bobbs-Merrill, 1958), Ch. 18, 1455b32–1456a5.

The tragedy of suffering, or, as I prefer to call it, the tragedy of endurance and decline, exhibits inevitability in a different way from the tragedy of complex action. The inevitability derives from forces clearly distinct from the protagonist's will and intention, and therefore a distinctive literary form is allowable—perhaps the literary form is *required* by plot structure. One of the liberties this kind of plot permits is to be found in the coda at the end of the novel in which we learn what happens after the Prince's death. This structural peculiarity is a function of the tragic subject. In contrast, a tragedy of reversal and recognition cannot allow itself the excess of an afterthought, a literary coda. The structural boundaries of the tragedy of suffering are, in this case, established quite differently from those imposed by reversal and recognition, and these differences are in themselves an interesting problem for inquiry that I cannot pursue here.

The tragedy of endurance and decline has its rules and its limitations just as the tragedy of reversal and recognition does. One of its problems is to show that the suffering self is a function of a larger order, which I will call the political; thus the subject of the tragedy of suffering, most broadly stated, is the relation of soul states to history. Their interdependence is one of the themes of *The Leopard*. Beneath the accidents of time, there is a constancy of the self in its forms and developmental phases, just as there is a constancy in the forms and progressions of the state. Here the state is Sicily, whose spirit survives in all the political orders impressed upon her.

Lampedusa's technique for bringing together the self and the state is the great house of Donnafugata, which stands at once as ancestral and intimately personal history for the Prince. Through the house the novel establishes parities of self and reality which define what the characters are. Donnafugata, its hidden rooms revealing the inner lives of past generations, especially their religious and erotic sufferings, its muteness symbolizing the inevitability of death, first establishes parity between the Prince and the generations of his family; second, between the family and the history of the state of Sicily; finally, Donnafugata is the link between the human and the governing rhythm of the cosmic order.

From the observatory of his house, the Prince searches for the source of order and inevitability in the stars. The flux of daily experience hides the orders of life from us, but when we recognize heavenly constancies we begin to suspect, as the Prince does, that all of nature, including our own seemingly chaotic experience, is orderly and ultimately understandable as well. The heavens he studies with scientific detachment help him to see himself; yet his awareness of an analogy between the cosmic order and human life does not lead him to postulate a Dantean universe presided over by a personal eminence; rather, it leads him to reaffirm the order of life that Sicily and his family seem naturally to foster, an order of totemic scientific naturalism indigenous to the pagan past. The conflict within the Prince and his Sicily is powerfully stated at the very beginning of the book where, following the Catholic service,

the divinities frescoed on the ceiling awoke. The troops of Tritons and Dryads, hurtling across from hill and sea amid clouds of cyclamen pink toward a transfigured Conca d'Oro, and bent on glorifying the House of Salina, seemed suddenly so overwhelmed with exaltation as to discard the most elementary rules of perspective; meanwhile the major Gods and Goddesses, the Princes among Gods, thunderous Jove and frowning Mars and languid Venus, had already preceded the mob of minor deities and were amiably supporting the blue armorial shield of the Leopard. [P. 16]

Out of the pagan past the Prince of Salina plucks his armorial identity, a totem beast boastfully representing those qualities the Prince would find in himself, ruthlessness, power, and wiliness. None of the Prince's fellow "beasts" has his nobility, and none who come after him can command the esteem he enjoys. "We were the Leopards, the Lions," says Don Fabrizio; "those who will take our place will be little jackals, hyenas; and the whole lot of us, leopards, jackals and sheep, we'll all go on thinking ourselves the salt of the earth" (p. 214).

When the story opens, Fabrizio is the last noble animal isolated on an island of lesser beasts. Here is a fine comic possibility exploited throughout the novel. For example, as the Prince watches the women at a ball he

felt like a keeper in a zoo set to look after a hundred female monkeys; he expected at any moment to see them clamber up the chandeliers and hang by their tails, swinging to and fro, showing off their behinds and loosing a stream of nuts, shrieks, and grins at pacific visitors below. [P. 255]

The dancing men remind him "of crows veering to and fro above lost valleys in search of putrid prey" (p. 258).

But the identification with animals is not simply a metaphorical issue in the book; it grows out of a natural condition of life in the tradition the Prince represents, for he lives close to the wild animals he both nurtures and hunts:

190

It was a wild rabbit; its dun-colored coat had not been able to save it. Horrible wounds lacerated snout and chest. Don Fabrizio found himself stared at by big black eyes soon over-laid by a glaucous veil; they were looking at him with no re-proof, but full of tortured amazement at the whole order of things; the velvety ears were already cold, the vigorous paws contracting in rhythm, still-living symbols of useless flight; the animal had died tortured by anxious hopes of salvation, imagining it could still escape when it was already caught, just like so many human beings. [P. 123]

The dying rabbit is at least offered a moment of com-passion, but what of the men everywhere dying for the king, or for the new Italy? Don Fabrizio recalls that a dead soldier was found in the garden of his house in Pa-lermo. The mutilated body fills him with disgust and anxi-ety: "But the image of that gutted corpse often recurred, as if asking to be given peace in the only possible way the Prince could give it: by justifying the last agony on grounds of general necessity" (p. 22). The Prince can give no such justification in the terms that come lightly to the lips of his contemporaries: one dies for the king, an ideal, for duty. Dying is more mysterious than that, and it is his search after the mystery of death which leads Don Fabri-zio on his daily hunt. For hunting and stargazing are like activities inquiring into the ways of nature. Hunting, as Machiavelli points out, is the physical counterpart to the mind's search for understanding.

On his hunting expeditions the Prince is accompanied by his dog Bendicò, a central "character" of the story, for Bendicò opens the book and closes it. He brings life and vigor into the deadening routine of prayers; he is the last image of the Salina house:

As the carcass was dragged off, the glass eyes stared at her with the humble reproach of things that are thrown away, that are being annulled. A few minutes later what remained of Bendicò was flung into a corner of the courtyard visited every day by the dustman. During the flight down from the window his form recomposed itself for an instant; in the air one could have seen dancing a quadruped with long whiskers, and its right foreleg seemed to be raised in imprecation. Then all found peace in a heap of livid dust. [P. 320]

Bendicò's end simply reaffirms a quality of animal life that allows the novel to treat its central theme of death the more fully, for in their dumbness animals are like death, and in their closeness to us they are a sometimes comforting, more often disquieting, reminder of our own mortality.

But there is a crucial difference between the animal and man, a difference simply but relevantly stated by Wordsworth in "The Fountain":

> The blackbird amid leafy trees,
> The lark above the hill,
> Let loose their carols when they please,
> Are quiet when they will.
>
> With Nature never do *they* wage
> A foolish strife; they see
> A happy youth, and their old age
> Is beautiful and free:
>
> But we are pressed by heavy laws;
> And often, glad no more,
> We wear a face of joy because
> We have been glad of yore.

Because Bendicò is an animal, lives in a bestial time parenthesis, the author can use him to make ironic comments on the relation of a living form to its fate. Bendicò, in a grotesque literalness, survives death—indeed he remains with the House of Salina long after the Prince is gone, but the dog's presence is a stuffed one, and his end but trash.

Bendicò helps us to see another aspect of our lives more clearly: In Sicily particularly, because of its ambivalence of pagan and modern, the human finds it hard to realize and assert itself above the animal conditions of life. No matter how civilized a man may be—the Prince is, among his family and his countrymen, most civilized— what is human in him must suffer the coercion of the bestial.

One way to cope with this force in the self is to exercise one's animal compulsion in adversary relationships; but the Prince cannot find one among his peers able to meet his physical and intellectual powers. Therefore he is lonely, forced to pit himself against the only forces that at all come up to him: rude nature and death. The Leopard has not the objects of prey upon which to exercise his potency; on an island of fowls and jackals, he is alone. His physical and intellectual powers untested, the Prince lives as if the ordinary world is vulgar and witless. The best he can do is to sharpen his manners on his family and his yokel tenants; his intellect seeks its match in the totally otherworldly pursuit of astronomy. The consequence for the Prince is sad, and herein lies one of the grounds for asserting that this is a tragedy of suffering. In both manners and intellect, the Prince is less impressive and developed than he might be were there a social and intellectual world worthy of his talents.

The Prince cannot help but misunderstand himself in this setting, and the story makes clear the extent to which the man Don Fabrizio is misled, almost distorted, one might say, by the impoverishment of his realm. When two British naval officers ask Don Fabrizio what the Garibaldini hope to accomplish, he answers (in English): "They are coming to teach us good manners, but they won't succeed, because we are gods." [4]

The Prince's comment on himself is at once true and filled with misunderstanding, for he has indeed manners and a godlike mien, but they are absolutely of no account in affecting political events. His misapprehension follows from his belief that a man ought not to care to affect events, that the best for an individual is understanding. And yet his purpose in understanding is, covertly, to be able to control events. The Prince is not aware, but we are aware, of the manifest and latent wishes he expresses.

Manifestly, the Prince has in the heavens his escape and his superior, for they in their simple intelligibility and might are worthy of a person's total yielding of himself.

The soul of the Prince yearned out toward them, toward the intangible, the unreachable, which gave joy without being able to ask for anything in return; as many other times, he tried to imagine himself in those icy reaches, a pure intellect armed with a notebook for calculations: difficult calculations, but ones which would always work out. "They're the only really genuine, the only really decent being" [*Esse sono le sole pure, le sole persone perbene*], thought he, in his worldly formulae. [P. 101]

---

[4] There is a curious distortion here in the English translation of the book. This sentence, in English in the original, comes out in the translation as "because *we think* we are gods" [emphasis added]. I believe the grammatical simplicity and sureness of "because we are gods" are intended.

The escape and pleasure afforded by astronomical calculation, the feeling of power derived from observing the stars "docile to his calculations, just the contrary to human beings," is an activity of sublimation very like death. The Prince thinks,

Let's leave the Bendicòs down there running after rustic prey, and the cooks' knives chopping the flesh of innocent beasts. Above this observatory the bluster of the one and the blood of the other merge into tranquil harmony. The real problem is how to go on living this life of the spirit in its most sublimated moments [*momenti piu sublimati*], those moments that are most like death. [P. 54]

Yet the stars are not wholly independent of human affairs; there must be a meaningful relationship between human caprice and cosmic order. The fact of a mirroring is suggested in the names of two women—the Prince's wife, Stella, and Tancredi's fiancée, Angelica. The astronomical order is somehow linked with the sensual world of love. Love and death are related, and to discover how they are related is the truth pursued by the Prince.

Crudely stated, the answer the Prince finds is that death unites the woman of earthly longing with the woman of heavenly aspiration, the two Aphrodites of whom Plato speaks in the *Symposium*. In terms of the life of the Prince, this means that in death he is able at last to unite sensuality and intellect (the seemingly contradictory aspects of the self) with the apparent inconsistency of feminine qualities, for women are at once attractive and troublesome, promising peace but bringing more often restlessness and dissatisfaction. Only in death does a woman fulfill the promise of peaceful sensuality. In the

o

treatment of this difficult theme Lampedusa combines two traditions, one romantically poetic, the other introspectively psychological. Romantically, the theme finds its purest expression in Keats' "Bright Star," which brings love, death, and heavenly power into one grand gratification completing and closing a life.

Bright star! would I were steadfast as thou art—
   Not in lone splendor hung aloft the night
And watching, with eternal lids apart,
   Like nature's patient, sleeping Eremite,
The moving waters at their priestlike task
   Of pure ablution round earth's human shores,
Or gazing on the new soft fallen mask
   Of snow upon the mountains and the moors—
No—yet still steadfast, still unchangeable,
   Pillowed upon my fair love's ripening breast,
To feel forever its soft fall and swell,
   Awake forever in a sweet unrest,
Still, still to hear her tender-taken breath,
   And so live ever—or else swoon to death.

I believe it is this poetic statement which best opens up to us the meaning of Don Fabrizio's final vision, the moving description of which closes Chapter 7.

II

Yet this is not the source of Lampedusa's theme, for the treatment he accords it is obviously dependent upon another, far less poetic inquiry, part of Freud's speculation on love and death. The final revelation of the Prince's character grows out of a somewhat unsatisfactory but deeply insightful essay written by Freud in 1913, "The Theme of the Three Caskets," [5] in which Freud explores a recurrent literary situation: the choice by a man of one of three women. Examples are to be found in myth (Paris' choice of Aphrodite), in fairy tales, and in literature, especially in Shakespeare's *The Merchant of Venice* and *King Lear*. In all the examples cited by Freud, one pattern emerges: the fairest, the truest, the most desirable is the youngest. Yet choosing her and possessing her are fraught with difficulties. Success in settling the selection brings with it apparent happiness, but often death as well. The significance Freud finds in the theme is that it unites the preoccupation of men with love and death through depicting the three women in the life of every man, the mother, the mistress, and finally the woman who receives him at the end of his life, death or "Mother Earth." That the third is represented as the most desirable is a displacement; the successful suitor *chooses* the beautiful one because in this way the ugly inevitability of death is transformed into the freely chosen gratification of one's most intimate desires.

Lampedusa has self-consciously provided another literary instance of this theme, and yet has done it without forcing the didactic issue because the symbolism works within the world constructed and the characters' relationship to one another. That I trace the theme in this way does not imply that I find the treatment artificial or superimposed gratuitously upon the story. Rather, the life and

[5] Sigmund Freud, "The Theme of the Three Caskets," *Standard Edition* (London: Hogarth Press, 1958), 12: 289–301.

death of Don Fabrizio allow an alliance with an ancient and recurring literary subject because his life is defined by an ideological ambience peculiar to Sicily in whose past and present, in whose social and political affairs, we see the violent efforts to cope with an essentially pagan antiquity. It is against the pagan tradition and its conflict with Christianity that the Prince's relationship to women must be seen.

In his wife, Stella, and his daughter-in-law to be, Angelica, the Prince imagines that he might find the Venus of his rational deliberations and the Venus of erotic love respectively. But in his wife he finds repressed sensuality which subordinates pleasure to the restraint of Christian superstition; in his daughter-in-law, the appearance of unbridled sensuality without the ability to give or receive gratification. Although he longs for a relationship of complete superiority and subjection or, alternatively, of mutual dependence, he finds that there is no sympathetic understanding that would make either possible. These women suggest to the Prince the two sides of wifely decorum and sensuous abandon that a man might seek in his mistress.

They are possible objects of heavenly quest and earthly love, would they but fit the fantasy. They cannot, nor can a man ever find in fact the real counterparts of the ideal Uranian and Pandemian Aphrodite. Every woman the Prince encounters—including his mistress, Mariannina—is something of a travesty on what he seeks among the stars and in his house. Only the one who comes for him at death realizes the perfect mating he longs for. That he happily departs with her is proof of his having lived as a pagan with the object of dying well. But much of his life was devoted to the proud, defensive belief that women of Christian charity might protect him and save him from death as if he were a child and they his mother.

This illusion of protection is sustained by his proprietary attitude toward the nuns of Donnafugata. Once a year, coincident with his return to his ancestral house, he visits the convent, access to which is allowed only to him and the King of Naples, a privilege of which "he was both jealous and proud." Toward the nuns, his feelings are those of a child toward the inviolable and consoling mother. They complete the trinity of women in the Prince's life, and indirectly suggest that King and Prince, that is father and son, share access to the mother.

His deeply complex involvement with woman, so carefully drawn in the novel, is contrasted with the cavalier, violating behavior of Tancredi who, we are told, was party to an assault on a convent.[6] The Prince is shocked at this, not only because it is ungentlemanly, but also because it disturbs the delicate weighting of pagan and Christian so necessary to the preservation of Sicily. The Prince defends a tradition that depends upon the ambiguity of pagan and Christian conflict; Tancredi announces the new politics of revolutionary freedom. Tancredi's violations extend further than that, however, for he, with his fiancée, Angelica, makes an assault on the Prince's deepest self, the family past of the Salinas. Together the lovers penetrate the most secret rooms and corridors of Donnafugata, discovering hints of licentious perversions which excite their passion. The ancient house preserves the family unconscious; Tancredi would expose to light what has

---

[6] See pp. 99–101. Later we learn that this story was one of Tancredi's many fantasies.

so far remained hidden. In this, his attempt at love, as in politics, he would deny ambiguity and complexity, seeking for the explicitly direct in libidinous expression. Therefore he and Angelica can find in their explorations no cease to their physical craving. And, indeed, the omniscient author tells us that they will never find satisfaction in love. But this is a way of saying, also, that the revolutionaries cannot create a world fit for men of possible greatness, like the Prince.

That the Prince does have greatness near him is suggested by the fact that he can consider the new revolutionary state without feeling that it denies *him*. He can examine the claims of the Garibaldini because they promise resolution of conflict; but he sees through the unreality of such a longing, and naïve social program. Yet *his* sense of political reality allows him to see that the new order must be given its place, just as paganism had to yield a place to the naïvetés of Catholicism. Acceptance, however, is not acquiescence, and in this the Prince exhibits greatness of soul.

We are old, Chevalley, very old. For more than twenty-five centuries we've been bearing the weight of a superb and heterogeneous civilization, all from outside, none made by ourselves, none that we could call our own. . . .

Sleep, my dear Chevalley, sleep, that is what Sicilians want, and they will always hate anyone who tries to wake them, even in order to bring them the most wonderful of gifts; and I must say, between ourselves, I have strong doubts whether the new Kingdom will have many gifts for us in its luggage. All Sicilian expression, even the most violent, is really wish-fulfillment [oniriche]: our sensuality is a hankering for oblivion, our shooting and knifing a hankering for death; our lazi-

ness, our spiced and drugged sherbets, a hankering for
voluptuous immobility, that is, for death, again; our medita-
tive air is that of a void wanting to scrutinize the enigmas of
nirvana. [Pp. 205–206]

With his sense of the past, and the eternal indifference
of the true pagan to "progress" and the power of law to
rule [Chevalley, a bureaucratic friend, says, "But, Prince,
the Senate is the High Chamber of the Kingdom! In it
the flower of Italy's politicians [*uomini politici italiani*],
chosen by the wisdom of the Sovereign, will examine, discuss, approve, or disapprove the laws proposed by the
Government for the progress of the country; it functions
at the same time as spur and as brake: it incites good actions and prevents bad ones" (p. 203)], the Prince can
recommend to his peasants that they vote for the unification, though they in their atavistic shrewdness believe he
is insincere. What does it matter if one or another rules?
The Prince is far more interested in the stars than in
states, more committed to death than to power. He suggests that Don Calogero, one far beneath him in rank, be
named to the Senate.

The Prince is able to accept the modern renovation,
just as, at some distant time, an ancestor of his was able
to accept the proclaimed regeneration of Christianity.
The Prince inherited from that compromise his duties to
the church, which he meets in full; he supports Father Pirrone as his confessor and spiritual guide, but without
conviction; and for his part Father Pirrone recognizes the
ultimate hopelessness of his effort to "save" the Prince. He
sees that the Prince belongs to "a class difficult to sup-
press because it's in continual renewal and because if

needs be it can die well, that is it can throw out a seed at the moment of death" (p. 230). The church has found no more than toleration in the noble families, and Father Pirrone cannot triumph over the stars.

During those moments of abstraction he seemed more intimately absolved, in the sense of being linked anew with the universe, than by any blessing of Father Pirrone. For half an hour that morning the gods of the ceilings and the monkeys on the walls were again put to silence. But in the drawing room no one noticed. [P. 55]

No one noticed because the others have lost the sense of the pagan past that haunts the Prince. But the Prince's house is dedicated to the survival of the pagan world. No sooner does the afternoon prayer end than

the divinities frescoed on the ceiling awoke. The troops of Tritons and Dryads, hurtling across from hill and sea amid clouds of cyclamen pink towards a transfigured Conca d'Oro, and bent on glorifying the House of Salina, seemed suddenly so overwhelmed with exhaltation as to discard the most elementary rules of perspective; meanwhile the major Gods and Goddesses, the Princes among gods, thunderous Jove and frowning Mars and languid Venus, had already preceded the mob of minor deities and were amiably supporting the blue armorial shield of the Leopard. They knew that for the next twenty-three and a half hours they would be lords of the villa once again. On the walls the monkeys went back to pulling faces at the cockatoos. [P. 16]

The Prince and the priest are each effective in his own world, guiding their families, settling disputes, acting as lawmakers. But between them there can be only the tie of a modest friendship, which survives the strained rela-

tionship of sponsor and spiritual adviser. Whatever conflicts there are between the first and second estates have
been mitigated by years of living together. Yet that cannot survive the Risorgimento, which will strike at the
foundation not only of the nobility springing from the
pagan world, but also at the church. To preserve itself
after the Risorgimento, the nobility must become allied
with the new monied class, as Tancredi does with Angelica, joining the Salinas to the Calogeros; and the church
must become bureaucratic. Each lapses into its more
primitive self: the family of Salina into erotic paganism,
venerating false relics and dubious paintings in a hide-
ously decorated chapel; the church into smug literalism.
Under the scrutiny of a young priest, trained in the Vati-
can School of Paleography, the relics collected by the sur-
viving daughters of the Prince are declared fakes.

But the meddlesome interest of the church in the private devotions of the Salinas is not hurtful to the three
old princesses; the effect of social change is seen in the
personal suffering it causes. More disturbing than the enforced renovation and reconsecration of the chapel is the
past that the censure awakens for Concetta, who so long
ago hoped to marry Tancredi.

The concluding chapter of the book, taking place twen-
ty-two years after the death of the Prince, carries us back
to the vital moments of a family, now no more than dim
memories distorted by wishes and unfulfilled desires. A
dominant purpose of the story is here realized, for we see
the impotence of the past in setting an enduring pattern
for the future, yet we recognize the staying power and
print of the past on the reflections and memories of the
individuals who have lived through it. What really hap-

pened in those days when the Salina family was at Donna-fugata? What really moved the Prince to deny Tancredi entrance to the convent? What was Tancredi's feeling to-ward Concetta? What does a man seek in revolution and in love?

Nowhere has truth so short a life as in Sicily; a fact has scarcely happened five minutes before its genuine kernel has vanished, been camouflaged, embellished, disfigured, squashed, annihilated by imagination and self-interest; shame, fear, generosity, malice, opportunism, charity, all the pas-sions, good as well as evil, fling themselves onto the fact and tear it to pieces; very soon it has vanished altogether. And poor Concetta was hoping to find the truth of feelings that had never been expressed but only glimpsed half a century before! The truth no longer existed. Precarious fact, though, had been replaced by irrefutable pain. [P. 314]

There is in all human life the tragic conflict between the self and the larger events of which it is a part. What really was "the Risorgimento"? How can we understand it? Only through those who were part of it. But what was it to them?—not a historical period summed up in a para-graph, but part of a life endured, part of a reality lived through and coped with, the focus of reason's cunning, the ground of instinct's conditioning. The "truth" about the past is to be found in the persons who lived it; yet their selves are forever hidden from us, only possibly re-constructed through fiction. Outwardly, in historical statements proper, what is the difference between a so-ciety in which the peasants serve the Prince, or one in which the Prince serves the peasants? Either way, inde-pendent feudalism or bureaucratic statism, the historical description hides the suffering selves.

The key to understanding changes such as the Risorgimento is in the nature of the persons who submitted and suffered. Yet they elude us unless they can be given life in art. Of the many art forms in which this possibility might be realized, the so-called historical novel is peculiar for it permits a revivifying that no other literary form can realize, the reciprocal relationship of the self and the state, or, in Plato's terms, the interdependence of souls and constitutions. History, Lampedusa wants us to see, is a succession of soul states.

This theme, repeated again and again in the scenes of encounter between the Prince and those who act or would act in the political world, leads inevitably to the conclusion drawn by the Prince: There is no political role for him, because his person and the new state cannot be coordinated. When he is asked to serve as a Senator, the Prince declares his incompetence and, as he talks, breaks the cross upon the little model of St. Peter's, a gesture that conveys the impotence of an institution as a coordinate decline to his own. In historical terms, there is never the perishing of a self without the perishing of a political counterpart; never the passing of an institution without the destruction of persons. The era of manners has come to an end. We begin to see how much is contained in that single term *manners*. But the polity and soul-type to succeed are already on the scene, in the persons of Tancredi and Angelica. They shall be politically potent, the story seems to say, in proportion as they are impotent between themselves, while in the life of the Prince, political power is directly related to his success in intimate relationships.

Looked at in the light of a Platonic theory of *psuche-politeia*, the historical novel becomes an interesting and somewhat troublesome genre. Ordinarily, what we think of as the historical novel reconstructs history as events; it is a form of melodrama. But the historical novel realized in its capacity as a way to understand human action is far different, re-creating the historical by means of the personal. This is the great discovery of Stendhal, and the reason why, I believe, *The Leopard* is so close to *The Charterhouse of Parma* in its emphasis not only on the essential subjectivity of historical events, but in its theory of how the past is to be recaptured.[7]

In *The Leopard*, then, the changes that occurred in Sicily, to which we give the empty name *Risorgimento*, begin to take on the qualities of persons, and the events which we think of as "historical" are seen to be reorganizations of personal qualities—if we want to be Platonic, we say that one soul-type is succeeded by another soul-type.

This treatment of change is brought out clearly in Chapter 6, "Going to a Ball," for here two generations meet and are seen in their stark contrast: fading ancestral tradition succeeded by waxing revolutionary progress. Everything in the scene is decadent: the setting of the old house, the effort to perpetuate a social milieu now dead, the remnants of the aristocracy:

[7] This may be a clue to the bestowing of the name *Fabrizio* upon the Prince. See Note 8.

. . . in recent years the consequence of the frequent marriages between cousins due to sexual lethargy and territorial
calculations, of the dearth of proteins and overabundance of
starch in the food, of the total lack of fresh air and movement, had filled the drawing rooms with a mob of girls incred-
ibly short, unsuitably dark, unbearably giggly. [P. 255]

This is not only unreal to the Prince ["The crowd of danc-
ers, among whom he could count so many near to him in
blood if not in heart, began to seem unreal, made up of
that material from which are woven lapsed memories,
more elusive than the stuff of disturbing dreams"], but it
suddenly becomes shockingly anachronistic to us:

From the ceiling the gods, reclining on gilded couches, gazed
down smiling and inexorable as a summer sky. They thought
themselves eternal; but a bomb manufactured in Pittsburgh,
Pennsylvania, was to prove the contrary in 1943. [P. 258]

Lampedusa here has worked another trick of historical
omniscience which takes *The Leopard* beyond anything
Stendhal would have thought appropriate, although we
may find the innovation in poor taste. The point, I think,
is to force upon us the radical nature of the political and
psychic change which occurred in the proper time of historical narration, by jumping its limitations to our own
violence, our own passively accepted destruction. We are
the descendants of those unlovely creatures upon whom
the Prince looks with disgust.

The revulsion the Prince feels, and presumably the revulsion we may feel toward ourselves as we recognize
ourselves, is soothed by the consolation of human mortality. The Prince recalls the little procession, seen on the

way to the ball, of a priest and an acolyte, ringing the bell of death as they go to bestow the Last Sacrament on a dying man. All will come to this. At the thought the Prince is calmed, for, "when all was said and done, his own death would in the first place mean that of the whole world" (p. 261). The death of a man is always, whatever the political condition of his day, the end of the world.

Is the Prince's death any more a finality now, now that his family in his form shall not survive? Is not every Duke of Salina the last one, in his death? However much the Duke loves Donnafugata, it disappears with him, though the residue of dusty rooms, so intimately searched by Tancredi and Angelica, will yield up their obscene impressions to others. Whatever Donnafugata is to the Prince, we see that it is far different to his heirs. The past is possessed by each in the exploration of it, but what is apprehended by each differs. This is the hard necessity of death: that the world ends with oneself, that the seeming permanence of history is an illusion. When the Prince recognizes this—and the novel exhibits to us his coming to this recognition—he is, as much as any man ever is, ready for death.

Within the flux of social change the Prince discerns a necessity as hard as that of the heavens; his awareness of the unpredictable necessity of the earthly is joined to his awe in the predictable necessity of the heavens. Heretofore, the Prince has regarded the heavens as peculiarly "his" realm, for we are told, "In his mind, now, pride and mathematical analysis were so linked as to give him an illusion that the stars obeyed his calculations too (as in fact they seemed to be doing) . . ." (p. 19). Consequently, he loves them:

The soul of the Prince yearned out toward them, toward the intangible, the unreachable, which gave joy without being able to ask for anything in return; as many other times he tried to imagine himself in those icy reaches, a pure intellect armed with a notebook for calculations: difficult calculations, but ones which would always work out. "They're the only really genuine, the only really decent beings," thought he, in his worldly formulae. [P. 101]

While he has lived with the happy illusion that somehow the stars obey him, though he knows they do not, he has until recently lived with the belief that the terrestrial order does obey him, for he is the Prince whose domains are his by immemorial right. However, where he is supposed in fact to govern he is least puissant. Growing old, approaching death, he realizes that the earthly realm is no more his to rule in accordance with his will than the heavenly; both obey laws beyond human desire. The Prince ends his life more keenly and more self-consciously aware of the necessities in both earth and heaven.

It is this recognition that brings him before us as possibly a tragic figure. Although not tragic in the sense of the hero of reversal and recognition, he is tragic in the sense already stated, of that kind of tragedy we find more often—the tragedy of suffering. Pathos marks every aspect of the Prince's actions, for he is aloof, remote, removed: events are known through his reaction to them rather than through an effort to define the events themselves. Of course, this is part of Lampedusa's commitment to a vision of history that makes reversal and recognition in the historical context beyond the novel's grasp. What comes thereby centrally within the novel's grasp is the subject of dying.

The necessity of death enters the Prince's awareness with his realization that he commands little, and is subject to the necessity of unpredictable forces. The bond of affection which the Prince would have forged with other persons is never possible for him; rather his affect is directed to nature, to animals, and to his own end. In this simple sense a tragedy of reversal and recognition is irrelevant to the story because, as Aristotle noted, that requires two persons between whom there is a bond of love or hate. *The Leopard*, in its concentration on dying, forges the bond of affect between the hero and those impersonal, nonhuman aspects of reality to which he, like all living things, must succumb.

In this sense, then, it seems to me appropriate to speak of *The Leopard* as a philosophical novel, for its concern is the relationship between human actions and nature. If this is a theme that has an established genre, as I believe it does, then we can evaluate Plato's comment in the *Laws* to the effect that philosophers would necessarily make the best tragedians; they might be writers of pathetic tragedy, but they could not sustain the vision of a Sophocles.

The necessities that make the Prince a hero of tragic suffering are not nobly met with by the other characters, who fall far below the Prince. Tancredi might have been a political leader, were he not lazy and passive, content with conferred power in a new order. Angelica might die for love, were she not sensually self-conscious, incapable of giving herself to another. Concetta might have realized the Salina potentiality for fineness, if she were not dominated by the past; she lives her life with the stuffed carcass of Bendicò in her room, preserving around her the

false memories of having been wronged. Too late she realizes that "there had been no enemies, just one single adversary, herself; her future had been killed by her own
impudence, by the rash Salina pride (p. 313)." She has
had no time to live life because she has been unable to
face death.

Only in the Prince is the man of contemplation strong
enough not to be overwhelmed by the demands of scientific observation, and the man of natural appetite not
overwhelmed by religious asceticism. These are characteristics that make him pathetically fit for the endurance
of suffering. Unlike the hero of conventional tragedy, the
pathetic hero must have a stability and inner power to
persevere that set him apart from other fragile persons,
and from the weight of events. Pagan and empiricistic by
nature, autocratic and domineering by fortune of birth,
the Prince is able to cultivate manners. Thus protected,
he can come to know himself. There is here a "moral" as
urgent as that we associate with the more shocking tragedy of reversal and recognition.

The proper mise en scène of the tragedy of suffering is
history, and it may be that the historical novel is the only
genre to perpetuate this tragic possibility. Whether this
be so or not, the tragedy of suffering in historical contexts
such as those of *The Leopard* shows us important truths
about the past and the future as it relates to our lives.

The past can exercise upon us a charm, promising
peace and security, while the future threatens with its
dangers and uncertainties. Being always next to the future, we must try to give it form and meaning, and one
way of doing this is to make it the harbinger of better
times. In fact, however, the future holds our death; no

P

matter how we promise ourselves the ease of betterment, we fear the future. Thus we turn once again toward the past, endowing it with all the grace, charm, unreal felicity we would find in the future. The human longing to possess the past in all its specificity and reality is in fact the impossible demand to know the future.

Only in art can we join nostalgia and omniscience; the tragedy of suffering, in the context of history, is this strange creation. Human longing to transcend the bounds of historical accident is realized in the acceptance of death, for to learn how to die one must honor the past for its qualities of life, and yet know that these are intensely, inevitably private. The tragedy of suffering then is, unlike other kinds of tragedy, sadly solipsistic: its private visions are its only realities.

Suddenly amid the group appeared a young woman, slim, in brown travelling dress and wide bustle, with a straw hat trimmed by a speckled veil which could not hide the sly charm of her face. She slid a little suede-gloved hand between one elbow and another of the weeping kneelers, apologized, drew closer. It was she, the creature forever yearned for, coming to fetch him; strange that one so young should yield to him; the time for the train's departure must be very close. When she was face to face with him she raised her veil, and there, modest, but ready to be possessed, she looked lovelier than she ever had when glimpsed in stellar space. [P. 292]

The corollary to Freud's assertion that in literature we still find people who know how to die is that in literature we may learn something of our death. In *The Leopard* we are presented with the fact that life is but a moment, "the tiny ray of light granted . . . between two shades, before the cradle, after the last spasms" (p. 259).

This is a banal truth, to which all would assent, but the literary work in which the statement appears is at once a consolation and a shock, for through it we vault the blinding urgencies of our actual present to inhabit, for a moment, the wider necessities of the past and future of the Salina house. We see in the Prince's life the spindle of necessity and the consequences of choice. This vision, which lasts only as long as the book, cannot endure the importunate moments of everyday life. Back in our time-coerced lives, where the future threatens, we lose the value of death because we fear it, while in the novel that denies the usual temporal order we see that to deny time is to make death a part of life and thereby to confer upon life the only survival possible. This is to render life art-like, and that Lampedusa has done. In this way the literary arts survive modernity, which dealt an almost fatal blow to story in denying the stable truthfulness of the past.[8]

[8] I have puzzled a good bit over the similarity between the names *Don Fabrizio* in *The Leopard* and *Fabrizio* (Fabrice) in Stendhal's *La Chartreuse de Parme*. I cannot assert that there is a dependency of Lampedusa's Prince upon Stendhal's character, but they certainly inhabit the same fictional space, and I have found making comparisons meaningful. For what it is worth, then, I shall note a few interesting similarities. They lead me to a final point about Don Fabrizio as a literary creation.

The emphasis in both novels is upon what we term "character," and Stendhal has made note of what he understands by that term in words that are relevant to Don Fabrizio as well as to Fabrice del Dongo: "J'appelle caractère d'un homme sa manière habituelle d'aller à la chasse du bonheur, en termes plus claires, mais moins qualificatifs, l'ensemble de ses habitudes morales" (*La Chartreuse de Parme* [Paris: Editions Garnier, 1961], p. 149). So considered, both characters are "determined" by their relationship to religion and the stars. On this ground a significant comparison takes shape, for while Don Fabrizio is an astronomer, to whom the stars are symbolic of order and freedom and ultimately extensions of his sense of power through willing, Fabrice del Dongo is superstitious, a religious person by vocation only, and, like the Sicilian Prince, forced to endure a Jesuitical interference.

Both Father Pirrone and Prior Blanes are as it were "confessors," but in the first case Pirrone stands for the limitations of the church, while in the second Blanes stands for the heresy of presage in astrology. Both heroes have an escape in the stars, but for Fabrice they foretell wonders; for Fabrizio they exhibit wholly impersonal rationality.

Astronomy in both cases is the counterweight to religion, leading in the first case to simple superstition, belief in signs, hopefulness about one's future, and in the second toward rationalism. Religion is undermined by both. But more, religion would direct attention away from the self, and both heroes are deeply self-involved. Stendhal, with his usual sharpness, puts it this way: "religion *ôte le courage de penser aux choses inaccoutumées*, et defend surtout *l'examen personnel*, comme le plus enorme des péchés; c'est un pas vers le protestantisme" (p. 195. Italics in original).

The heroes are alike in their search into themselves and the effort each makes to establish traditional (that is, ancient) virtues in the face of the modern affective and moral reevaluation of those qualities. Significantly, the world they live in is counterpoised against the mythic past and remnants of myth in the present. Fabrice would join it in his astrological naïveté; Fabrizio would reuse it for his achievement as the great-souled man. Both must fail because of modernity; each must fail in the inevitability of his death. Thus both novels could be said to concern themselves with the theme of personal integrity in the modern world.

Chapter 6

Philosophy as a Form of Art

The analysis of two modern literary works, **Resurrection** and *The Leopard,* reveals a persistent concern in which we participate: that the literary statement be capable of saying the truth, that literary performance be endowed with values other than the aesthetic, however much the aesthetic be fundamental. In order to affirm powers of a broad kind, we must be able to show how literary statements refer to the world; both Tolstoy and Lampedusa are preoccupied with the problem of how a novel reflects or shapes or makes understandable the reality we possess. They are concerned to show that their works have conceptual content as well as aesthetic shape: Tolstoy compels the reader to listen to his ideas as they come through the mouths of characters, and as they exist in editorial pas-

215

sages; Lampedusa insists that the psychological reality of his hero's experience constitutes *the reality* of this world, and is therefore more truthful than any historical narrative. The reader, if he wants to find himself, can do so only in the books; there is no life for him outside the book, for life, whatever that means, is the mirror of art.

That art constitutes reality, in the only meaningful sense we can give the term "reality," satisfies Tolstoy and Lampedusa because they believe their art is true. But human beings utter sentences outside novels as well as within, and we are not much helped in dealing with our everyday talk by theories about art.

Inquiries into the way language means and how it is structured have been a central interest of philosophy, and therefore we may hope to find something about the way literary language works by listening to philosophers. The dominant schools of our time—positivism, structuralism, phenomenology, and analytic philosophy—puzzle over the same problems that novelists take up in their writing; and a community of linguistic interest has been established in our own time as firmly as ever in the past. Indeed, the close sharing of methods and visions may be more marked now than ever before. As philosophy inquired into the way language works, writers have struggled with the use of language for the creation of new kinds of experience. Linguistic structures which create new literary worlds have been carved out as philosophers have worked on problems of meaning with increasing subtlety and sophistication.[1] We might expect that here,

[1] Contemporary French literary critics and historians have thought about these problems in some detail. See Jacques Derrida, *De la grammatologie* (Paris: Les éditions de Minuit, 1967); Philippe Sollers, *Logiques* (Paris: Éditions du Seuil, 1968); Pierre Macherey, *Pour une théorie de la production littéraire* (Paris: François Maspero, 1966).

as in other times, philosophy and literature would exhibit common methods and shared conclusions. I shall show that in one small part of the contemporary scene a remarkable participation in a shared set of problems has gone on. One side of it, which we term "symbolism" and "imagism," has received considerable attention; the other, the philosophical work of Wittgenstein as it contributes to a general theory of literary language, has not. The young, thoughtful Wittgenstein grew up in and contributed to the literary realm in which we still have our home.

The appearance of the *Tractatus Logico-Philosophicus* (in German, *Logisch-philosophische Abhandlung*) was a philosophical event of a unique kind, but from our perspective now it is an event sharing many characteristics with other publications of its time. Of course, in substance it replies, refines, and tries to correct the logical thought of Russell, Whitehead, and Frege. But in its form it finds a much wider company, for it is, in a sense proper to the early twentieth century, a *text*. As such it has a rigorous form, exactitude of detail, finickiness of fidelity that is uncommon in documents up to that time. One of the questions the *Tractatus* asks, and one of the questions it most labors to answer, is "What is a text?" This has importance both to philosophers and to literary writers, for the finished work goes into the world with the assurance of conformation to the intention of the creator. Wittgenstein we know from various accounts of his life was compulsively concerned that his thoughts be printed exactly as written. And he threatened to let the *Tractatus* languish unpublished if it could not be reproduced to the least detail of his manuscript. In this sense, then, a text is a document faithfully reproduced from an original.

This implies that a reader can follow out the document with assurance of its accuracy, and will find interpretive assistance in the details of exposition. The text is an adequate representation of itself. Odd as this sounds, it makes sense because texts are reproduced documents existing in various editions, printings, translations, and redactions. Thus there must be *the* text against which to measure all others. Wittgenstein created that in every edition of his work by insisting that the original German text be printed alongside any translation. And this has been faithfully followed out in every edition of the *Tractatus*. The text in this case then is a manuscript in German, each of whose sentences is clearly distinct, each part of which is numbered by a decimal system so that every edition of the text can be collated with the original. It is worth noting that about the time the *Tractatus* was published, other works, with equal concern for fidelity, were reproduced. I mention the *Principia Mathematica* of Russell and Whitehead, T. S. Eliot's *The Waste Land*, and the aphoristic writings of Nietzsche. The *Tractatus* fancies itself both a *Principia* and a *Waste Land*, possessing the logical rigor of the first and the poetic vision of the second. Wittgenstein created a linguistic form that was at once argument and performance, like the philosophical and literary texts. That is why it stands close to, yet ambiguously far from, its contemporary writings, and that is one reason why it is so difficult to understand. In that respect, as an hermetic document, it reminds me of Mallarmé's *Un Coup de dés*.

In addition to establishing their own authority, texts of this sort created in this milieu exhibit structural organization of great clarity, realized by a numerical and a topographical relationship among sections of the text, and by a collation of materials which, in Wittgenstein's case, derives from both Nietzsche and *Principia Mathematica*. There is evidence that Wittgenstein's method of composition was "zettelistic," compilation of pieces or scraps upon which propositions were inscribed (*Zettel*, German for scrap of paper). While he believed there was internal coherence and evident cross-references, the actual order of the text was not so much determined by logic as it was by imagination. To be sure, sections of the *Tractatus* are related to one another as propositions in a logical system are related, but the subjects dealt with are contrapuntally developed in the text as a whole. In the *Tractatus* the unutterable is a part of what is uttered. Inscribing propositions on slips of paper suggests that there might be one right order for them to be put into, but also that chance or accident might order them. Indeed, many readers of the *Tractatus* complain that the topics do not carry through, but are thrown up over and over again, as if one were to reach into a box and pull out slips at random, and then consider each slip as it appears, returning to it if it turns up again. Wittgenstein achieves two conditions this way: any order is a possible order where a text is concerned, and therefore whatever order is established can stand by itself for any order. The linguistic world contains or possesses the same set of tokens no matter how ordered, and the sense of the tokens can be discovered no matter what way they are apprehended by the reader. But a certain order is selected by the writer for reasons of a somewhat literary kind: they realize a performance as well as an argument, and therefore make special demands on the reader. This organization, at first glance obvious, soon reveals itself as complex and devious, requiring an act of interpretation as demanding as any in the tradition. To share the text with another, one must be able to interpret it. The method of interpretation is not metaphysical, as Hegel's method was, nor affective in the gestalt manner, nor psychological, but rather appears to be a reading of symbols in a sense that is peculiar to Wittgenstein. The symbols in the text do not refer to other orders of reality, nor to a private fantasy system of the writer, but rather to the structure and the ultimate meaning to be found in the text itself. The symbols of the *Tractatus* are to be explicated into their own actualized meaning. The language of the text—that is, the language which *is* the text—is a language about itself because it explores how and in what way what it offers may be meaningful. And it considers seriously the possibility that it itself may be without meaning. One purpose of the text then is to provide evidence for its own meaningfulness, and that implies offering to the reader a method for reading. Wittgenstein's preoccupation with reading and understanding becomes explicitly stated in his later, more self-conscious notes published posthumously as *Philosophical Investigations,* which along with the *Tractatus* can be seen as a text about texts and how to interpret a text.[2]

One further characteristic of the *Tractatus* as text should be pointed out: it has the appearance of a residue from a much longer written work, the worthwhile, salvaged from much that is worthless and to be disposed of. Indeed we now see the larger matrix from which the

[2] Wittgenstein, *Philosophical Investigations* (Oxford: Basil Blackwell, 1953), Sections 156 ff., 526 ff.

Tractatus was separated in the *Notebooks* of 1914–1916. Not only did this separating out of meritorious from worthless constitute a major creative activity on Wittgenstein's part, it becomes a part of the text itself which declares that very little can meaningfully be said. Extremely high standards of workmanship are insisted upon, and the text itself frequently gives way to the wanhope of intellectual inadequacy. These feelings are not peculiar to the *Tractatus*, for they are expressed by many of Wittgenstein's contemporaries for whom theoretical formulations became important. And where actual artistic making was undertaken, the need for explanatory accounts was openly stated. Wittgenstein was fascinated by both the theoretical and the artistic sides of his cultural world, and while trying to realize greatness in both aspects of it, believed he had failed. All achievements worth anything seemed to him almost beyond reach, and while he admired those of his contemporaries who wrote, painted, and built, he found little in their world of absolute excellence, and such excellence was his goal. His preoccupation with intellectual and artistic perfection helps us to understand the way the *Tractatus* was written, for it seeks to be meaningful with consummate clarity and therefore is obsessively concerned with how language and the world can be related. So difficult is this traditional philosophical problem that the *Tractatus* takes on the care and compulsive delicacy of a poem.

Therefore it is both literally and analogically true that the language of the *Tractatus* is creative; through language the author creates the world. The writer of the *Tractatus* is the *divine* creator, for his forming power *makes* the world. And should he fail in any respect, should his "blueprint" of creation be defective, then the world would not be right. There is in the *Tractatus* divine pride. As in God's creation, there is in the *Tractatus* a higher, secret realm to which access is granted only to the saved. For beyond the created world of language is that which cannot be spoken. And its reality is above, perhaps even sacred, in comparison to what is written. There is thus in the *Tractatus* a supreme irony: it is the book of God, but what *only* God can say. In comparison the Bible is false for it tells, or pretends to tell, ultimate truths. But just as the ultimate meaning of the Bible is discovered through an act of interpretation, so the meaning of the world is discovered through an act of interpreting the text. But those who "expound" the Bible believe they can say the unsayable; in the *Tractatus* it is recognized that this cannot be the case. The unsayable is just that; and what is not in the text could never be part of a text; the text is a fragment of what absolutely is, but only a fragment—the bare bones of language—suggesting a fleshed-out totality.

It may be that Wittgenstein's interest in St. Augustine is connected with the theory of interpretation Augustine worked out as well as with his wonder at language. But the two interests go together, for philosophers who wonder how language is possible also wonder how language can be interpreted. To speak, to hear, to write, to read, to understand—all these are coordinate processes. Could we penetrate their mystery we would understand as much as it is allotted to man to understand. Augustine and Wittgenstein share this curiosity, as well as a sense that what they can know is sharply circumscribed.

An Augustinian hermeneutic is relevant to the text

Wittgenstein created, since he suggests that for the world to exist it must be created in language. Augustine considered the sacred texts as revelatory of God's will and analogically symbolic of the divine intellect. But what Augustine created as an interpretation of the text stood to the original text in an ambiguous relationship: is the interpretation the meaning of the text? Is it the reality which the text approximates? Or is it itself to be interpreted as another text? The mystery of the received text, as Augustine describes it, is similar to the mystery of the text as Wittgenstein created it. I believe that Wittgenstein consciously struggled with the problem of interpretation, as it was formulated by Augustine, because the conception of language Augustine worked out was philosophically powerful, but dependent upon assumptions about language that Wittgenstein was forced to challenge. That challenge grew out of philosophical reflections on language as well as upon literary developments in poetry to which Wittgenstein was sensitive. Therefore, the two philosophers differ on a basic issue: Augustine regards all writing and speaking—all language—as imitation of divine order and number, whereas Wittgenstein finds reality, insofar as we can manage it through language, only partly reflected in language. The rest is only an intimation, and beyond language. Of course Augustine believed too that there were vast realms of creation that were not and could never be reflected in language, but he did believe that language could capture something of beauty and number which are God's magnificent essence. I don't think Wittgenstein ever granted us that much insight; yet what he saw as the power of language is far more precise, and now, from our logical point of view, far more impressive than anything Augustine dreamed about. But that is a result of developments in symbol systems of which Augustine could know nothing. For all that, there is a compelling similarity in Augustine and Wittgenstein —a similarity Wittgenstein must have recognized, because it is said that the one author he read all his life, the one author whose works were always in evidence in his rooms, was Augustine. In examining Wittgenstein's theory of language we may come closer to seeing this similarity.

In trying to set out what Wittgenstein's theory of language is, I think one ought to begin with his formalism, his belief that somehow language in its structure *is* the world—at least the world insofar as there can be a world for human beings. When Wittgenstein says that the world is the totality of facts, he is speaking in one way about language, for facts exist in "logical space" (*logische Raum*, as he calls it), but those facts do not exist alone; they maintain, or ought to be seen to maintain, a relationship to events. Thus, the world and language relate to one another as the thing and the representation of the thing. On first reading the *Tractatus* one seems to entertain once more an imitation theory of meaning much like Plato's. But it is actually a reversed Platonism, for Wittgenstein develops a theory in which, as Max Black puts it, "the universe . . . is a projection of what he finds in language." [3] Language exhibits a structure of facts; this structure ought to be a mirror of the world (events). But there is only one way into the structuring and that is logic. Logical studies enable us to articulate the fact structure which is at the same time the event structure.

[3] *A Companion to Wittgenstein's Tractatus* (Cambridge: Cambridge University Press, 1964), p. 35.

We see that Wittgenstein's theory of language suggests an ontology as surely as does Plato's, but the ontology remained forever a possibility to be somehow glimpsed but never apprehended directly. All that is *mystical* embraces this ultimate reality, but the mystical is at best a human peep at the divine. What we can see, and see straight on, in all its clarity, is logical space. That must be the focus of philosophical analysis.

Wittgenstein's coining of the phrase "logical space" and his contention that this ought to be the focus of philosophical analysis bring him close to "symbolism" as a theory of poetic meaning. The symbolist theory of poetry insisted that the internal, self-referring "poetic form" defined the linguistic world. What use was made of this kind of formalism depended upon the calling of the writer; Wittgenstein cannot be said to participate in the symbolist ideology directly, but he shares with Valéry a concern for textual self-sufficiency worked out through careful thought about linguistic possibilities. Despite the differences of Wittgenstein's and Valéry's temperaments and callings, they shared beliefs about the power of language. Valéry, following the thought of Poincaré, believed that an exact, beautiful structure characterized the language of both poetry and science, and that reconstructive analysis of their languages would somehow bring them together. Wittgenstein attempts a similar reconstruction through logic, since logic is the key to all possible linguistic meaning. The unification of human awareness through understanding the power of language, and the benefits to follow in casting out nonsense, remained the goal of logical and symbolist efforts to understand how language functions. Of course, in the writing of a

225

great poet like Mallarmé the achievement is not theoretical but actual. However, there was far more thought about symbolic theory than there was artistic success in the symbolist mode. As poet, Valéry shared in the limited but dense success; as philosopher, Wittgenstein produced a work contributing both to theory and to a symbolist structure. In Valéry's terms Wittgenstein comes closer to realizing unified consciousness than did Valéry himself for whom the poetic and the theoretic modes of statement were quite distinct. In terms of the symbolist movement as a theory about and an actual structuring of language, the *Tractatus* deserves recognition; it carries out for philosophy what symbolist theory hoped to see in other modes of statement.

Linguistic forms fascinated both Valéry and Wittgenstein, and the possibility that language might achieve necessity in that it produced sentences held together by bonds of absolute security and irrevocability operates in the logical forms of the *Tractatus* as it does in Valéry's art. A poem, Valéry believed, must be wrought with such necessity of part to part, such fastness of interior design, that the reader may have absolute confidence in it, and be compelled by his reading to recognize all the implications of the sentences. That suggests that a literary statement, like a musical composition, exists as a stimulation to elaboration. Valéry makes a comparison between poetry and music which conveys the sense in which he sees poetic language as compelling the anticipation of implications:

. . . I should be tempted (if I followed my inclinations) to engage poets to produce, like musicians, a diversity of variants or solutions of the same subject. Nothing would seem to

226

me more consistent with the idea I like to hold of a poet and poetry.[4]

This sense of fecundity has another aspect which Valéry relates to the poetic mechanism, for we are compelled to see implications and possibilities by the way poetic language, when organized into a whole poem, works.

A poem is really a kind of machine for producing the poetic state of mind by means of words. The effect of this machine is uncertain, for nothing is certain about action on other minds. But whatever may be the result, in its uncertainty, the construction of the machine demands the solution of many problems. If the term *machine* shocks you, if my mechanical comparison seems crude, please notice that while the composition of even a very short poem may absorb years, the action of the poem on the reader will take only a few minutes.[5]

Valéry's idea that a poem is a machine for producing poetic states is analogous to Wittgenstein's idea that logic is a machine for making sense, that there exists a structure which is the structure of possible meanings. "If a sign is *useless* it is meaningless." [6] Like the poem as machine, logic as the structure of language and of the world opens up to us all the possibilities that there are, for as logic is the determination of the boundaries of my world, so to entertain sentences in a language is to seize hold of the means for exploring and defining that world.

[4] "Concerning *Le Cimetière marin*," *The Collected Works of Paul Valéry*, ed. Jackson Mathews and trans. Denise Folliot (London: Routledge & Kegan Paul, 1958), 7: 145. All translations are taken from this edition.

[5] "Poetry and Abstract Thought," p. 79.

[6] Ludwig Wittgenstein, *Tractatus Logico-Philosophicus*, trans. D. F. Pears and B. F. McGuinness (London: Routledge & Kegan Paul, 1961), 3.328. All subsequent quotations are from this edition.

Q

5.5563   In fact, all the propositions of our everyday language, just as they stand, are in perfect logical order. —That utterly simple thing, which we have to formulate here, is not an image of the truth, but the truth itself in its entirety.

(Our problems are not abstract, but perhaps the most concrete that there are.)

This sense of the specificity of language, when considered in its basic structure through logic, enables us to see the possibilities of language for the hardest, densest, clearest formulations. Knowing language this way is analogous to the knowledge given to us, according to Valéry, by the poetic experience. Like Valéry, Wittgenstein values the kind of experience we derive from knowing language in this way. He repeated his observation of 5.5563 in his later writing:

97.   Thought is surrounded by a halo. —Its essence, logic, presents an order, in fact the a priori order of the world: that is, the order of *possibilities*, which must be common to both world and thought. But this order, it seems, must be *utterly simple*. It is *prior* to all experience, must run through all experience; no empirical cloudiness or uncertainty can be allowed to affect it. —It must rather be of the purest crystal. But this crystal does not appear as an abstraction; but as something concrete, indeed, as the most concrete, as it were the *hardest* thing there is (*Tractatus Logico-Philosophicus* No. 5.5563).[7]

To Valéry the poet is like an engineer, accurate, precise, in full control of his language, aiming at total control of the reader's experience. To Wittgenstein, analogously, the philosopher controls with absolute clarity and preci-

[7] *Philosophical Investigations*, pp. 44, 44e.

sion the propositions he formulates by means of a crystal-clear language structure, and through his text gains control of the least movement of his readers' thoughts. Of course there is the possibility of an extralinguistic event, a vision, but both Wittgenstein and Valéry agree that this by-product is not the purpose of language in either its poetic or philosophical form. Rather, such states are due to an inevitability of human nature, for there will be intimations of further realms to which language points, but realms it cannot describe. That is the province of the "unutterable," toward which Valéry and Wittgenstein had similar attitudes and for which, oddly, the poet may have had more suspicion and contempt than the philosopher. But they agree it cannot be the aim of language as a meaningful poetic or philosophical instrument.

In "Concerning *Le Cimetière marin*," Valéry describes a theoretical poetic exactitude which the forms of his poems often failed to imitate, but this possibility, that the poetic form be a representation, sententially and orthographically, of a poetic goal and principle of necessity was explored by Mallarmé. With his last overwhelming work, *Un Coup de dés*, Mallarmé experimented with a logic of poetic composition, setting out the poem on pages of squared paper, with specifications to the printer on typography. The movement of the poem on the page is the movement of thought in the speaker and reader; the text is an imitation of itself. Something of this kind we know to have been an ideal of Wittgenstein's in the production of the *Tractatus*.

But the other side of the *Tractatus* is its concern for *logical* form as the self-referring, self-representing language. Here Wittgenstein is much closer to Valéry, for whom poetic language, in its developed and controlled state, was like, if not rival to, mathematical language. Valéry notes that for Mallarmé, poetry was a kind of algebra, and for himself a kind of arithmetic. But these are at best poetic metaphors; the important point is the search for an adequate language in poetry, just as the search for an adequate language went on in philosophy. In both undertakings, the search for a self-fulfilling and a self-representative medium, a language purged of all values save the values of formal elegance, defines the modern. A poetry and a philosophy whose utterances would be a world, as the utterances of music are a world, comes close to what Valéry and Wittgenstein wanted to achieve. They use different metaphors to convey their hopes. Valéry speaks in this way:

The poetic universe of which I was speaking arises from the number, or rather from the density, of images, figures, consonances, dissonances, from the linking of turns of speech and rhythms—the essential being constantly to avoid anything that would lead back to prose, either by making it regretted or by following the *idea* exclusively. . . .

In short, the more a poem conforms to Poetry, the less it can be thought in prose without perishing. To summarize a poem or put it into prose is quite simply to misunderstand the essence of an art. Poetic necessity is inseparable from material form, and the thoughts uttered or suggested by the text of a poem are by no means the unique and chief objects of its discourse—but *means* which combine *equally* with the sounds, cadences, meter, and ornaments to produce and sustain a particular tension or exaltation, to engender within us a *world*, or *mode of existence,* of complete harmony.[8]

8 "Concerning *Le Cimitière marin*," 7: 147.

Valéry returns to the problem of poetic meaning, its peculiar power and difficulty, in the aphoristic *Mauvaises pensées:*

To love, to admire, to adore, have as expressions of their truth the negative signs of the power to express oneself. Further, everything that is strong in feeling and everything that excites a sudden reaction from a remote source immediately dislocates the complex mechanism of language: silence, the exclamation, or the cliché are the eloquence of the moment.

Obscurity is the inevitable reward of one who responds to things deeply and who feels himself to be in intimate union with those very things.

For light does not penetrate more than a few cubits below the surface.[9]

The distinction between clarity and obscurity, a problem Valéry entertains in his greatest poetry as well as in his comments upon the nature of art, is expressed in metaphors of water, whereas the imagery that comes most readily to Wittgenstein has to do with space.

"Logical space" embraces all things, and what we conceive a thing to be cannot be entertained without the space within which it occurs. Although Wittgenstein says at one point that he can imagine an empty space, it is hard to understand what he means here, for he makes it clear elsewhere that "thing" and "space" refer to coordinate concepts. Each is necessary for the other (2.013). This has wide applicability in a theory of language, and its possibility is extended somewhat in a comment Wittgenstein made in the *Notebooks*, working papers pub-

[9] "Mauvaises pensées" (Paris: Gallimard, 1943), pp. 83, 15. In *The Poetics of Paul Valéry*, trans. Jean Hytier (New York: Anchor Books, 1966).

lished after his death. "Each thing modifies the whole logical world, and the whole of logical space, so to speak" (7-10-16).[10] This seems to me to be a translation of an essentially Newtonian notion into linguistic terms. It was taken as basic by Newton that space and objects are coordinate concepts, and all objects have infinite reach in cosmic space. This notion of reciprocity was developed by Newton in such a way that he concluded space could be postulated, in absolute terms, as distinct from objects. But the Leibnizian and the Kantian correction of this separation led to a post-Newtonian emphasis on a unified cosmology in which space and matter were coordinate concepts each necessary to the definition of the other. Newton, however, had brought to philosophical attention the necessity for a theory of matter in which all events related somehow to other events.

In transferring this conception of reciprocity to language, Wittgenstein is able to formulate a theory of meaning which is truly contextual. That is, the meaning of linguistic units depends upon all the other units in the logical space. No meaning is assigned to or determined for a unit alone. He develops this idea of reciprocity as the necessary condition for meaning in language (3.4 and 3.42): "A proposition can determine only one place in logical space: nevertheless the whole of logical space must already be given by it. . . . The force of a proposition reaches through the whole of logical space" (3.42). Meaning is determined by the place of a proposition in logical space and by its relationships to other propositions.

[10] All references are to *Notebooks 1914–1916*, ed. G. H. von Wright and G. E. M. Anscombe (New York: Harper Torchbooks, 1969). Hyphenated number refers to the date of entry.

Now a problem arises to which Wittgenstein has no satisfactory solution, or which perhaps he did not consider. In logical space, all locations are equally efficacious, that is, ultimately all propositions are related to all other propositions. Of course some are axioms and some are theorems proved by deductive inference, but Wittgenstein seems to want to establish a theory of meaning which would enable us to think of propositions as all disposed in a space analogous to points in a Cartesian space. Of course there are nodes of influence that are potent, and those less efficacious. This relativity of meaning potency becomes clearer when we think of meaning in a philosophical or poetic work—for example, in the *Tractatus* itself. Some propositions are centers from which meaning emanates powerfully, and others are mere dependencies, gaining their meaning from the relationship they have to the central propositions. Like a solar system, there are centers and edges, gravitational pulls of considerable force and weak energies drawing from the larger masses. In other words, every text has its anchorings to events in the world. While Wittgenstein readily agrees to this at first, he soon moves to a formalistic conception of language that would treat it as a total system, every part of which radiates a force to every other part in equal degree. However, the cosmic analogy is carried further by Wittgenstein and specified for location in logical space to some extent.

The way he does that is as follows: in logical space, as in Newtonian space, there are objects. "The possibility of its occurring in states of affairs is the form of an object" (2.0141). Every object possesses, as it were, logical form which can be thought of as power, as a capacity to combine with other objects in atomic facts. Objects are thought of, following out the analogy, as having "logical shapes" (Max Black's phrase), and these shapes fit into one another. In this addition to the above notion of reciprocity a necessary limitation is put on the logical power of propositions: they will fit with some but not all other propositions. Which ones will and which ones won't fit depends on their shapes, and the shapes are defined in part by the system as a whole, its ordering and starting point. This implies that there are some impossible or non-existent propositions for every logical space. As Wittgenstein puts it: "The totality of existing states of affairs also determines which states of affairs do not exist" (2.05).

Application of this concept to literary language is helpful for we can think of every literary text as a logical space within which there are fitted propositions whose shapes preclude the occurrence of certain other shapes because they will not "fit." We can think of a logical space in which every proposition will fit with every other (tautologies) and spaces in which no propositions will fit with any others (contradictions). In between are all the meaningful logical spaces, or language orders, the realities of which are established by existing texts. If we think, as Wittgenstein does, of logical space as a play space (*Spielraum*, 4.463) then we can state an interesting spatial analogy for the theory of meaning: "A tautology leaves open to reality the whole—the infinite whole—of logical space: a contradiction fills the whole of logical space leaving no point of it for reality. Thus neither of them can determine reality in any way" (4.463). A tautology is compatible with every state of affairs, hence occupies no part of logical space (that is, has no determined location), whereas a contradiction allows for everything as possible, and therefore occupies every point in logical space.

All finite literary statements determine a structure of the sort Wittgenstein describes for language as a whole. Within any finite structure there are possibilities for tautologies, contradictions, and "shaped" propositions of many kinds whose "fit" is determined by the lexical system established by the artist. There are boundaries of meaning, centers of meaning power, peripheries of meaning, and consequences which are not explicitly stated in the work. Not all inferences of a language system are made within the system, and one aim of literary works is to make inferences possible, but not necessarily obvious, for the reader. Thus every language structure participates in the organization Wittgenstein assumes for his explication of logic. His effort in the *Tractatus* is to create a theory of linguistic meaning in general (and I believe he has done so), but the implications of his analysis for literary statement must be made explicit. One critical issue for Wittgenstein's theory of meaning as it might be applied to literary art is the detachment of work from world which it implies. Like imagism, its closest literary analogue, it inadvertently ends up in linguistic subjectivism, that is, in an effort to make all meaning internal and to deny the necessity of referring language to the world. Of course there is "the out there," but what matters "out there" is not capturable in language.

Logical space as a controlling metaphor endangers Wittgenstein's effort at realism; he does not want to retreat to a radical formalism of meaning, for he proposes early in the *Tractatus* that to understand how language means we must think of it in relationship to the world of events and objects. Yet he makes it clear that events follow from language, and that it is not the case that language follows from events. "Pictorial form is the possibility that things are related to one another in the same way as the elements of the picture" (2.151). Reality is known through the language picture. This means that when language functions in a truth-telling way, it has the same form as reality, and when it functions falsely it somehow misshapes reality. But since the reality we know is known through language, it seems to be the case that Wittgenstein is proposing a contextualistic theory of meaning, language gives a true picture of the world when it itself (language) is orderly, structured logically, and adheres to canons of well-formed formulae as defined through the analysis of propositional functions.

Wittgenstein's ambivalence about language and reality infects contemporary poetic theory too. If the poet's linguistic universe is well structured, it makes a world. To ask if it represents a world antecedently so structured is ridiculous; but then to ask if the poetry is "true" in the sense of "representative of an external reality" becomes something of a problem. "Is true" becomes meaningful on logical grounds of internal order, consistency, and meaningful structure of the sort Wittgenstein tries to describe. And the discomfort at rejecting realism becomes less and less as the linguistic structure, embodied in a text, becomes itself more and more entrancing. We ask little on behalf of "poetic truth" if the poem is greatly interesting in itself, and we ask more as it fails in its linguistic or, if you will, "aesthetic" adequacy. Thus logical space is analogous somehow to notions we have of aesthetic adequacy and artistic interest. Stylistic excellence leaves us satisfied: "that," we say, "is reality." Artistic crudity leaves us aware of how much the world impinges upon us and makes language unfit. So too with philosophical language, one boundary of which is the formal system of logical relationships. But in poetry as in logic, there is no independent avenue to verification: the meaning of the linguistic space is determined by its constituents, and we would be foolish to ask if we could enter that space by some other route, or see it as it were from outside in order to compare it with things as they *really* are. To get at things as they really are we make language systems; the system is reality.

Of course there is another reality; to it Wittgenstein gives the name "the mystical." Kant called it the noumenal realm; Hume called it "the secret Springs and Principles of Nature." Poets have a variety of names for it, but it is for all writers what cannot appear in language and literary or logical space. But it is, Wittgenstein maintained, a felt presence against which all language gains the power to "say." I think this applies both to philosophy and to literary uses of language as well. The interdependent nature of linguistic elements, whose meaning as a whole becomes clear only when they are joined together, is articulated by Wittgenstein in one of his mordant observations: "Man possesses an innate capacity for con structing symbols with which *some* sense can be expressed, without having the slightest idea what each word signifies" (*Notes on Logic* (95).[11] This is essentially a literary observation; the impulse to thrash out meaning comes with the compulsion to wrench linguistic elements into some kind of meaningful order. But that order

---

[11] "Notes on Logic" is an Appendix to the *Notebooks 1914–1916*.

emerges from the struggle, and is not antecedently "out there" to be captured. So considered, the "picture theory of meaning" becomes ambiguous, and at best misleading. It is a theory of meaning which assumes not a reality to which language conforms, but a reality shaped as language is shaped in making propositions. Thus, the truly creative person is the one who makes a world. I presume Wittgenstein would include both poets and philosophers as world creators. He did, we know, have a close interest in poetic forms, especially those of Trakl and Rilke. But I think it is fair to say that in his own thinking about language he made clear, philosophically, what had existed as an unarticulated aesthetic and which continues to exist as *the* modern theory of literary meaning.

The picture theory of meaning is further refined in Wittgenstein's discussion, and these refinements are of some importance if we are to see the full extent of his contribution to modernity in literary matters. He labors to clarify a distinction that is central to his theory of meaning: a proposition has two aspects which must be appreciated, for it both *says* and *shows*. But what it says is not the same as what it shows, and a confusion of saying with showing vitiates not only much linguistic theory, but also much literary practice. Propositions are *not* about their form. Thus ~ p is not about negation as if negation were an object; negation is already anticipated or defined by affirmation (5.44). "Logical constants," he says elsewhere, "are not representatives" (4.0312). Most deeply stated it takes this form: "What finds its reflection in language, language cannot represent" (4.121). I believe Wittgenstein is trying in this way to explain how language relates to that reality which language cannot talk about. There is an aspect of the picture theory of meaning which I think is profound and difficult to state. What propositions picture is not the world in the ordinary sense of what I experience through my senses in everyday routine, but rather they are altogether part of a language in which we find an imbedded structure that is an *exhibit* that cannot *tell* us anything. That is, if I am correct, language is the greatest symbolic possibility for man, not as fragments which relate to events, but as a whole whose totality as symbolic possibility we must grasp. The only way we can grasp it is through studying its form, and the most clearly articulated form of language is logic. So logic is justified, beyond its beauty and rigor, by its providing a way into the nature of language as such, and this means by providing us with the first tool by which we can pry open that totality to which we as symbolizing creatures have access. Language reflects or shows something overall—something crucial for us as human, "the mystical," as Wittgenstein calls it. But I do not like to return to that overused and misunderstood term. It is something which I think is more readily approached through poetry than logic, but understood in poetry because of what Wittgenstein has said about logic.

As I reflect on this idea I am brought to disagree with Wittgenstein, for it seems to me that in much poetry and in some philosophy the form of the sentences making up a text is what the text is about. There is an explicit relationship between saying and showing which Wittgenstein denies. I think it can better be stated this way: Language expresses relationships but does not in expressing them talk explicitly about them. But the sentences exist so that the relationships be expressed, and do not exist for the talking that they do. It may be that much literary state-

239

ment is a talking or saying so that there may be a show-ing. Somehow in using language to show something, that is, what language as a whole is a symbol of, we approach a conception of philosophy that Wittgenstein wanted to establish in his first book. Philosophy, in its considerations of language, sets limits to what can be thought and hence to what cannot be thought (4.114). In this way it talks about something which poetry only shows. And it may be that the relationship between saying and showing which Wittgenstein labored to clarify is taken care of by different uses of language. That is, what can be said about language is philosophy's job to say: philosophical language is essentially a saying language, but it is periph-erally a showing language, and can lead to intimation of a symbol theory of meaning which Wittgenstein touched on now and then in the *Tractatus*. On the other side is poetic statement whose main power, because of its logical order, is showing, and only occasionally saying. Thus po-etic statement functions as symbol in this wide sense, while it makes statements of a more specific kind periph-erally. The boundaries that philosophy gives to language are transgressed by poetry not in saying, but rather in showing.

As he puzzles over the distinction between saying and showing, Wittgenstein opens up the possibility for a novel way of considering linguistic meaning. In the terms I have elaborated earlier, I should say that the showing power of language is realized and explored in perform-ance; the saying power of language is realized and ex-plored in argument and in experiment. But there is a continuum of reference which I believe Wittgenstein was sensitive to. Argumentation is midway between performance and experiment, for it shows us logical forms as an imbedded linguistic structure, and can talk about these without any reference to the world of physical events and processes. Experiment, on the other hand, deals only with these "things" as the "out there" and the independently processing, while performance can, if it wills, be wholly "in here," the self-expressing and alluding whereby we move outside of argument and experiment. There is a linguistic order which is poetic, structured in terms that Valéry tries to describe, and for which he can find only the analogy of music. But that will not quite carry the burden of poetic accomplishment, because poetry, unlike logic, refers to events in the world. Considering the variability of poetic language as compared with argument and experiment, I am tempted to see their relationships as more complex than that represented by a continuum; rather, they stand to one another not only linearly, but geometrically. They are in a space of many dimensions, participating in, and excluding one another in a variety of parameters depending upon the kinds of structures they explore.

For Wordsworth as for Hegel, mind and nature are somehow mysteriously fitted to one another, but this optimistic romanticism and philosophically logical idealism find no place in modern linguistic theory. Philosophical and literary statements, formulated in the self-consciousness of a new way of thinking about language, and themselves constituting that new way of thinking, insist upon the reality of mind being the language in which thought is cast; the natural order "out there" to which idealism makes a corresponding thought copy becomes with analytic philosophy and imagistic and symbolistic poetry the awareness of persons as they make their world in their language. Spirit no longer can be postulated as the waiting-to-be actualized thought stuff, but consciousness is postulated as a prime matter to which a great variety of shapes can be given by the languages we inherit and develop ourselves. Philosophy and poetry are thought of as instruments both of discovery and of invention.

The closest approach to this way of thinking about philosophy and literary statement is to be found in the imagist aesthetic of poetic language in which a "logic of imagination" was worked out. And it does seem to be a differentiating property of a philosophical work like the *Tractatus,* and a literary work like a poem or novel, that there is a coherence in the first which we might, following T. S. Eliot, call "conceptual," and a coherence in the second we might call "imaginational." While a philosophical argument is repeatable and transferable—one can carry it in one's head, as it were—this is not the case with literary language unless it is exactly memorized and then "performed." The logic of imagination needs to be realized in performance; the logic of concepts works its way through inferential steps each of which can be formulated in a variety of ways. There is only in a remote sense a "style" of logical affirmations, but there is in an immediate, qualitatively definite and identifiable sense a style of literary language. In fact, that language *is* literary reveals itself to us in style. So that what literary statements say is in part what they show; and while philosophical statements do show us something—they carry personalized qualities—they are evaluated for what they say.

Philosophical and literary language both "refer to" the world, but are themselves the world they refer to. This is not so odd a way to talk about language if we think of it as the creation of a world in the sense that Wittgenstein wanted to establish when he concluded his reflections in the *Tractatus*. His sense of linguistic structure in this ultimate statement is very like the sense of poetic structure asserted by imagism. "*The limits of my language* mean the limits of my world" (5.6).

In a curious way, the capacity to have and use language hides reality. Since logic presents the form of our consciousness as human, the deeper understanding and penetration of our own consciousness lead us away from the mystical. There is a duality in Wittgenstein's sense of what it is to possess human awareness which appears as the *Tractatus* develops. While we become increasingly aware of how much eludes language and lies outside it, we become more sensitive to the outsideness of the most important values—ethical, aesthetic, and religious. Understanding what it is to have language is at once recognition of how little we have of substantial value in possessing language. Yet the way to saying anything is through the power of language. As saying increases its hold on our consciousness, as we move more deeply into what it is to say, so showing recedes from us. An inverse relationship of saying and showing is implied in the *Tractatus*. Conversely, as we appreciate the penumbra of the shown, we are struck dumb. Human consciousness is endowed with two powers: a sensitivity to ultimate mystery and a cognitive refinement of conceptual clarity. As the latter comes into sharper focus, the former becomes blurred; as we seem to have the former in focus, speech falls into silence.

Logic is the structure of my world insofar as I can possess a world; but it is alien to *the* world. Does ultimate

R

reality have a structure too? We cannot even ask that question, for to ask it is to import logic into the extralogical, just as, for Kant, to ask if the noumenal "makes sense" is to attempt to apply the categories of the understanding, valid within experience, outside experience. A true Kantian in this respect, Wittgenstein has reasserted the Kantian mystery, but has no way out of the intellectual blinders it imposes. No deduction of value categories is possible, but the values of reality are represented to us through a dim sense of otherness, an apprehension of "the mystical."

II

Wittgenstein shares with the writers of his time a reaction against theories of symbolism which would make all modes of expression interpretable. In this he reacts against the Hegelian tradition and returns to a superrefined Kantianism. So too his thought is closer to surrealism and imagism than it is to the interpretive elaboration of post-Hegelian idealism as found most particularly in psychoanalysis. Wittgenstein retained to the end of his life a strong antipathy to the interpretive theories of Freud. But in taking his stand there, he was working out a theory of language that was not peculiar to him. Indeed, the interest in symbolic modes of communication other than ordinary words was pursued by imagist, vorticist, and futurist aesthetics. Pound, T. E. Hulme, Mallarmé, all sought a language of "dead" images whose certainty and specificity would overcome the vagaries and ambiguities of words taken from ordinary language and set into literary patterns. Successful poetic statement required a new set of counters; but where would they be found? As poets, of course, Pound and Mallarmé were forced to use language, but as a philosopher and logician Wittgenstein had the advantage of access to a purely "dead" language. His discussion of logic's power as a mode of statement in which one's world is created sounds very like the longings expressed by imagism for a new poetic symbolism. It is no wonder that both philosopher and poet at the turn of the century sought a new language; the old philosophical talk, coming out of eighteenth- and nineteenth-century romanticism was overblown, empty, bombastic. A purging of all talk was felt to be the first need if anything was to be said ever again. Both poetry and philosophy started off trying to speak in the new language of purified symbolism. But one must recognize the sense of this new kind of symbolism: both idealism as philosophical metaphysics, and poetic statement as romanticism related to the external world by stating reality's order and composition. To speak as philosopher or poet was to reveal the truth "out there," not the structure "in here." And it was supposed that what could be said was referentially unencumbered—language got from *here* to *there*, and reported in appropriate symbols what was *there* by means of a structure *here*. However, what the relationship of language to reality might be, what the deliverance of systems structured in words concerning a world structured in events might be, remained deeply puzzling. The literary way out was sought in a new conception of symbolism; the philosophical way out in a new symbolization

245

of concepts. The first we refer to as "imagism," the second as symbolic logic.

Imagism stifled the natural discursiveness of language; logic inhibits the natural tendency to conflation in language. While both imagistic poetry and logically tight philosophy may allow interpretations carrying one beyond the given order of terms on a page, the focus of attention is on the structure itself. In this respect, the linguistic commitments I have been describing realize the aestheticizing of language and deny the moralizing of language. They are, historically considered, linear developments in a process that has been going on now for over two hundred years, and Wittgenstein's cryptic comment: "*The limits of my language* mean the limits of my world" (5.6) can be seen as the terminal position to which the interest in language has led.

This statement sounds as if it were merely a reiteration of traditional *solipsism,* and it is solipsistic with a serious reservation:

5.62   This remark provides the key to the problem, how much truth there is in solipsism.
For what the solipsist *means* is quite correct; only it cannot be *said,* but makes itself manifest.

And to this extent it is correct to say:

5.621   The world and life are one.

But to follow this out brings us to the conclusion that:

5.64 . . . solipsism, when its implications are followed out strictly, coincides with pure realism.

This is the implicit argument, I believe, underlying imagism and symbolism, for language is our world, and what poets say is the way things are. It is not the case that poets say in order to describe a separate reality; nor do they wish to have their words "interpreted" so that they emerge translated into another set of statements. The immediate givenness of the poetic is the meaning of the poem. And its construction must be such that the reader rests with the given, and is not driven to search for "ultimate" meaning. I think Wittgenstein states this way of looking at poetic language in a letter he wrote to Paul Engelmann in which he comments on a poem by Uhland:

9-4-17

Many thanks for your kind letter and the books. The poem by Uhland is really magnificent. And this is how it is: if only you do not try to utter what is unutterable, then *nothing* gets lost. But the unutterable will be—unutterably—*contained* in what has been uttered.

As for Brahms's Handel Variations—I do know them. Uncanny—About your changeable mood: it is like this: We are asleep. (I have said this once before to Mr. Groag, and it is true.) *Our* life is like a dream. But in our better hours we wake up just enough to realize that we are dreaming. Most of the time, though, we are fast asleep. I cannot awaken myself! I am trying hard, my dream body moves, but my real one *does not stir.* This, alas, is how it is!

Yours

Wittgenstein [12]

A late construction of imagist theory is offered by T. S. Eliot in his introduction to the poem "Anabasis" by St. J. Perse. In directing the attention of the reader to the difficulties in the poem he says:

[12] Paul Engelmann, *Letters from Ludwig Wittgenstein* (Oxford: Basil Blackwell, 1967), p. 7.

The reader has to allow the images to fall into his memory successively without questioning the reasonableness of each at the moment; so that, at the end, a total effect is produced.

Such a selection of a sequence of images and ideas has nothing chaotic about it. There is a logic of the imagination as well as a logic of concepts. People who do not appreciate poetry always find it difficult to distinguish between order and chaos in the arrangement of images; and even those who are capable of appreciating poetry cannot depend upon first impressions.[13]

Eliot has brushed against the issue so laboriously worked at by his Continental predecessors: "What kind of logic is the order of poetic language?" "How do the literary and the philosophical differ?" To these questions I believe Wittgenstein gave an answer, yet without joining the issue directly since his concern was with the orders of language appropriate to argument rather than to performance. In each linguistic use there is a structure whose space and whose space events define the things that can be said, and what cannot be said. Every linguistic order implies other orders lying outside it. But the orders lying outside are mysterious worlds, whose presence is felt, or intimations of which are received indirectly, but whose reality in a linguistic sense remains mysterious. Those are the "unutterables" to which utterables make oblique reference.

Imagism, as formulated by Pound (*phanopoeia*, he called it, to avoid its being identified with the imagism of Amy Lowell) aimed at direct presentation in the most economical medium. This accounts for his interest in Chinese ideograms and the strength he drew from Fenol-

[13] London: Faber and Faber, 1930, p. 8.

losa's commentary on the nature of Chinese writing. Poetry, like the symbolism of the new logic, sought to be clear, self-evident, and powerful. The linguistic reorientation explored by imagism is the complement to Wittgenstein's efforts to explain how language can be meaningful. One section of the *Tractatus*, that numbered 4 ff., amplifies imagist poetic theory. A close look at Wittgenstein's theory of language discovers a philosophical and literary renovation whose influence is felt in midcentury texts. Section 4 asserts that "A thought is a proposition with a sense" ("Der Gedanke ist der sinnvolle Satz"), and the totality of propositions constitutes language (4.001). The curious fact is that with the ability to use language, we possess an instrument with which we can express every possible sense, yet without knowing how each word comes to mean, and without knowing exactly what the meanings of individual words are—that is to say, meanings evolve and take shape in the course of linguistic usage. In all linguistic performances, meaning is in some way or other "discovered" in the process of language use. This certainly applies to literary uses of language, and as part of a philosophical theory of language is itself subject to its own rule: the idea that language becomes meaningful in context applies to the statement "Language becomes meaningful in context." So what Wittgenstein understands by that assertion comes clear as the *Tractatus* develops and as it introduces notions of "showing," "mirroring," and "saying." We recognize a difference between showing and saying without being able to articulate clearly exactly what we are getting at in language use. But we recognize that sentences have several dimensions, some of which remain vague in any effort to say what a sentence means. Those vague aspects are exploited by poetry, and they must be accounted for by a philosophical theory of language. The sentences numbered 4 ff. in the *Tractatus* try to give an account of language in these various capacities.

A metaphor of great power, in Wittgenstein's conceptualization of how language relates to meaning, is the one he introduces in section 4.011; it is a metaphor that he shares with the imagist poets.

4.011 At first sight a proposition—one set out on the printed page, for example—does not seem to be a picture of the reality with which it is concerned. But no more does musical notation at first sight seem to be a picture of music, nor our phonetic notation (the alphabet) to be a picture of our speech.

And yet these sign-languages prove to be pictures, even in the ordinary sense, of what they represent.

4.014 A gramophone record, the musical idea, the written notes, and the sound-waves, all stand to one another in the same internal relation of depicting that holds between language and the world.

And after that, another metaphor, again one shared with the imagist poets, is called upon to help clarify the relationship of language to the world:

4.016 In order to understand the essential nature of a proposition, we should consider hieroglyphic script, which depicts the facts that it describes.

And alphabet script developed out of it without losing what was essential to depiction.

Of course, Pound differs from Wittgenstein in the assessment each gives of the power of alphabet script as compared with hieroglyphic figures, for Pound believed that the alphabet lost the depicting property and that Chinese ideograms retain that property; hence his dedication to the essay by Fenollosa, published by Pound after Fenollosa's death.[14]

Pound believed that imagist poetry, in its economical construction of word images, re-creates the ideogrammic power to say and show at once, and believed the power of poetry to lie in that comprehensive dual function. Wittgenstein, however, believed that the alphabet if understood could be seen to retain the ideogrammic power, but felt, with Pound, that the power could be actualized if language were "purified" in the sense of stripped down to its essential relational first elements. And for Wittgenstein this skeletal structure could be revealed if one were to introduce logical functions; then how language is meaningful would be revealed, and that it is meaningful understood with a clarity that has eluded us. Both Pound and Wittgenstein see musical notation as a paradigm for language that is clearly meaningful, but for Wittgenstein the notation appropriate to philosophical statement is logical notation, whereas for Pound it is the poetic image composed with an economy of words.

Both imagism and the linguistic objectivism Wittgenstein struggled to create depend upon a primitive theory of linguistic meaning. The theory is presented by Wittgenstein's distinction between *showing* and *saying*.

4.022 A proposition *shows* its sense.

A proposition *shows* how things stand *if* it is true. And it *says that* they do so stand.

[14] *The Chinese Written Character as a Medium for Poetry: An Ars Poetica*, Ezra Pound (San Francisco: City Lights Books, 1936).

4.121 Propositions cannot represent logical form: it is mirrored in them.

What finds its reflection in language, language cannot represent.

What expresses *itself* in language, *we* cannot express by means of language.

Propositions *show* the logical form of reality.

They display it.

This distinction is essentially poetic, for it insists that there are two dimensions of language: philosophy *says* what they are, while poetry *shows* them in use. Of course Wittgenstein does not put it this way; I observe this historical parallelism which emerges in the years when the *Tractatus* was being composed, for imagism as a poetic movement asserts the same linguistic dualism and presents it in the poetry it created. *Language* expresses *itself;* and *we use* language to express thoughts. *Language* possesses expressive power; *we* possess an instrument, language, whose expressive power we wonder at, and also use to say things about the world and about ourselves; but in saying what is or is not the case we also show what there is to be shown in language. But the wonder is that language expresses *itself*. This mysterious linguistic power is merely asserted by Wittgenstein; it is explored on behalf of art by symbolist and imagist poets.

When we *use* language to assert or deny a state of affairs, we are performing in somewhat the way a composer performs when he writes out a musical notation. That notation must be "played," translated back into sound by an instrument. So we, in reading, translate the linguistic symbols back into the images which were the initiating events to which language was the response. Yet as we *use* language in this way, we also come to see that the language we *use* expresses *itself*, and its expressing itself is a *showing*, not a *saying*. Were it a saying, language would talk about its own shape, but it cannot do that. It can talk about events; it can show what its structure is as it talks, but it cannot talk about what it shows; yet every talking about is at once a showing. It is as if we were to ask if we can always articulate the affective tone of what we articulate. And of course we cannot. For in articulating one set of tones, another set is created. Wittgenstein puts it in this way:

4.124 The existence of an internal property of a possible situation is not expressed by means of a proposition: rather, it expresses itself in the proposition representing the situation, by means of an internal property of that proposition.

Although this statement is introduced on behalf of the logical structure which shows itself in propositions, the linguistic dimension thereby revealed is of central importance to all linguistic usage.

Poetic use of language relies upon a dimension Wittgenstein would consciously reject as irrelevant to the philosophical uses he explores, but I believe both the *Tractatus* and the imagist poetry of its time make use of a similar technique which broadens the distinction Wittgenstein makes between saying and showing. Sentences show their internal structure, and they cannot say what they show; we have already examined this position. Now I enlarge that by introducing another linguistic dimension, that of traditional linguistic uses which a writer takes up into his sentences, and which then become elements of showing. A discourse upon the text—for example, a commentary on the *Tractatus,* or an analysis of a poem by Pound—can bring out these elements of show, but the original text cannot say what it shows in this sense, in part because every text unconsciously exhibits elements over which it could not make statements. In the case of imagism, and of symbolism as it developed in the French school, elements from the past were taken up into the present. Eliot's *The Waste Land* and Pound's *Mauber-ley,* Rilke's *Elegies* and *Sonnets,* Valéry's musical poetry all take up into themselves bits of past linguistic assertion, transmitted in a new context. In this respect the *Tractatus* is a work of its time, for all the terms used in the *Tractatus* have traditional usages in German philosophy, and are here represented with new connotations and new interpretations. The *Tractatus* is as revolutionary in respect to its metaphysical tradition as symbolism is to its; both affirm that language creates the world, and that our exploration of linguistic structures constitutes for us the enlargement of human awareness. However much the past has been devoted to *things,* however much poets and philosophers believed they talked about what is out there, the liberating discovery of poetry and philosophy in the contemporary world consists in tearing away the veil of reality. While idealism claimed to have torn asunder "the veil of Maya" as Schopenhauer so romantically put it, what idealism began linguistic objectivism finished: the final dispersion of that unnecessary duplication, the external world. While Descartes believed he could reconstitute it from a logical argument, Wittgenstein boldly asserts that what Descartes "made" was but a system of linguistic "events" whose structure we can study through the logical instruments of Frege and Russell. Indeed, the "world" that poets and philosophers create *exists as a text.*

254

III

If the world exists as a text, what becomes of me? Both philosophical analysis of language, as worked out in the *Tractatus*, and poetic analysis of language as explored by Valéry stress the critical issue of the self. What has language to do with the "I" of experience and consciousness when it is used to speak about the world and about experience? Explaining the way the self, subject, or "I" participates in and defines experience is a problem to which both Wittgenstein and Valéry gave thought. Responding to this interest, Wittgenstein interrupts the logical inquiry of the *Tractatus* with this assertion:

5.632 The subject does not belong to the world: rather, it is a limit of the world.

As the eye does not see itself, and nothing in the visual field demonstrates that it is seen by the eye, so the "I" of consciousness is not an object of consciousness. The only way the self legitimately gets into philosophy is through the notion of "the world" for

5.641 What brings the self into philosophy is the fact that "the world is my world."

The philosophical self is not the human being, the human body, or the human soul, with which psychology deals, but rather the metaphysical subject, the limit of the world—not a part of it.

Wittgenstein's effort to define a concept, "the philosophical self," to be distinguished from "the psychological self" and presumably other interpretations of "self," intro-

255

duces a philosophical theme essential to his interpretation of experience. The self is the limit of my world, and my world is an interconnected series of linguistic events; therefore, the whole issue of the self falls outside philosophy, into that realm of the "unutterable" to which the *Tractatus* consigns the most important questions insofar as they have to do with our moral, aesthetic, and religious values. As we might expect, values fall outside the philosophical world too.

6.4   All propositions are of equal value.

6.41   The sense of the world must lie outside the world. In the world everything is as it is, and everything happens as it does happen: *in* it no value exists—and if it did, it would have no value.

If there is any value that does have value, it must lie outside the whole sphere of what happens and is the case. For all that happens and is the case is accidental.

The consequences are simple: There are no propositions of ethics, because they specify necessity, and all in the world is accidental; my will can alter the limits of the world, but not the events which constitute the world; death is simply an ending, not an event in life; and religious values are outside the world, for God cannot reveal himself in the world. The *Tractatus* concludes with a remarkably concise ontology of negation whose appeal to successive generations of philosophers has been, for some, curative and clarifying, for others, blinding and stupefying. But the philosophical intention is worth considering, because it reveals at last the interpretation of experience the *Tractatus* affords us.

I shall come to that interpretation of experience by means of symbolist analogues, since they make it clear by giving it the content which Wittgenstein, because of his dedication to linguistic purity, and because of his belief in the unutterability of certain felt aspects of experience, thought a philosophical text could not explore without contradicting itself. But Wittgenstein's sense of where the self can be "found" is of some importance. Wittgenstein interprets the world:

6.374 Even if all that we wish for were to happen, still this would only be a favor granted by fate, so to speak: for there is no *logical* connexion between the will and the world, which would guarantee it, and the supposed physical connexion itself is surely not something that we could will.

Detaching will from world, as Wittgenstein does, drives thought into the self, for only in my consciousness does willing make any difference, and therefore what I can will in regard to the world is the limit of the world, but not its content. I take this to mean that my interests in the world, as a valuing, judging person, are realized in the development I give to logic, for in extending the inquiry of philosophy so interpreted, I enlarge and articulate the order of the world, though not its content. The only difference this makes to me is in the shape—or, if you will, the extent of the boundaries—of the world.

6.43 If good or bad acts of will do alter the world, it can only be the limits of the world that they alter, not the facts, not what can be expressed by means of language.

The world of the happy man is a different one from that of the unhappy man.

I take this statement to be a reply, with agreement in part, to the interpretation of experience developed by Schopenhauer, for Wittgenstein accepts Schopenhauer's deterministic view of events, but refuses to go along with the romantic interest in will that his predecessor defended. When Schopenhauer says: "Every one knows only *one* being quite immediately—his own will in self-consciousness; everything else he knows only indirectly and judges it analogously with this," [15] Wittgenstein agrees that the illusion of events prevents us from penetrating to inner consciousness, but he insists that events are structures of logical possibilities, existing in language, and not projections of will. Where we can talk about will is in relation to the outer edges of events. For Schopenhauer, will projects itself into all philosophy. We can think of the *Tractatus* as a logical voluntarism, to be contrasted with the psychological voluntarism of Schopenhauer. In this connection, I think it is worth mentioning the fact that Schopenhauer's views were important to the early literary exploration of Thomas Mann; that in the German world of letters at the turn of the century when Wittgenstein's thoughts were taking shape, Schopenhauer was a thinker to reckon with, and the *Tractatus* is a way of disposing of that philosophical pressure as surely as Mann's criticism of Schopenhauer in his stories of the early 1900's is a rejection of the lugubrious "pessimism" of the most painfully suffering German philosopher. Mann's interest in Schopenhauer, whether serious or ironic, remained throughout his life, and the book he was working on when he died, *Confessions of Felix Krull*, contains long passages in which Schopenhauer's thought is parodied.

The poetic interpretation of language temperamentally closest to Wittgenstein's is that of Paul Valéry, whose in-

[15] Schopenhauer, Supplement to Book II of *World as Will and Idea*. Ch. XXV.

terest in a poetic theory of linguistic objectivism I have already alluded to. It will be useful at this point once again to consider Valéry's conception of poetic language, for here a sense of the self analogous to Wittgenstein's is explored.

. . . the poetic state or emotion seems to me to consist in a dawning perception, a tendency toward perceiving a *world*, or complete system of relations, in which beings, things, events, and acts, although they may resemble, *each to each*, those which fill and form the tangible world—the immediate world from which they are borrowed—stand, however, in an indefinable, but wonderfully accurate, relationship to the modes and laws of our general sensibility. So, the value of these well-known objects and beings is in some way altered. They respond to each other and combine quite otherwise than in ordinary conditions. They become—if you will allow the expression—*musicalized*, somehow commensurable, echoing each other. The poetic universe defined in this way bears a strong analogy to the universe of dream.[16]

Valéry's verse creates a "musicalized" self-sufficient universe of the kind he alludes to in the essay. His poetry might be thought of as an incantation, a linguistic evocation of the self, bringing it into its reality from the edges of the world where it resides. The self comes out of negation and nothingness (see *La Jeune Parque*) and lives, if at all, in the poetry created by its violent fight against the negativity of existence. It is as if Valéry answers the *Tractatus* by saying that the self of philosophy, that which exists as a limit upon the world, can be brought into experience by a use of language which shows that the self is

[16] "Remarks on Poetry," in *The Art of Poetry*, trans. Denise Folliot Vol. 7 (London: Routledge & Kegan Paul, 1958), p. 198.

S

part of a single, unified, and, in the sense of Zeno of Elia, a motionless wholeness. But that is the underlying, hidden structure; superimposed upon it is the fantastical poetic world of dreams and myth, a violent picture world contrasting shockingly with that of the *Tractatus*. No two modes of using language could be more at odds than the rich imagery of *Le Cimetière marin* and the stark factual language of the *Tractatus*. But each seeks to establish a linguistic order in which the experience which constitutes human awareness will be interpreted, the suffering self and the external order will be brought into a wholeness. In doing this, the typical alienation of self from world will be overcome by offering a reconstruction of what one undergoes.

The reconstruction is of two kinds: in the *Tractatus* it is theory of language in which the logical structure of what can be said is contrasted with what cannot be (meaningfully) said. There is no logically constructed language of feeling and of human consciousness of values; therefore they belong outside language and exist as the unutterable. Yet that world is in effect the world Valéry imagines as a prose world into which poetry has not penetrated. With the creation of poetic language, all that the *Tractatus* pushes to the periphery comes into the world, not to displace the logical, but to exploit it in its total formalism, to create a musicalized use of language as precise in its way as the logical language of symbols is in its. Ultimately, then, symbolism in this version denies the vision of the *Tractatus*, not by saying the unutterable, but by creating a language which can in its imagistic force show what Wittgenstein assumed it could not show. Poetic language reverses the relationship of saying and showing, for

by showing, it says, if there is a competent reader to respond to the images. But this response is itself a redupli-
cation of the form. Poetry then is a kind of language "in
which a form reproduces itself." I take this sense of
Valéry's to be that what the poet creates is in effect a
piece like a musical work, whose notation is words. This
notation, full of strange images and connecting links of
image to image, finally reproduces itself in the mind of
the reader as a reconstruction. Poetic language, like logical symbolism, is a notation of relationships whose order
reconstitutes itself in individual minds. What we mean by
"reality" is mental content plus notation. Anything beyond that is speculative metaphysics. In this sense Wittgenstein and Valéry share a conception of language; but
in another sense, namely, what it is language can be
"about" they differ profoundly.

I V

Looking across the philosophical and literary works of
our time back to the *Tractatus* and to symbolism, we can
see a likeness of the recent past to the more remote, a
continuity and development in the conception of philosopher established by Wittgenstein, and the conception of
literary artist imagined by Pound, Valéry, Trakl, and
Mann. While philosophers reiterate the belief in the independence and autonomy of philosophy, and literary artists create more and more on the basis of art itself, the
two urgently independent activities complement each

other now as they did in their early modern establishment. Outside the logical, become a part of mathematical inquiry, the interests of philosophy and literature remain close, and no more so than at this moment when conceptions of experience, self, and action dominate contemporary philosophical thought.

Similarity of concern characterizes philosophy and literary art today in an obvious sense, that they participate in our wonder about experience, especially experience in a time of cultural fragmentation. I am struck by the extensive, detailed, argumentative attention given to the *Tractatus* as a text. As much ingenuity has gone into interpreting the *Tractatus* as has gone into the poetry of Pound, or Valéry, or T. S. Eliot, or Rilke. Textually the *Tractatus* confronts us with ambiguities, difficulties, allusiveness, uncertainties as great as any in those poetic documents we prize so highly. Its difficulty does not come merely from hermetic writing; it comes as well from the ideas it struggles to get out, and of those ideas, the most intriguing have to do with ultimate philosophical questions: God, freedom, immortality, for they are the issues alluded to at the end of the book. Wittgenstein represents fairly the fundamental philosophical wonder to which all philosophers respond, no matter how much they consciously refuse to enter into these issues.

We can ask therefore whether or not there is, no matter how vaguely, an ultimate point of view represented and *shown* in the *Tractatus*, something we, its readers, see in it. And just as we can characterize poetic points of view, such as those of Valéry or Mallarmé who use language in somewhat the way Wittgenstein does, so we can look through the language of the *Tractatus* to the shadow

262

it casts as a whole. In doing this, we see that the conclusion of the book is a series of statements of how we feel and think about the world, the totality of facts, insofar as we are affective, striving, human beings. The totality of propositions which constructs *my* world is at the same time something toward which I feel, strive, wonder, and hope. How can we make a place for this side of awareness? In answering this question Wittgenstein introduces an interpretation of experience that is fundamentally poetic. The ethical and aesthetical perspectives, which in themselves change nothing, for the world is as it is, yet *create the consciousness of the happy man* as against the consciousness of the unhappy man. Their worlds are different worlds, not because their worlds are constructed factually in varying ways, but because they maintain different attitudes of wonder, awe, hope, and fear toward what is. In essence, Wittgenstein's beliefs about the power of art and morality derive from Schopenhauer. That he gathered much from Schopenhauer is evident from the notebooks he kept at the time he was writing the *Tractatus;* in them we see all the emotion to which all thought is subject, yet emotion which the philosopher tries to distill out of his language, as the poet tries to find objective correlatives for it in his language. In both uses of language, however, the affective drama of composition and inquiry is revealed as something shown, not said. We are helped in finding what the *Tractatus* shows by those much fuller assertions in the *Notebooks* that Wittgenstein never allowed to penetrate his finished text. His own working method illustrates so well another side of his philosophical doctrine of saying and showing. Somehow the writer, the producer of texts, must hide what he feels.

And the very effort to hide that side of thought, so strenuously exhibited in the *Tractatus,* leads us to sense something beyond the text, as God and the self lie beyond the world of facts. All of the creative thinker's mystical reality lies outside the text, as the mystical lies outside the world. In both the unutterable is, in this sense, contained in what is uttered.

At this point we encounter Wittgenstein's philosophic self in its most artistic identity, for ethical and artistic feelings, intimations, longings express that side of human nature which asserts the existence of the unutterable. The good life, in the classical sense of the life of the great-souled man, the happy man who accepts what is with equanimity and love, can be realized in the philosophic world of the *Tractatus.* In his *Notebooks* (7-10-16) Wittgenstein asserts that "The work of art is the object seen *sub specie aeternitatis;* and the good life is the world seen *sub specie aeternitatis,*" a simple but by no means irrelevant way of looking at human products and human actions. In the world of the *Tractatus* art and the good life have this sort of being, and so seen, so interpreted, the aesthetic and the ethical remain simple sorts of pleasures, realizations for the suffering thinker who hammers out a viable space. When Wittgenstein defends his world against the overelaborations of idealism and the impoverishments of simple empiricism, he resorts to a vision which is that of Spinoza and Schopenhauer. Perhaps those predecessors together with Augustine showed him his philosophic way.

It is here, in the sense of life's sufferings, that Wittgenstein's logical and ethical doctrines touch, for the need to clarify language, to move out of the murkiness of everyday conceptual ambiguity into the realm of purified conceptualization with a system remote, formally satisfying, unambiguous, and above all settled to the perceiving intellect, so that all minds should agree on the meaning of propositions—all this, with Leibnizian fervor—was the vision Wittgenstein tried to construct. "The life of knowledge is the life that is happy in spite of the misery of the world" (*Notebooks*, 13-8-16). If only the life of knowledge could be constructed with the purity of and with the satisfaction to be derived from the aesthetic. For behind the drive to logical clarity lies the assertion of the individual will; Wittgenstein, like Schopenhauer, sees the world as a creation of the self. "What has history to do with me? Mine is the first and only world!" ("Was geht mich die Geschichte an? Meine Welt ist die erste und einzige!") (*Notebooks*, 2-9-16). This cry of distress is the same as that of the novel, *The Leopard*, whose hero, like Wittgenstein himself, lives a double life of intellectual abstractedness and purity, alongside the affective confusion of human desire. Indeed, Lampedusa's hero, the Prince of Salina, exists as a fictional analogue to the real life of the philosopher Wittgenstein.

But unlike Fabrizio, Wittgenstein lacked the ability to yield to the instinctual and erected a strong defense against the intrusion of physical, affective, and volitional needs. His separation of the person into a self and an other, that is, the physical presence, is strikingly asserted in the *Notebooks;* after a paragraph which went into the *Tractatus* intact (see 5.641) there is the revealing comment which was separated out:

The philosophical I is not the human being, not the human body or the human soul with the psychological properties, but the metaphysical subject, the boundary (not a part) of the world. The human body, however, my body in particular, is a part of the world among others, among animals, plants, stones, etc., etc.

Whoever realizes this will not want to procure a pre-eminent place for his own body or for the human body.

He will regard humans and animals quite naively as objects which are similar and which belong together. [*Notebooks*, 2-9-16]

Therefore, the salvation of the self consists in its creating the order, purity, and perspicaciousness that is symbolized by the work of art.

Despite the apparent disorder of the world, there is an order that can be found, and the drive of intellect has always been toward a method to realize this inner structure.

Mankind has always looked for a science in which *simplex sigillum veri* holds.

. . . In every possible world there is an order even if it is a complicated one . . .

Art is a kind of expression.

Good art is complete expression. [*Notebooks*, 19-9-16]

The work of art has a wider connotation than that, for it stands as the paradigm for logical constructions, and the method of truth, which for Wittgenstein is the logical system he accepts and refines from Frege and from Russell, can be symbolized by the interrelationships that obtain in art:

The work of art is the object seen *sub specie aeternitatis;* and the good life is the world seen *sub specie aeternitatis*. This is the connexion between art and ethics.

The usual way of looking at things sees objects as it were

266

from the midst of them, the view *sub specie aeternitatis* from outside.

In such a way that they have the whole world as background.

Is this it perhaps—in this view the object is seen *together with* space and time instead of *in* space and time?

Each thing modifies the whole logical world, the whole of logical space, so to speak.

(The thought forces itself upon one): The thing seen *sub specie aeternitatis* is the thing seen together with the whole logical space. [*Notebooks,* 7-10-16]

As the artist creates his work out of himself, and thereby achieves a view of "the world" *sub specie aeternitatis,* so the philosopher comes to realize that *the* world for everyone is his willful creation: "Things acquire 'significance' only through their relationship to my will" (*Notebooks,* 15-10-16).

But the will felt and known by the individual is identical with the world will, for, "As my idea is the world, in the same way my will is the world-will" (*Notebooks,* 17-10-16). Therefore, the identity of myself is in a peculiar, and, I should say, in an essentially *artistic* way bound up with the identity of every other thing. Wittgenstein comes to this realization in a remarkable passage—one of the longest in his *Notebooks*—which states an artistic conception of the self and the world, a consciousness in which all things parallel all other things, and therefore a world that allows *metamorphosis.* Philosophy, as Wittgenstein comes to understand it in this rumination, is a bringing into awareness and a making articulate the truth which artistic expression and ethical reflection have long recognized but never been able to say with philosophical

267

precision. The truth Wittgenstein *as philosopher* can now see is that the self is interchangeable with all other forms, that there is a unity to reality which depends upon the sustenance of consciousness. The same realization was expressed by the poet Yeats who regarded poetic contemplation as a study of soul deliverance, not in the sense of escape, but in the sense of metamorphosis:

> Now shall I make my soul,
> Compelling it to study
> In a learned school
> Till the wreck of body,
> Slow decay of blood,
> Testy delirium
> Or dull decrepitude,
> Or what worse evil come—
> The death of friends, or death
> Of every brilliant eye
> That made a catch in the breath—
> Seem but the clouds of the sky
> When the horizon fades;
> Or a bird's sleepy cry
> Among the deepening shades.[17]

Artistic transformations then "state" a deep truth: that miraculously the world exists; that miraculously all is one. "Aesthetically, the miracle is that the world exists. That what exists does exist" (*Notebooks*, 20-10-16).

But this way to formulate what there is still leaves out of account the forcefulness and the dynamic quality of the world. Ultimately what we mean by "force," "change," "movement" can be traced back to the will.

[17] Last stanza of "The Tower," *The Collected Poems of W. B. Yeats* (New York: The Macmillan Company, 1942), pp. 230–231.

The remaining problem then is how, since the world is what it is, I act, bring about change, and can even be said somehow to effect events? The problem that puzzles Wittgenstein, like that which makes the experience of the Prince of Salina so troublesome, is this: "What am *I* to the course of events in the world; what are *events* to me?" For if my consciousness is the world, then I am either impotently but an event, or I must consider some explanation of my intervening in the world. That theory of how there can be a willing self which "interrupts the world" is just the question Wittgenstein worried over all his life. It is expressed in that sad exclamation: "Was geht mich die Geschichte an? Meine Welt ist die erste und einzige!" (*Notebooks*, 2-9-16).

His answer, insofar as he gropes for one in the *Notebooks*, is essentially the answer of art: although in common awareness we distinguish events close to me and far from me, and although we say some things are under my control and some are not, the truth must be otherwise. Here is the puzzle:

But, of course, it is undeniable that in a popular sense there are things that I do, and other things not done by me.

In this way then the will would not confront the world as its equivalent, which must be impossible. [*Notebooks*, 4-11-16]

Resolution for a philosopher lies in a retreat to the comfort of logic: for logic teaches us that, theoretically at least, "every possible form of proposition must be FORE-SEEABLE" (21-11-16), and this is a consequence of a primitive logical property, that is, all signs are constructed according to a rule, and that rule is one of structural similarity. All propositions are transformable by series of operations into other propositions. Language, which is the world, is therefore a congery of transformational sentences whose fundamental property we might call, borrowing the mythic term, "metamorphosis." But metamorphosis, we have already seen, is the property of the world insofar as we think of it as the projection of, or content of, awareness of the self. There is a root parallelism among all things:

> This parallelism, then, really exists between my spirit, that is, between spirit and the world.
>
> Only remember that the spirit of the snake, of the lion, is *your* spirit. For it is only from yourself that you are acquainted with spirit at all. [*Notebooks*, 15-10-16]

Logic is the philosopher's school for his soul. Wittgenstein has come to the point where the study of logical relations opens up to him all that philosophy need be concerned with, the realm of primitive values. And he sees that as art expresses the beautiful organization which is the world, and in its synoptic, inclusive vision sees it as gay ("Ernst ist das Leben, heiter ist die Kunst," [18] he quotes from Schiller) so philosophy sees the sad and oppressive reason for the similitude, for the philosopher is infected by the anxiety of existence, while the artist celebrates its wonder. I believe that here is the critical *Weltanschauung* of Wittgenstein's philosophy, one that he inherited from Schopenhauer and Nietzsche, and one that suited his unhappy life. The fragment of his *Notebooks* ends, strangely enough, with just the question philosophy can never resolve, the question to which Wittgenstein's life was dedicated:

[18] Life is serious, art is gay.

If suicide is allowed then everything is allowed.
If anything is not allowed, then suicide is not allowed.

Or is even suicide in itself neither good nor evil? [*Notebooks*, 10-1-17]

Suicide is the one act in which the self can be changed in a radical way; suicide is the metamorphosis of one's being and the end of the world. But the thought of suicide, which is in reality the thought that one might control and master death, is the philosopher's way of thinking about the way to control all events. The terror of radical determinism, a feeling, an emotion deeply embedded in the *Tractatus* can be overcome only if there is a way to alter events in a primitive way, that is a way which is at once the control of events and the altering of events so that it really makes a difference in how the world runs. If my language is my world, and if I cannot conceive of will except as existing on the periphery of linguistic space, then by one act I can bring it into the world, namely, in the act of annihilating the world. Therefore suicide becomes the truly *philosophical* act, and as such possibly *the* act without a value. Mysteriously, the end of my world is something I am allowed to long for.

At this moment, the moment when reflection on the *Tractatus* must end, we reach a mythical primitivism, the primitivism whose forms are first stated in the stories of metamorphoses of gods and men. Wittgenstein shows us that to the philosophic mind the most powerful metaphor is that of metamorphosis, the changing of forms, both those of consciousness and those of physical shape. Language, the stuff out of which we make the world, is at bottom this fluidity of metamorphosis, an articulation of

271

the passing of shape into shape, of being into being, of consciousness into consciousness, and ultimately of consciousness into the negation of consciousness, of death. As this poetic act consists in creating forms through images, the philosophic act is the annihilation of forms through the uprooting of consciousness. Here we confront the difference between philosopher and poet, the difference for which Plato argued in so many ways: the poet is forever a maker of worlds; to him language can never be exhausted. The philosopher is the analyzer of one world, the structure of consciousness, and when that has been exhaustively explored, there is nothing left but its negation, the end of that world. Of course philosophy must end in silence, as the *Tractatus* asserts: "Wovon man nicht sprechen kann, darüber muss man schweigen." [19] The poet sings throughout the night.

[19] What we cannot speak about we must consign to silence.

Index